D1594733

The Passions of Christ in High-Medieval Thought

OXFORD STUDIES IN HISTORICAL THEOLOGY
Series Editor
David C. Steinmetz, Duke University

Editorial Board
Irena Backus, Université de Genève
Robert C. Gregg, Stanford University
George M. Marsden, University of Notre Dame
Wayne A. Meeks, Yale University
Gerhard Sauter, Rheinische Friedrich-Wilhelms-Universität Bonn
Susan E. Schreiner, University of Chicago
John Van Engen, University of Notre Dame
Geoffrey Wainwright, Duke University
Robert L. Wilken, University of Virginia

The Passions of Christ in High-Medieval Thought

An Essay on Christological Development

KEVIN MADIGAN

OXFORD
UNIVERSITY PRESS

2007

BT
198
.M297
2007

OXFORD
UNIVERSITY PRESS

Oxford University Press, Inc., publishes works that further
Oxford University's objective of excellence
in research, scholarship, and education.

Oxford   New York
Auckland   Cape Town   Dar es Salaam   Hong Kong   Karachi
Kuala Lumpur   Madrid   Melbourne   Mexico City   Nairobi
New Delhi   Shanghai   Taipei   Toronto

With offices in
Argentina   Austria   Brazil   Chile   Czech Republic   France   Greece
Guatemala   Hungary   Italy   Japan   Poland   Portugal   Singapore
South Korea   Switzerland   Thailand   Turkey   Ukraine   Vietnam

Copyright © 2007 by Oxford University Press, Inc.

Published by Oxford University Press, Inc.
198 Madison Avenue, New York, New York 10016

www.oup.com

Oxford is a registered trademark of Oxford University Press

All rights reserved. No part of this publication may be reproduced,
stored in a retrieval system, or transmitted, in any form or by any means,
electronic, mechanical, photocopying, recording, or otherwise,
without the prior permission of Oxford University Press.

Library of Congress Cataloging-in-Publication Data
Madigan, Kevin, 1960–
   The passions of Christ in high-medieval thought : an essay on christological
development / Kevin Madigan.
      p. cm.—(Oxford studies in historical theology)
Includes bibliographical references and index.
ISBN 978-0-19-532274-3
   1. Jesus Christ—History of doctrines—Middle Ages, 600–1500.   I. Title.
BT198.M297 2007
232'.809—dc22   2006025928

9 8 7 6 5 4 3 2 1

Printed in the United States of America
on acid-free paper

To Bernard McGinn
magistro optimo et amico fideli

Acknowledgments

Special thanks to the National Endowment for the Humanities for a Prize Fellowship awarded in 2002–2003, without which the publication of this book would have been much delayed. I would like to thank my colleagues at Harvard Divinity School for their kind encouragement. Let me particularly thank Amy Hollywood and Sarah Coakley for having read through the entire manuscript before publication and for invaluable advice. I am grateful to Jon Levenson for his continuous support, intellectual companionship and wit. Portions of this book were drafted when I was on the faculty of Catholic Theological Union (CTU) for six happy years in Chicago. I wish to thank Don Senior, its omnicompetent president, for friendship and release time. To my many other friends at CTU, especially John Pawlikowski and Paul Wadell, I am grateful. I have benefitted greatly from the good humor and faithful friendship of John van Engen and David Burr. Many thanks to my research assistant, Zach Matus, for keeping me supplied with books with such good humor. Thanks too, to my faculty assistants over the past six years—Eric Unverzagt, Kristin Gunst and Kathy Lou—all of whom provided invaluable assistance with manuscript preparation. Thanks to Cynthia Read, my editor at Oxford University Press, and her very able assistants Theo Calderara and Julia TerMaat. My wife Stephanie Paulsell and daughter Amanda Madigan were a constant support and source of humor, the latter especially when wondering, at age 4, when I'd be coming home from the "Vidinity School." I dedicate this book in gratitude and deep respect to my graduate school advisor and friend, Bernard McGinn.

Contents

Abbreviations

Sent. Peter Lombard, *Sententiae in IV libris distinctae* [3rd ed. rev.], Ed. I. Brady. 2 vols. Grottaferrata: Editiones Collegii S. Bonaventurae ad Claras Aquas, 1971–1981.

Albertus Magnus, *Commentarii in IV Sententiarum*, from *B. Alberti Magni Opera Omnia*, ed. E. Borgnet [38 vols.; Paris: Vivès, 1890–1895], 28.

Bonaventure, *Commentaria in Quatuor Libros Sententiarum*, from *S. Bonaventurae Opera Omnia*, 11 vols. (Ad Claras Aquas [Quaracchi]: Ex Typographia Collegii S. Bonaventurae, 1882–1902, 3: 322).

Thomas Aquinas, *Scriptum super Sententiis Magistri Petri Lombardi.* Ed. P. Mandonnet and M.F. Moos (4 vols.; Paris: P. Lethielleux, 1947–56), 3. Also referred to as *Scriptum.*

Summa: Summa Theologiae, in *Opera Omnia* [16 vols. to date; Rome: Typographia Polyglotta S.C. de Propaganda Fide, 1887–], vol. 11.

CSEL: Corpus Scriptorum Ecclesiasticorum Latinorum (Vienna, 1866–).

CCL: Corpus Christianorum, Series Latina (Turnhout, 1953–).

The Passions of Christ in
High-Medieval Thought

I

Introduction

In this study, I offer a meditation on a basic assumption all but universally accepted by historians of medieval thought: namely, that ancient and medieval christological thought are essentially in doctrinal (if not formulaic or verbal) continuity with one another. Most historians of medieval thought have perceived profound continuity between scholastic theological and exegetical thought and the patristic authorities with which such thought characteristically began. I argue here that high-medieval thinkers on the possible aspects of Christ's human nature—fear, sorrow, apparent ignorance and so forth—more often rupture such putative conceptual links and erase much or all dogmatic continuity with the very figures whose thought they seem to want to preserve or, in many cases, to rehabilitate. This argument has implications for the much larger theme of continuity and discontinuity in the history of Christian thought.

Discussion of what came to be called the possible dimensions of Christ's humanity did not begin in the medieval university or even in the worlds of ancient Christian writing. It began within the texts of the New Testament itself. Indeed—especially in light of classical Christian assumptions about divinity and the metaphysics of the incarnation—one of the curious features of the gospels, especially the three Synoptic Gospels is that each includes incidents in which Jesus at times clearly is, or at least certainly appears to be, in doubt, error, or ignorance. He makes statements that reveal uncertainty, utters prophecies that go unfulfilled, and asks questions demonstrating that he does not know things known by "his Father" or even by his followers.

In other episodes in the Synoptics, Jesus appears to be overcome with profound and sometimes violent emotion. The last hours of his life especially seem marked, not by serene assurance of divine oversight, but rather by terror, grief, and uncertainty. Such emotions are rarely more poignantly inscribed in the gospels than in the puzzled query of dereliction that, in Mark and Matthew, punctuates the long ordeal of his passion: "My God, my God," Jesus exclaims, "why have you forsaken me?" (Mark 15:34; Matt 27:46, NRSV). Jesus seems, thus, to distinguish himself, not by his immunity to the passions, but by the often-cruel intensity with which he appears to experience them.

Still other parts of the Gospels appear to suggest that Jesus was, at times, powerless to execute his own will and even in disharmony with his Father's. Jesus' nocturnal vigil in Gethsemane, for example, is marked not by sovereign control of his destiny but by helplessness, not by quiet surrender to the divine will but repeated resistance to it. Thus the gospels present us with a figure who is at least occasionally ignorant, passible, powerless, and recalcitrant. What makes this fact worthy of further inquiry is that Christian theologians in the premodern era have inevitably identified with the Incarnate Word, and especially his divinity, the opposite qualities of omniscience, impassibility, omnipotence, and obedience.

The first Christian theologians to show anxiety about Jesus' human ignorance, passion, and will were the later Gospel writers.[1] Among the most difficult and embarrassing texts for later Christian theologians to manipulate was Jesus' candid acknowledgment that he was ignorant of the time at which the Son of Man would return in glory. Jesus concludes the Apocalyptic Discourse in Mark by declaring that "about that day and hour no one knows, neither the angels in heaven, *nor the Son,* but only the Father (Mark 13:32; emphasis supplied). In this case, Matthew reflects no obvious discomfort with the version of the story he inherited from Mark and delivers the verse in essentially unaltered form (Matt 24:36). Interestingly enough, however, there are ancient manuscripts of the Gospel of Matthew whose scribes, perceiving a problem not recognized or acknowledged by the evangelist himself, dared to edit out the words "nor the Son."[2] The difficulty does not escape Luke's attention. He is so uncomfortable with the verse that he does not even attempt to edit it. Instead, he expunges it altogether from his account of the Discourse (Luke 21:25–37).

A second category of scriptural texts relating to Jesus' human knowledge are the many questions he asks in the Gospels, particularly in Mark. In Mark, after a woman with a hemorrhage touches Jesus' garments in the hopes of being cured, Jesus turns and asks, "Who touched my clothes" (Mark 5:30)? Receiving no satisfactory answer from his disciples, Jesus, still apparently ignorant, looks "all around" (Mark 5:31) to see who had touched him. Here Matthew modifies the story bequeathed by Mark. In the Matthean version of the story, Jesus is touched, turns and instantly recognizes the woman who had sought his cure (Matt 9:22). Any hint of ignorance is erased.

It is more usually the case that both Matthew and Luke rewrite texts inherited from Mark (or a source they all used) in which Jesus appears to be ignorant. In Mark 9 the disciples, arguing with a group of scribes, are asked by Jesus, "What are you discussing with them?" (Mark 9:16). In their versions of the story, Matthew and Luke both edit out the questions Jesus asks (see Matt 17:14). Somewhat later in Mark 9, the disciples, on the way to Capernaum, argue about who among them is "greatest" (Mark 9:34). When they arrive in Capernaum, Jesus asks them, "What were you arguing about on the way" (Mark 9:33)? Again, both Matthew and Luke omit the question posed to the disciples and, in their rendering of the story, Jesus marvelously knows the content of their discussion (Matt 18:1; Luke 9:47). Luke explicitly states that Jesus was able "to perceive the thought of their hearts" (Luke 9:47). In this case, Matthew and Luke do not simply edit out an embarrassing piece of the received story. They also transform a Markan pericope that incidentally alludes to Jesus' ignorance of some things into a story that intentionally reveals his extraordinary knowledge of many or all things.

Just as problematic for the later gospel writers are texts in which Jesus appears to experience and even to be overcome by turbulent emotion. In the Markan account of the passion, Jesus arrives at the Garden of Gethsemane and "begins to be terrified and troubled" (Mark 14:33). Apparently tormented, he poignantly announces to his disciples that he is "deeply grieved" (Mark 14:34). Matthew transmits this part of the story in essentially unaltered form (Matt 26:38). Luke, however, expurgates from the Markan narrative any reference to Jesus' terror or agony (Luke 22:39). Moreover, he subtly transfers the sorrow present in the original story from Jesus to the disciples. The disciples, Luke tells us, are sleeping "because of their grief" (Luke 22:62). Indeed, in order to keep the disciples from being vanquished by their sorrow, Jesus must sharply command them to "get up and pray" (Luke 22:46). The discomfort with Mark in Luke becomes outright denial in John. The author of the Fourth Gospel borrows from Mark (or a common source), it seems, only to mock his picture of a vulnerable and frightened Jesus. Where the Markan Jesus implores his Father three times to "let this cup pass," John's Jesus practically ridicules this possibility: "What shall I say," he sarcastically inquires, " 'Father save me from this hour'? No, it is for this reason that I have come to this hour" (John 11:27). In the Fourth Gospel, Jesus experiences no fear and little sorrow at the prospect of his death. There is no tension between the will of the Son and the will of the Father. Only in the noncanonical gospels do we find a figure so immune to human vicissitude, passion, and finitude. Had this picture of Jesus triumphed decisively over Mark's, his victory may have saved later Christian exegetes much embarrassment, anxiety, and labor.

There is perhaps no more pathetic episode in the Gospels than Jesus' anguished cry of dereliction at the moment of his death (Mark 16:34). Again, Luke is uncomfortable with the note of grief, complaint, and perplexity sounded here. True, he allows Jesus to cry at the moment of his death, but in his version of the story, Jesus cries, "Father, into your hands I commend my spirit" (Luke 23:46). Luke drains Jesus' final cry of the sorrow and doubt with which Mark had drenched it. Where in Mark, Jesus is the object of his Father's action (abandonment), here he is the subject of the action. In Luke, it is Jesus who stoically superintends the conclusion of his own death.

A similar pattern of embarrassed editorializing occurs in the transmission of those parts of Mark in which Jesus seems to be in disharmony with the divine will. In Mark, Jesus arrive at Gethsemane and announces that he is "grieved even to death" (Mark 14:34) and begs his father three times to "let this cup pass" (Mark 14:36, 39, 41). Matthew transmits this part of the story with almost complete fidelity to Mark (Matt 26:39, 42, 44). The insistence with which the Markan Jesus presses this request was, perhaps, too strong to allow Luke to strike out these passages entirely from his Passion Narrative. Yet Luke has Jesus ask this question only once (Luke 22:42). Moreover, he emphasizes more than both Mark and Matthew the unity of Jesus' will with his Father's. Where in Matthew, Jesus begins his prayer by saying, "Father, if it be *possible*, let this cup pass from me" (Matt 26:39), the Lukan Jesus begins his prayer, "Father, if you are *willing*..." (Luke 22: 42). Just as Luke's Jesus is sovereign over the passions, so too is his will in near-perfect accord with the Father's. Taken together, these texts in the Synoptics reveal there was significant discomfort with the genuinely human dimensions of Jesus' experience as early as the second generation of Gospel writers. It is an anxiety that, in different contexts and in slightly different forms, would be felt in Christian theological writing for at least the next thirteen centuries.

Yet not all early Christian groups were made anxious by such texts. In fact, the fourth-century "Arians"[3] found them most convincing proof of their conviction that the Son of God was a creature or lesser deity. It was these very texts to which, over and over, they pointed their "orthodox" opponents' eyes. In the study that follows I analyze how the Arians, their orthodox opponents, and three high-medieval theologians and exegetes—Peter Lombard, Thomas Aquinas, and Bonaventure—interpreted these problematic scriptural texts and how they understood Christ's human passions. As I move through the following chapters, it will be observed that the exegetical maneuvers that the ancient fathers needed in order—not to put too fine a point on it—to make the scriptures sing an orthodox tune is then mirrored, many centuries later, by the high-medieval authors' tacit manipulation of their patristic authorities, which was intended both to make their patristic authorities both coherent with one another and orthodox in content. Second, it will become clear that the problematics first raised in the "Arian controversy" continued to haunt the writings of the high-medieval scholastics long after Arianism had disappeared as a concrete social and historical force. This is in part because the ancient fathers with whom high-medieval authors began their reflections—Hilary of Poitiers, Ambrose of Milan, Jerome, Augustine of Hippo, and others—themselves were involved in literary polemic against "Arians" they knew or knew of. But it is also because Arian exegesis posed the most difficult threat to orthodox understanding of Jesus' passions, and that *theological* threat remained real for many centuries, even when unmoored from the specific ecclesial, social, and polemical context in which it originated. Finally, juxtaposition and comparison of patristic and high-scholastic interpretations of the scriptural texts considered in this study reveals that, under the guise of unchanging assimilation, incorporation, and transmission of a unanimous tradition, fissures and discontinuities actually forcefully separate the two bodies of thought, ancient and medieval, in such as way as to make continuing talk of dogmatic continuity deeply problematic.

It seems especially appropriate to address these questions of continuity and change now, in a time of renewed interest in the reception of the fathers in Latin theology, signaled so spectacularly by the recently-published *The Reception of the Church Fathers in the West*.[4] Several of the essays collected in these two volumes take up the problem I address here. Some essay, for example, acknowledge that high-medieval commentators had to "explain" or "interpret" dubious or problematic patristic opinion.[5] But none makes the argument that I advance here, namely, that such "explanation" or "interpretation" could and often did involve quite radical distortion of patristic opinion. What I see rather than organic change, exposition, interpretation, or correction is novelty, erasure, and eisegesis.

In the end, then, this new book is about an ancient theme in the history of Christian thought, namely, the problem of doctrinal change and continuity. Like all historical theologians, I have read and wrestled with the great Cardinal Newman's elegant, profound, and learned essay on doctrinal development.[6] It is with great respect and with a sense of the gravity of what I am saying when I state that, while Cardinal Newman explains much, his theory tells us very little indeed about the history of interpretation of Christ's passions, which is not a history of continuity, or even organic development, but of often radical discontinuity, trial, novelty, and even heterodoxy.

Late in the composition of this work—indeed, after all but the introduction and conclusion were drafted—I encountered Paul Gondreau's massive and fine study of the treatment of the passions of Christ's soul in Thomas's *Summa*. Gondreau's volume is certainly, as Richard Cross has declared, "the first place than an English-speaker would look for a thorough account of this anthropological question."[7]

In this volume, I have not aimed for the sort of thorough account of Thomas's account of the passions of Christ in Thomas's *Summa* which Gondreau has so splendidly achieved, though I have done my best to note where his arguments intersect with my own. Instead, I have concentrated on the use of patristic authorities in Peter Lombard's *Sentences* and on the commentaries on the *Sentences* by Bonaventure and Thomas Aquinas. My aim is not simply to talk about Thomas, though he looms large in this study, nor do I wish to concentrate on his *Summa*, though I do not ignore it. Rather I concentrate in the Sentence commentary on a genre of literature that was, in its day, in many ways more important than any other genre of high-medieval theological literature.

I concentrate, secondly, on *both* Thomas and Bonaventure's Sentence commentaries (with occasional references to Albert the Great) because, as Thomas is known to rely on Bonaventure as well as on the commentary of his teacher Albertus Magnus (though not slavishly),[8] the two can be considered together for the purposes of understanding a more or less common way of approaching the Lombard's *Sentences*. In particular, the way in which each uses, appropriates, shapes, and transmits his inherited patristic authorities is, so I shall argue, all but indistinguishable from one another and, more important, *entirely characteristic of the era in which they wrote*. Through much of the thirteenth century, it is quite possible to talk of a common "scholastic" approach to problems in commentaries on the *Sentences* (and I shall want to talk, throughout this book, about that common approach. This is not, needless to say, to go the next step and say the outcomes were inevitably common.) But at some point—put authoritatively right around 1285 in a brilliant new essay by Russell Friedman[9]—theological "schools," especially the Franciscan, Dominican, and Augustinian, develop in ways that make it impossible to talk any more of a single sort of approach to the problem of Christ's passions. But in the mid-thirteenth century, these schools had not yet developed. It is, I repeat, possible and even advisable to speak of a common high-scholastic approach shared by the figures under consideration in this study. Indeed, I hope to convince the specialist reader that the conclusions I defend here have implications for the nature of central- or high-medieval theological and exegetical thought as such.

Let me say a word about organization. In the second chapter, I talk about Arian, including less well known Latin Arian sources, using some of the problematic texts I have described above. I attempt to analyze how the Arians interpreted these texts, show why they thought it theologically necessary to analyze them as they did, and to hint at the dismay caused in the developing pro-Nicene party. This chapter is the foundation of my argument that the Arians, long after they ceased to be a political or social force in Western Europe, served as silent interlocutors for the great medieval authors under consideration here.[10]

The following five chapters then treat ancient and medieval orthodox responses to five of the major issues raised by the Arians. Chapter three treats the interpretation of Luke 2:52, which states that "Jesus progressed in wisdom," an immensely problematic text for patristic writers, as was Mark 13:32, in which Jesus appears to avow his ignorance of the day of judgment, a topic I treat in chapter three. In chapter five, I examine Hilary of Poitier's attempt to neutralize Arian subordinationism by arguing that Christ felt no physical pain in his passion and death. It is in this chapter that the wide gap between patristic and high-medieval interpretation of the same text is especially obvious, as is the high-medieval anxiety to make Hilary say something he quite evidently did not intend to say. In chapter six, I study the interpretation of the Gethsemane pericope and the ways in which Christian authors dealt with Christ's sorrow and fear. In chapter seven, I examine reflection on the act of Christ's praying (as distinct from the passions he expresses while praying). Here we will see that the Arians made much of his submission to the supreme Deity, his apparent powerlessness, his doubt, his praying for himself, and God not, apparently, answering his prayer.

The medieval figures discussed here are by many often (and rightly) regarded as theological saints. Their ideas are, for some readers, of existential and religious as well as intellectual interest. I understand this. Nonetheless, I have felt I have had to make my case, in places, quite vigorously. I hope my respect for the medieval authors, of whose staggering erudition and achievements I simply stand in awe, is never obscured. But one must distinguish between respect and idolatry. I remain convinced that the beginning of error in this realm of historical inquiry is to accept uncritically the actors' own description of their procedures and, in particular, their views, as expressed in actual theological and exegetical *practice*, of the authority of the past and its continuity with the present. I also remain confident that scholars of Thomas, especially, have been predisposed to gloss over or minimize the degree of their hero's intellectual discontinuity with the patristic past. To make an argument such as this and to determine whether it sheds any light on the past demands, of course, that the evidence be presented convincingly. That is my job; I doubt I will convince everyone. But it also requires that the arguments put forward be heard with open minds, and discussed with thoughtfulness and, above all, civility.

2

Humanity, Divinity, and Biblical Exegesis in Early Arian Thought

As is now widely recognized, the Scriptures and their interpretation were not mere embroidery in a larger theological dispute during the "Arian controversy."[1] In fact, the relationship between theological discourse and the Scriptures is rather the reverse of the one often assumed. Far from being fodder for proof-texting of already-established theological positions, the theological language was in fact the fruit of reflection and argument over key scriptural passages. It may well be true that the controversy stemmed from dispute over the meaning of only a dozen or so such texts. Instructive here is Aloys Grillmeier's remark on the role played by a few select texts in controversy: "However much the whole of Scripture continued to be read, theological polemics, precisely in trinitarian and christological discussion, restricted themselves to a certain number of important or disputed scriptural texts."[2] That is true. But that is very different from suggesting that the Scriptures functioned as mere proof-text to what was central, namely philosophically-informed theological argument. These scriptural texts were the initial and abiding source of the quarrel. Examining both genuine Arian and Nicene sources in this chapter, we will identify which scriptural texts were crucial in the dispute. We will also briefly gesture toward the ways in which they were interpreted by the early Arian writers. But first a word on sources.

Sources

It is now almost idle to observe that, in the history of Christian thought, our information about movements deemed "heretical" derives, for the most part, from hostile, not wholly reliable observations of victorious or "orthodox" parties. For that reason, we must be particularly careful to maintain a critical, sometimes agnostic point of view on "orthodox" perception and judgment. Naturally, this principle applies to early Arianism as well. In this case, as in analogous ones, it remains true that the bulk of our knowledge of this heretical movement comes from writers—Athanasius, Hilary of Poitiers, Ambrose of Milan, the Cappadocian fathers, and others less familiar—intensely and, in cases, ferociously opposed to it. Not surprisingly, the anti-Arian writings these thinkers produce rarely can be trusted entirely. Nonetheless, they are hardly without importance or use. For one thing, it would have been pointless for the pro-Nicene party to refute only arguments the "Arians" did not in fact assert. Thus, we can learn quite a lot, particularly about what scriptural texts the Arians used, and how they interpreted them, from biased sources.

Fortunately, we are not entirely wanting in genuine sources for early Arianism, particularly for the late-fourth and early-fifth centuries. Indeed, we have something like a dozen or so authentic sources for Arianism during this period. These sources take a whole variety of literary forms: conciliar *acta* and glosses, commentaries, (including the very lengthy and valuable Pseudo-Chrysostom *Opus Imperfectum in Matthaeum*),[3] an unfinished fifth-century commentary on the First Gospel (with "orthodox" emendation) and, interestingly, two commentaries on Job,[4] as well as homilies, creeds, letters, liturgies, church orders, and a few other fragmentary writings.[5] Putting together materials from both these orthodox and non-orthodox sources, we can achieve a remarkably clear picture about which scriptural texts were considered important in the controversy, as well as of how such texts were interpreted by the early "Arians." Before discussing these, however, we must first analyze the crucial soteriological motivations the Arians had for interpreting the Scriptures as they did.

Soteriology and Anthropology in Early Arianism

One of the curiosities of scholarly work on the Arians is that, for the first eight decades of the twentieth century, few, if any, scholars perceived that either Arius or the Arians had compelling soteriological reasons for emphasizing that the Son was a creature or a reduced, inferior, or imperfect divinity. Most scholars viewed the Arians—at least those who do not dismiss them as self-evidently heretical[6] or even heathenish[7]—as logicians, cosmologists, rigid syllogists, or as thinkers whose interests were otherwise largely philosophical or obsessively focused on the monarchy of God. Harnack is quite representative of early twentieth-century work on Arianism in this respect. He not only fails to talk about Arian soteriology; he denies that it had any.[8] More recently, R. D. Williams has contended that, whatever else it was, Arianism was surely not a theology of salvation.[9] In some ways these views are quite excusable. Virtually all of the extant writings of Arius himself concern the ontological relation of Father and Son (and many of the texts we now have were not edited when Harnack was writing).[10] On the other hand, it still can be maintained justly that Harnack, Williams, and others focused too intently on the writings of Arius and insufficiently on the writings of the early Arians. When scholars began to examine the latter more carefully, a very different picture came into view.

One of the main reasons Hanson rightly designates Gregg and Groh's *Early Arianism: A View of Salvation* a "milestone in the study of Arianism"[11] is that, as their title explicitly implies:

> Gregg and Groh maintain emphatically that Arius and Arianism
> had a soteriology, that the Arian Christ was specifically designed to be
> a Saviour and that neither Arius nor Arianism can be understood
> until this point is realised.[12]

This "welcome and timely" emphasis upon the soteriology of Arianism," Hanson emphasized was in "strong contrast to almost everybody who preceded them in the field."[13] Part of Gregg and Groh's achievement derived from their willingness to examine not only the writings of Arius himself but of the early Arians. Having scrutinized those writings, Gregg and Groh came to the conclusion that "one of the most important keys to unlocking Arian Christology and soteriology is to be found in Stoic-influenced ethical theory," especially that of late Stoicism.[14] More specifically, Gregg and Groh argued that the Arian Christ was improvable, capable of advance in virtue and knowledge, ever moving toward perfection. If the Savior were mutable, as the Arians insisted he was, it was because he was capable of progress in knowledge, love, and virtue. As such, he could serve as an example of to his imperfect and sinful human followers. In the Arian view, then, Christ the Savior's redemptive work was to educate humanity in moral *paideia*. As Gregg and Groh sum up their argument, "Arians are arguing not for the stratification of the universe but for the dynamics of redemption whereby creatures, in emulation of the creature of perfect discipline, may be themselves begotten as equals to the Son."[15]

While commending the general emphasis on soteriology given by Gregg and Groh, Hanson has argued against the particular soteriology they attribute to the Arians. Essentially, Hanson criticizes Gregg and Groh on three points. First of all, Hanson argues (convincingly) that Arian soteriology is not indebted to the terms and thought-world of Stoicism. If the early Arians wished to depict a mutable or improvable Son, as Hanson certainly conceded (if for reasons other than those suggested by Gregg and Groh) they did, "the language of the Bible was sufficient." Second, while some Arian writers are, in fact, anxious to depict a Son who can progress toward moral perfection, other Arian writers (particularly late ones) seem less comfortable with such a Son. Finally:

> The third and most serious objection to the account of Arianism given by Gregg and Groh is that the Son cannot give an exam-ple of human achievement of perfection, because he is precisely not a man. The Son assumed a *soma apsychon,* a body without a human mind or soul.... The Word incarnate in the Arian scheme may give some sort of example, but certainly not that of a human being making moral progress.[16]

The doctrine of a "soulless body" (σῶμα ἄψυχον) was, as Hanson has emphasized, crucial to the soteriology of the Arians. Essentially, this is because the exemplarist ethical soteriology emphasized by Gregg and Groh was far less important to early Arian writers than was the notion of a suffering God.[17] This idea Hanson identifies, again quite accurately, as "the heart of Arianism."[18] In Arian eyes, humanity is redeemed only if God suffers.[19] At the same time, the Arians were quite loath to assign suffering (or change of any kind) to the Su-preme God. Thus, in the Arian system, the Son functions to perform the suffering required for human redemption. The Arians, in effect, (as Hanson has plainly put it) taught "two unequal gods, a High God incapable of human experiences, and a lesser God who, so to speak, did his dirty work for him."[20]

This sort of redemptive work, it cannot be overemphasized, was possible, in the Arian view, *only* if the Son lacked a human soul or mind. If the Son had taken on a complete human nature, with soul and mind (as the Arians vigor-ously denied), it would have been quite easy to shield the Logos (as the pro-Nicene party constantly attempted to do) from human finitude, limitation, and suffering. One would need only to assign these quintessentially human expe-riences to the human soul, or even (if more awkwardly) to the human flesh, of Christ. The Arian doctrine of *soma apsyschon* effectively blocked this ploy. For if the Logos assumed a body without a soul, it followed remorselessly that the Logos *must* have been the subject of these experiences, including suffering. In fact, the Arians argued that *if* the Logos had been screened from the human experience of suffering, humanity had not been redeemed. Thus, the anonymous author of the *Opus Imperfectum in Matthaeum* (*Unfinished Work on Matthew*), complains that if it were a "mere man" (*purum hominem*) who suffered on the cross, humanity was doomed. "The death of a man," he concludes bluntly, "does not save us."[21] God had to suffer.

Once we begin to comprehend the motives and nature of Arian soteriology, it becomes obvious why the Arians were so anxious to comb the Scriptures, especially the Gospels, for proof of the Son's ontological inequality to the Father. In this they were impressively skilled. In fact, one of the features of Arian theology that caused its orthodox opponents special distress was the Arian eagerness and talent for searching the Gospels, especially, but not only the Synoptics, for proof of the inferiority of Christ's divine nature. As Gregg and Groh have observed, "the picture of Arius as a logician and dialectician" has been so "firmly entrenched in all our minds that it has been easy to overlook the degree to which appeal to the Scriptures was fundamental for Arius" and, it might be added, the later Arians.[22] Hanson, too, is on the mark when he states, "the dispute was about the interpretation of the Bible" and that the philosophical language used by Athanasius was "all devoted to what was ultimately a Scriptural argument."[23] Actually, this observation applies with equal force to the Arians and the orthodox. Scriptural warrant and support were essential for both.

In addition, it may be observed that, hermeneutically, however they differed in interpretation of specific texts, both sides approached the scriptural text atomistically. Both lifted certain key texts (and both sides agreed to a remarkable degree about which were the pertinent ones) and attempted to interpret them, often in radically decontextualized fashion. This is certainly not to fault them for not being modern. It is simply to observe that, however incompatible, even contradictory their interpretation of specific texts, their basic approach and exegetical assumptions—particularly the "atomic" principle of interpretation—were quite indistinguishable.[24] "All of the antagonists," concludes T. E. Pollard, "were primarily interested in the literal interpretation of Scripture, and it was on this ground that the battles were fought."[25]

Following Athanasius too closely, some modern scholars have argued that it was only the Arian side that so interpreted the scriptures. T. E. Pollard, for example, argues:

That the Arians were extreme literalists is borne out by Athanasius's criticism of them. He criticizes them, however, not because they interpret the Scriptures literally, but because they isolate carefully selected texts from their context and interpret them literally without any regard for their context or for the general teaching of Scripture.[26]

But the pro-Nicenes were no less capable than their counterparts of reading the text of Scripture in this decontextualized fashion. Indeed, it could be argued that the Arians were generally on much stronger ground when exegeting the Bible. Some critics have argued that the Nicenes so doctored the pertinent texts as to have practically intentionally falsified the meaning of Scripture. Hanson in particular has argued that "when arguing about the career and character of Jesus Christ himself as depicted in the Gospels," the Arians "are usually on much firmer ground than their opponents. Here both Athanasius and Hilary [of Poitiers] are driven to take refuge in the most unconvincing arguments."[27] Hanson would surely have agreed with Maximinus (whom he quotes), when he observed to Augustine, "the divine Scripture does not fare badly in our teaching so that it has to receive correction (emendationem) from us."[28] One does not have to be an Arian apologist to perceive that Hanson is often quite on the mark about the tortured character of Nicene biblical interpretation. Hanson observes of his attitude toward anti-Arian hermeneutics in his own book, "There is little denunciation or derision, little approval or dissent."[29] But there is in fact quite a lot of derision, possibly much of it quite justified, when it comes to Nicene exegesis. Be that as it may, it was over the Scriptures and their interpretation that this theological battle was fought. "All of the antagonists," concludes T. E. Pollard, "were primarily interested in the literal interpretation of Scripture, and it was on this ground that the battles were fought."[30]

Creaturely Limitation: The Key Biblical Texts and Their Meaning in Early Arianism

Despite the hermeneutical similarities, the Arians, both Eastern and Western, ruthlessly focused on texts that, in their eyes, indicated quite clearly that the Son of God had experienced pain, ignorance, sorrow, fear, abandonment, distress, need, and other sorts of creaturely limitation and weakness. As Hanson points out, "The Arian theologians whom [Athanasius] was opposing made...a great point of the infirmities, weaknesses and limitations of the historical Jesus...in order to argue that these frailties demonstrated that the pre-existent Son was inferior."[31] Gregg and Groh concur: "One of the best attested and most ignored aspects of early Arian Christology has to do precisely with the chronicling of the creaturely limitations of their redeemer."[32] This is evident from both Arian sources and, more fully, from orthodox sources, not least of all from Athanasius.

In his *Orations* against the Arians, Athanasius (296–373) complains bitterly that the Arians, their hearts hardened like that of Pharaoh, perceive only the Savior's "human characteristics" (τὰ ἀνθρώπινα).[33] He then proceeds to give a remarkably rich description of scriptural texts precious to the Arians, which can be organized into roughly five categories: texts that prove (in the Arian view) the radical ontological difference between Father and Son; texts that suggest the Son was overcome by irrational passion; texts that indicate the Incarnate Son was ignorant of some things; texts that show Jesus in prayer and, by implication, in a state of creaturely submission; and the texts in the Synoptics that establish Jesus' belief that he was finally forsaken by the Father.

To Athanasius, these Arian interpretations and ideas are all "irreligious concepts," evidence that the Arians had (again, like Pharaoh) willfully hardened their hearts. Nonetheless, he goes to some length to enumerate them. Of the many texts favored by the Arians to demonstrate the inferior nature of the Son, Athanasius observes that his opponents preferred Matt 28:18 ("All power is given to Me") and Luke 10:22 ("All things are delivered to me by the Father"). They also invoked three Johannine texts: John 5:22: "The Father . . . has committed all judgment to the Son"; John 3:35–36: "The Father loves the Son and has given all things into his hand"; and John 6:37: "All that the Father gives me will come to me." Athanasius and the pro-Nicenes in general were convinced that the Gospel of John was on their side; Athanasius once observed that it was the Fourth Gospel that "especially condemned" and "vanquished" the Arians.[34] But the Arians were able to exploit John as well, though, in general, they preferred the Synoptic Gospels to the fourth.

Referring both to the Synoptics and to John, the Arians were quick to point to texts in which the Incarnate Son appeared to be overwhelmed by uncontrollable passion, an infallible sign, in Arian eyes, of the vulnerability associated with the state of creaturehood. Thus the Arians, according to Athanasius, pointed their opponents' eyes to John 12:27, where Jesus, in agony, admits, "Now is my soul troubled" (τετάρακται), or to John 13:21, where he is described as "troubled in spirit." The Arians made much of the entire Passion and above all the Gethsemane pericope, especially the prayer by Jesus to "let this cup pass" (Matt 26:39) and his admission that his soul was "troubled unto death" (Matt 26:38). One of Arius's first opponents, Alexander of Alexandria, mordantly if quite accurately observed, "The Arians remember all the passages concerning the Savior's passion."[35] Hilary of Poitiers reports that the Arians interpret this admission to mean that the Son was:

far from the blessedness and incorruption of God, whose soul permits itself to be dominated by fear of imminent sorrow, who was so terrified by the necessity of death.[36]

Athanasius informs us that, based on such texts as these, the Arians would argue, "If he were truly the Father's power (δύναμις), he would not have felt any trouble or fear."[37]

It is here, perhaps, rather than in connection with the Arian soteriological view, that late Stoic philosophical thought influenced the controversy, particularly the notion of the impassibility of deity and the undesirability of violent emotion, which, both sides agreed, would incline one to error and sin. Both sides, Arian and Nicene, agreed that the Supreme God was immutable, and each concurred that a wise man (sophos) was one who had achieved freedom from passion (apatheia).[38] As Gregg and Groh note, "the primary mark of the sage was his ἀπάθεια or, as it was occasionally termed by a Platonist aiming at the same target...παντελὴς ἀπάθεια ('complete indifference')."[39] For the Nicenes, it was urgent to demonstrate that the Incarnate Son was not, as he appeared to be, overcome by desperate passion in Gethsemane. Jerome (ca. 342–420), ever irascible, is quite representative here. He sp[^]enetically denounces the Arians for suggesting Christ felt fear in the Garden: "Let those who think that the Savior feared death and in fear of his passion said, 'Let this cup pass from me'—let them turn pink with shame."[40]

If strong and potentially uncontrollable emotion made the Nicenes anxious, then the appearance of a nescient Jesus made them even more so. Naturally, no influential Greek philosophy of the pre-Christian or Christian period celebrated ignorance; even less did any regard it as compatible either with divinity or the achievement of wisdom. It is no wonder, then, that the Arians (as Athanasius tells us) delighted in observing that Jesus is often found asking questions. "Who do men say that I am?" (Matt 16:13). "Where had Lazarus been lain?" (John 11:34). "How many loaves had the disciples?" (Mark 6:38).

By far the text most frequently cited by the Arians in this connection was Mark 13:32: "No one knows about that day or hour, not even the angels in heaven, nor the Son, but only the Father." Here the Incarnate Son seems unambiguously to confess his ignorance of the eschatological day of judgment; it was a text that was to give the pro-Nicene party grave difficulty. In his work On the Holy Spirit (381), Ambrose explicitly ties the subordinationist reading of the text to the Arians.[41] Genuine Arian texts also demonstrate both to what extent and how it was used. In one of the Latin Arian fragments Gryson has edited, we see Mark 13.32 used as a scriptural reinforcement to support the radical ontological difference between Father and Son. The author of this fragment makes his point by positing a long set of antinomies between the Father and Son, each of which is intended to demonstrate that they are of two substances, not one. Thus, they are unequal in power. One is ungenerated, the other only begotten. There is one who commands and the other who accepts commands, one who sends and another who is sent, one who is impassible and one who suffered. And so on.[42] The fragment concludes with a supporting reference to Mark 13:32: "There is the Son who denies he knows that day and the Father who in his power can know it."[43] In the view of this Arian author, Mark 13:32 demonstrated unequivocally that the Son, deprived of knowledge the Father clearly had, was therefore unequal to the Father. "How, the Arians ask, is he able to be Logos or God who . . . had to learn by inquiry?"[44]

Against such a reading, orthodox contemporaries would attempt, none more vigorously than Ambrose of Milan (ca. 339–97) and Hilary of Poitiers (ca. 315–67), to show where the Arians had erred. We will consider their responses in detail below. Gregg and Groh observed that, for late-Stoicism, lack of knowledge meant the Son could not be considered *sophos,* a wise man. But the more important point here is that, for *both* sides, lack of knowledge would have meant the Son was not fully divine, and this, in turn, would have suggested to the pro-Nicene party that he could not have served as redeemer.[45]

Another text very often invoked by the Arians in this connection was Luke 2:52, which states that Jesus "increased in wisdom," a text that implies that the Son was not noetically or ontologically equal to Eternal Wisdom and that he was increasingly less ignorant over time, though never, presumably, omniscient. "How then," the Arians asked, "can he be the true Wisdom of God, who increased in wisdom and was ignorant of what he asked of others?"[46] This, too, is a question over which much orthodox ink would be spilt for the next millennium. We find Augustine (among other Latin pro-Nicene writers) wrestling with this text in his anti-Arian work *Against Maximinus,* written just two years before his death (428), by which time Arianism had arrived in North Africa.[47] His contemporary bishop, Ambrose of Milan, who was preoccupied with the Arians, returned to the text over and over in an attempt to combat the Arian exegesis of it.[48] In his *Treatise on the Psalms,* Jerome denounced the "insanity" of the heretical Arian interpretation of the text and furnished his own, different reading.[49] And this only scratches the surface of the scores of Latin exegetes who attempted to come to grips with this problematic text.

Other texts that demonstrated the creaturehood of the Word were those copious instances in which Jesus is pictured at prayer in a state of submission and need. Why the Arians ask, should the Son have any occasion to pray? If indeed he was of the very substance of the Father, then it rigorously follows that he should need nothing. It is necessary for creatures to require divine assistance. But since the Son also prayed for such, it follows that he "must be a creature and one of the things generated."[50]

Again, the Son utters words of supreme vulnerability, weakness, defeat, and dereliction on the cross: "My God, My God, why have you forsaken me?"

(Matt 27:46). How can such a Son be the Father's essential Word, "without whom the Father never was," if he uttered such a cry? "How," the Arians conclude, "can he be the Word of God, this Son who had slept, wept, and asked questions—just as ordinary men do?"[51] "This, then," Athanasius wearily concludes, "is what these irreligious men allege in their discourses."[52]

Likewise, in his *Theological Orations*, the Cappadocian theologian Gregory of Nyssa (ca. 330–ca. 395) lists those assertions about the Incarnate Logos that his theological opponents relished and which they insisted were given in the explicit sense of the Scriptures: Christ's ignorance; his subordination; that he prayed; that he asked questions; that he grew physically and in wisdom; that he was being perfected; that he experienced hunger and fatigue; that he was sorrowful, wept, and endured agony; and that he was submissive to his Father.[53] It would be otiose to describe them, but very similar catalogues of Arian arguments (and the Scriptures that inspired them) appear in the works of other Eastern anti-Arian writers.[54]

From the Western Nicene party, no writer took on the Arian exegesis of these problematic texts more vigorously than Hilary of Poitiers, particularly in his most important dogmatic work, *De Trinitate*. The anti-Arian animus and intent of *De Trinitate* is so pronounced that Jerome thought the work entitled *Adversos Arianos*.[55] Written while Hilary was in exile in Phrygia,[56] where he probably encountered Arianism in its homoiousian form, Hilary complains bitterly that his theological opponents have usurped the Scriptures of *our* faith (*fidei nostrae*)—that is, of the pro-Nicene party.[57] He then offers a very useful, compact catalogue of the sorts of scriptural passages which the Arians delighted in "seizing upon" (*rapiunt usurpationem*) and which the pro-Nicene party found so difficult to explain away.[58] Like Athanasius, Hilary emphasizes how fiercely the Arians exploited Mark 13:32, how insistently they contended that his ignorance of the day and hour of the eschatological judgment proved there was a real ontological distinction between Father and Son. This avowal of ignorance the Arians interpret as evidence of an inferior nature (*infirmam naturam*) and, in Hilary's words, an insult to his divinity (*contumeliam divinitatis*). Hilary contemptuously dismisses this "godless blasphemy" as part of the "most ridiculous arguments"(*stultissimis professionibus*) of the Arians.[59] Nonetheless, behind the rhetoric of contempt there seems to lie genuine anxiety about the Arian exegesis of the text.

Again, like Athanasius, Hilary emphasizes how vigorously the Arians focused on the passion of Jesus, particularly those texts in John (12:27) and Matthew (26:38, 39) in which Jesus "trembles with fear," acknowledges his soul to be filled with sorrow, and asks his Father if it is possible to avoid the "brutality of bodily punishment." Likewise, the Arians make much of the text in which

Jesus asks God, "why have you forsaken me?" (Matt 27:46)[60] and the text in Luke in which Jesus ends his life by saying, "Father, into your hands I commend my spirit" (Luke 23:46). Hilary tells us in De Trinitate 10.71 that Jesus' cry of dereliction and his commendation of spirit was, for the Arians, the "chief way to deny his divinity."[61] For the Arians, these scriptural texts indicate that the Son lacked divine "assurance of power" (potestatis securitate) and the incorruption of spirit that does not feel pain or fear bodily suffering (corporalis poenae). After all, the Arians (Hilary tells us) would argue, anxiety (anxietas), fear, and desolation are all incompatible with possessing a fully divine nature (and Hilary would agree).[62] So is the experience of pain (dolor) and of being abandoned and vanquished in the passion. All these scriptural texts thus prove, to the Arians, that the Son's nature is inferior to God the Father's (inferioris a Deo Patre naturae); they prove, in particular, that the Son did not possess the nature of the impassible God (inpassibilis Dei).[63] One genuine Arian theological text states that the Son commended his spirit to the Father in order, precisely, to demonstrate that he was always subject to or beneath (subiectum) him.[64]

Though Hilary of Poitiers does not make much of Matt 20:23 ("Jesus said to them, 'You will indeed drink from my cup, but to sit at my right or left is not for me to grant. These places belong to those for whom they have been prepared by my Father' "), it is quite clear from many other anti-Arian writers that this was a disputed text through the sixth century. From Ambrose in his fourth century De Fide to Pseudo-Vigilius of Thapse's Opus contra Uarimadum Arianum, quasi-catechetical polemical instructions are produced on "how to respond to the Arians if they say x," and both gave lengthy advice to their readers on how to respond if Matt 20:23 was used by their theological foes.[65] An early Arian sermon edited by C. H. Turner focuses very heavily on this verse and its implications of divine inequality.[66]

According to Hilary, the Arians also frequently resorted to Mark 10:18 ("Why do you call me good?" Jesus answered. "No one is good except God alone") to establish a metaphysical distinction between Father and Son.[67] One of the authentic Arian scoliae on the Council of Aquileia demonstrates how, precisely, many Arians (it is one of the few Arian texts to explicitly invoke Arius—in fact, "the divine teaching of Arius") liked to interpret this text (Eusebius is also named as one of many bishops who favored it). It declares that even the Son cannot bear comparison with "the one through whom goodness was made."[68] Just as a human being is not to be compared to Christ, so Christ cannot be compared to God.[69] John 14:28 ("You heard me say, 'I am going away and I am coming back to you.' If you loved me, you would be glad that I am going to the Father, for the Father is greater than I") was put to similar use by the Arians. Members of the pro-Nicene party would vigorously respond, in word and deed, to what they perceived as the extremely dangerous Arian use and exegesis of this text. Indeed, at the Council of Aquileia (381), Ambrose famously debated at length with Palladius of Ratiara over the meaning of this text and finally anathematized him for it (with a chorus of bishops echoing his curse).[70] As is well known, Palladius was condemned at the Council. Whether his exegesis of this text was less convincing than that of Ambrose, though, is another matter.

As is obvious, these sorts of catalogues of scriptural texts bear close resemblances to each other. Indeed, they were more or less the same, regardless of whether they were Western or Eastern in origin. The reason, of course, is that both Eastern and Western Arians seized upon the same biblical passages to prove their point of divine inferiority. Gregg and Groh summarize the issue nicely when commenting: "the Arians pieced together a picture of the earthly Christ which emphasized the existential and psychological aspects of creaturely existence in the ministry of Jesus."[71]

Those existential and psychological aspects of creaturely existence would, however, haunt both patristic and medieval writers. The Arian insistence upon those aspects of Jesus' existence, given, so far as they could see, plainly in the Gospels, would shape christological and exegetical writing for more than a millennium.

3

Christus Proficiens?

Did Christ "Progress in Wisdom"?

Iesus proficiebat sapientia aetate et gratia apud Deum et homines.

—Luke 2:52

In an essay entitled "Church History and the Bible," Karlfried Froehlich once distinguished between the many biblical texts that have *had* a history and the few which really had *made* history.[1] His point was that, in the history of their effects, the different books and even individual verses of the Bible have had a very uneven influence. Some have been relatively neutral or unproductive in their visible historical impact. Others can almost be said to have brought into being, or at least to have contributed profoundly to the creation of, whole movements, institutions, ideas, and conflicts.

In Luke 2:52 we have a single sentence of the New Testament that falls naturally into that second, influential category: "Jesus progressed in wisdom (Gk.: προέκοπτεν [ἐν τῇ] σοφίᾳ; Lat.: *proficiebat sapientia*) and age and grace, among God and men." As Zachary Hayes has observed, this is a "text that has tantalized theologians over the ages."[2] As we have seen, it helped to create and did much to sustain the Arian controversy; Arius and his fellow travelers apparently delighted in pointing their adversaries' eyes to it. The text played an important role in the Nestorian dispute as well. In the Middle Ages, it would be discussed extensively in the writings of the major scholastics of the twelfth and thirteenth centuries. Besides being handled routinely in commentaries on Luke, the text stimulated the production of a new cluster of theological *quaestiones* in the christological parts of high-medieval *summae* and commentaries on the Lombard's *Sentences*. *Did* Jesus grow in human knowledge?[3] *What*, if anything, did he learn in this way? Did he learn *everything* in this way? *How*, exactly, did he acquire human knowledge, if at all?

From the third century through the eighth, Christian exegetes (both Greek and Latin) were deeply divided on the issue of whether Jesus in fact progressed in human knowledge. However, from the eighth century to the thirteenth, almost all Latin expositors denied that Jesus truly so progressed. Indeed, affirmation of real progress in knowledge would be interpreted, by the mid-eighth century, as a mark of christological dualism. Therefore, one who maintained that Jesus did really grow in human knowledge could expect to be stigmatized, on this issue at least, as heterodox.

In this context, it is remarkable that Thomas Aquinas was willing to depart, late in his career, from his mendicant contemporaries and teachers, from the majority opinion of the fathers and, interestingly, from his own early interpretation of the text. In fact, in his *Summa*, Thomas delivered what, in ancient and medieval exegetical context, appears to be an emphatic endorsement of the position that Jesus did indeed progress in human knowledge. Although this question has not received much attention in recent scholarship, *that* Thomas advanced such an interpretation, and that he appears to have been the first medieval thinker to have done so, have already been established by several scholars.[4] However, there has been almost no discussion of *how* Thomas used and differed from his patristic sources and his contemporaries and *why* he arrived, finally, at the position he did. My purpose in this chapter is to address these questions; more specifically, I hope to advance our understanding of Thomas's mature position in four steps.

First, I wish to provide a rich exegetical context for Thomas's exegesis of Luke 2:52. Only in this context can the distinctiveness and originality of Thomas's mature position be appreciated. To that end, I will first sketch out the major Greek and Latin patristic positions on the question of whether Christ did in fact progress in human knowledge. Here I will argue that Thomas borrows elements from the interpretations of Ambrose of Milan and John of Damascus, the figures with whom Thomas begins his mature discussion, but differs from both in significant ways.

Having outlined the major patristic interpretations of the verse, I will then analyze the position of four major thinkers from the high-scholastic period (Peter Lombard, Albertus Magnus, Bonaventure, and the early Thomas himself). I wish to show here that all four thinkers denied that Christ progressed in knowledge, at least in the sense that he passed from utter ignorance of something to knowledge of it. More technically, none allows that Christ progressed in "habitual" or "essential" knowledge or in abstracting new universal ideas from the data of sense experience by exercise of his active intellect.[5]

Having outlined the dominant high-scholastic interpretation of the verse, I will then analyze Thomas's later position, where he explicitly repudiates his earlier opinion and that of his mendicant confreres. Here, I will show that he asserts, with some important qualifications, that Christ *did* acquire new knowledge as a result of abstracting new ideas from his empirical sense experience.

Finally, I wish to account, at least in a provisional way, for Thomas's disagreement with his patristic predecessors and his scholastic contemporaries. What explains his change of heart and the novelty of his position? Here I wish to make two arguments. First, Thomas was simply willing, late in his career, to take more seriously than most of his patristic predecessors and all of his scholastic contemporaries the implications of the hypostatic union, in particular the conviction that the Word had assumed and used all the normal activities of the human person, especially the uniquely human power of abstraction. Second, he was more anxious than contemporaries to acknowledge that Christ had progressed in knowledge because he was more thoroughgoingly Aristotelian than they in his understanding of human cognition. It was, I suggest, his mature fidelity to Aristotelian epistemological assumptions that encouraged, perhaps even compelled him, to grant that Christ had indeed acquired new knowledge in the course of his human experience.

Ancient Interpretations

Of the five major interpretations of Luke 2:52 advanced in the ancient church, two were conceived by the early Arians and by Athanasius.[6] Perhaps the boldest of the five, the Arian interpretation of the text depended, as we have seen, on the fundamental philosophical assumption that communication between divinity and humanity required some kind of "reduction" or "lowering" of the deity. If the incarnation were to occur at all, the Arians assumed, it had to be undertaken by a being who was not fully divine. In short, the incarnational metaphysics of the Arians required a mediator who, though worthy of veneration and imitation, was inferior to the eternal Father.

For Arius and his followers, the philosophical assumption of the divine inferiority of the λόγος was amply supported by the evidence of the Scriptures. As we have seen, the Arians made much of the experiences of suffering, change, weakness, and limitation—in short, of the πάθος of Jesus—documented (as they saw it) so copiously in the Gospels.[7] What is more, they maintained that it was the λόγος itself, *not* the body appropriated in the Incarnation, that was the subject of these experiences. True, the divine λόγος had taken to itself a human body. However, the Arians insisted that this body was a *soulless* physical organism (σῶμα ἄψυχον). This is a point of cardinal importance. From the mid-fourth century onward, some (though not all) in the pro-Nicene party would argue that Jesus' human *soul* was the subject of the human passions, ignorance, and infirmities described in the Gospels. By this maneuver, the pro-Nicenes were able to screen the λόγος from human defect and imperfection and, therefore, to preserve the perfection of the Son's divinity. According to the logic of Arian anthropology, however, a body without a soul *could* not be the subject of these experiences. Put plainly, there was no mental or emotional organ in the human body to "process" them. It followed, for the Arians, that it was the divine λόγος, not the human soul, which experienced the πάθος registered so voluminously in the New Testament. Given this line of thinking, it is not surprising that the Arians interpreted Luke 2:52 to mean that it was the λόγος itself that "progressed in wisdom."[8] It was this reading of the gospel text, along with others like it, that awoke Athanasius from his dogmatic slumbers.

Paradoxically, the nature of Athanasius's refutation of the Arian interpretation of Luke 2:52 depends on an anthropological assumption he shares with his heretical archenemies. Like the Arians, Athanasius (d. 373) assumed for most of his career—and, significantly, at the time of the composition of *Orations*—that Christ did not have a human soul.[9] Thus, though he will occasionally ascribe human weakness and limitation to the "human part" (τὸ ἀνθρώπινον)[10]—i.e., the body—of the Incarnate Word, the lack of a human soul will make this exegetical strategy awkward. How, after all, can a soulless body progress in wisdom or knowledge?[11]

Perhaps for that reason, much of the discussion in *Orations* 3.42–52[12] is dedicated to the argument that the "progress" alluded to in Luke 2:52 was either sheer physical growth or the gradual "manifestation" (φανέρωσις)[13] of the wisdom of the Deity. Because the wisdom of the Deity was continuously being revealed (Θεότης ἀπεκαλύπτετο),[14] it *appeared* to his auditors as if the λόγος progressed in wisdom. But Athanasius will not allow that the λόγος itself progressed. Indeed, he explicitly identifies the problem, as he sees it, with ascribing progress to the Word: "If he advanced when he became man, it is clear that, before he became man, he was imperfect" (ἀτελής)[15]—precisely the Arians' point. In fact, the λόγος did not—indeed could not[16]—progress in any respect whatsoever: "How," Athanasius asks, "can Wisdom progress in wisdom?"[17] True, the physical organism appropriated by God the Word—i.e., the body—advanced.[18] But if the Incarnate Word progressed at all, it was only in this limited physical sense. Athanasius's basic point, however, is that the human body was a mere vehicle or instrument for the gradual revelation of the wisdom of the λόγος. Thus, the "progress" reported by Luke occurs quite literally in the mind of Jesus' beholders.

For the depth of his involvement in the Arian controversy, Ambrose of Milan (d. 397) has been designated heir to Athanasius in the West. Six years of his career (375–81) were consumed, in large measure, by anti-Arian activity. At the request of the Emperor Gratian, Ambrose wrote an influential anti-Arian work, De Fide (381). This work was intended to refute the Arian view of the Son and to provide the Emperor with an understanding of orthodox Christology.[19] Ambrose also played an important role at the anti-Arian Council of Aquileia (381), where he tyrannized the Arian ecclesiastics present.[20] Much of his writing reveals acquaintance with Athanasius's anti-Arian literary corpus (including Orations III).[21] Despite his extensive dependence on Athanasius, however, Ambrose departs from the Alexandrian on one critical anthropological point.

Perhaps partly as a result of the Apollinarian controversy, Ambrose came to posit the existence of a human soul (anima) in Jesus, and he never implies, as Apollinaris had, that the Verbum replaced it or nullified its operations.[22] Indeed, Ambrose concedes that Jesus' human soul experienced the ordinary human physical and psychological passiones—hunger, sorrow, fear, and so forth.[23] Having admitted this point, however, Ambrose hastens to add that the human experience of the passions had no effect at all on the divine Word.[24] Ambrose insists that one must strictly distinguish experiences that can be predicated of the Word from those that Jesus experiences "as a human being" (quasi homo).[25] The Word does not cancel the operations of the human soul; neither is it affected by them.

Ambrose appeals to this strict distinction when he comes in De Fide to the texts dealing with the ignorance of Jesus. Jesus' questions, for example, are not evidence of the ignorance of the Son of God: "he asks as Son of Man, he gives commands as Son of God."[26] The Son of God could not be ignorant of the Day of Judgment (cf. Mark 13:32); he knows as Son of God.[27] Turning to Luke 2:52, Ambrose cites as possible the opinion of those who say that Jesus progressed as man. However, he cites other opinions as well and does not commit himself to any one position.[28]

In De Incarnationis Dominicae Sacramento (381–82), a treatise that deals extensively with the Incarnate Word's human nature in response to questions posed by two Arians,[29] Ambrose states quite bluntly that he "progressed in human wisdom" (proficiebat sapientia humana), and he adds that "God assumed the perfection of human nature in the flesh; he took on human perception" (Sensum ergo suscepit humanum).[30] Thus, for Ambrose, since Jesus assumed all the normal operations of the human soul, it is not at all improper to assign to his human soul (but not of course to the *Verbum*) "progress in wisdom."

Each of these latter two Ambrosian texts will figure importantly in the medieval discussion, though in oddly unintended ways. Most high-medieval figures from Peter Lombard on find Ambrose's position embarrassing and, as it stands, erroneous. Many go to awkward lengths to explain it away. Yet Ambrose was surely convinced that he had checked a much more dangerous and not unpopular interpretation of the text. The Arians had assigned progress in wisdom to the Word. Ambrose deftly channeled it to the human soul, safeguarding (so he thought) the perfection of the Son's divinity and, crucially important, securing the integrity of human salvation. All this is to say that an interpretation of Luke 2:52 that a Doctor of the Church had devised to neutralize heretical exegesis of it later became, without the benefit of benign interpretation, tainted with the stain of error.

Hardly less influential (if more safely orthodox) an interpretation of the text was that furnished by John of Damascus (d. 749) in his *De Fide Orthodoxa*.[31] A good student of the Cappadocian fathers, John's interpretation is explicitly intended to defeat the arguments of Nestorius. Today, it is notoriously difficult to determine what Nestorius actually did say, and historians are deeply divided over the question of whether or not he was a heretic.[32] Regardless of what his actual opinions were, however, his error in John's mind was to have divided the divine and human natures of Christ too sharply and to have spoken of the union as an "indwelling" of the λόγος in a human temple. In John's mind, this conception of the union meant that the λόγος had transcended the flesh and left it untouched. And if the flesh was left untransformed by the λόγος, it could progress in wisdom and grace.

Against this perceived christological dualism, John affirms, in a chapter in *De Fide Orthodoxa* dedicated to the exegesis of Luke 2:52 and written to correct those who have been misled by the "empty-headed Nestorius," that the flesh (σάρξ) was so thoroughly transformed by its union to God the Word that it enjoyed perfectly "every wisdom and grace" (πᾶσαν σοφίαν χαὶ χάριν) from the first instant of its existence.[33] That is, the flesh existed in such intimate proximity to the divine that the human soul came to share in its properties.[34] In short, it became omniscient as well. If Jesus progressed in any sense at all, John concludes, it was by progressively manifesting the wisdom that filled his transformed human soul.[35] Thus, where the Arians designated the λόγος the subject of the Lukan "progress in wisdom," and Ambrose Jesus' human soul, John of Damascus insists that *neither* truly progressed in such fashion. *Both* enjoyed a fullness of knowledge, the Word from all eternity and Jesus' human soul from the first moment of its conception.

The Damascene's interpretation of Luke 2:52 would have tremendous influence on exegesis of the text in the twelfth and thirteenth centuries. Indeed, in the writings of the prominent scholastics of the period, it became the preferred and perhaps "orthodox" interpretation of the text, as popular as Ambrose's was suspect.

High-Scholastic Interpretations

The most celebrated textbook of the period alludes to both *auctoritates*, Ambrose and John, in its discussion of the text. In his *Sententiae*, Peter Lombard declares that the Incarnate Word possessed both divine and human knowledge. It goes without saying that Christ did not progress in divine knowledge. But what about his human knowledge? Did he progress in this respect? To this question, the Master of the Sentences replies that Christ, "insofar as he was a man, received such a fullness (*plenitudinem*) of wisdom and grace, that God was not able to confer them upon him more fully" (*plenius*).[36] Indeed, to declare that he did progress in human wisdom is to suggest that he did not have "fullness of grace without measure."[37] Yet, as the Lombard recognizes uneasily, this is precisely what Ambrose appears to have implied: "Ambrose seems to propose openly (*aperte*) that Christ progressed in human perception (*secundum humanum sensum*)."[38] Startled, the Lombard replies that "the Church" does not accept Ambrose's interpretation of the text; neither do his other *auctoritates*.[39] The Lombard is forced to conclude that Ambrose was correct if he meant that Christ progressed, as many of the fathers had suggested, only in revealing himself (*secundum ostensionem*) to others and in the opinion of other human beings.[40] Yet that is clearly *not* what Ambrose meant, and the Lombard seems to have recognized it.

Though most of the major mendicant *Sentence* commentators will in fact concur with the Lombard's opinion that Christ did not progress in human knowledge—at least in the sense of moving from ignorance of something to knowledge of it—none is completely satisfied with the response he furnishes. Indeed, Albertus Magnus states quite explicitly that, "there is more truth in the words of Ambrose than the Master gets out of them."[41] In order to understand the mendicant response to the Lombard, however, we must first introduce some technical terms used by the friars.

Each of the mendicant commentators under consideration here maintains that the Incarnate Word had two general kinds of knowledge, each corresponding to one of his two complete natures. The Word has, of course, an uncreated divine knowledge. In addition, he has also a created human knowledge in his soul. That human knowledge is, in turn, distinguished into knowledge which Christ had *in Verbo,* knowledge which he had by miraculous "infusion" *(scientia indita/simplex)* and knowledge which he acquired from sensible experience *(scientia experimentalis/acquisita).* For our purposes, the latter two kinds of human knowledge are especially pertinent.

Christ's infused or "simple" knowledge is gained by the union of his human soul to a divine nature. As a consequence of the hypostatic union, the universal concepts and "species" (the Latin terms are *habitus* and *species*)[42] of *all* existing things are "infused" into the soul of Christ (more technically, into his passive intellect) from the first moment of its existence.[43] On the other hand, experiential or acquired knowledge is gained when Christ uses his exterior senses (e.g., sight) over the course of time in order to perceive new objects in his experience.[44] In short, infused knowledge is given instantaneously, by supernatural agency, and encompasses the full range of humanly possible knowledge. Acquired knowledge is, as its name suggests, gained (if at all) by the natural operation of the human soul over time and, because sense experience cannot be infinite, remains, potentially it would seem, forever partial.

Whatever his position with respect to the possibility of Christ's experiential progress in knowledge, no medieval scholastic ever allows that Christ progressed in "infused" or "simple" knowledge. Owing to a combination of divine supernatural power and the infinite goodness of God, Christ's soul was endowed with a fullness of knowledge that neither required nor was capable of augmentation or perfection. As Bonaventure puts it, "Because the habits and species were infused to the soul of Christ in complete fullness *(in omnimoda plenitudine),* Christ *could* not progress in simple knowledge."[45] In short, all medieval scholastics begin by guaranteeing the omniscience of Jesus' soul at the level of simple knowledge. None will concede that Jesus was ever ignorant in every respect of those things which he eventually came to experience. Bonaventure again: "Christ did not progress by coming to knowledge of something that was once unknown *(rei prius incognitae).*"[46]

Did Christ, then, progress on the level of acquired knowledge? Once more, the medieval scholastics under consideration begin by introducing a distinction, this time between an increase in acquired knowledge according to its essence *(secundum essentiam)* and an increase in knowledge according to experience *(secundum experientiam).* Each of the *Sentence* commentators here will allow only that Christ progressed in knowledge in the latter way, namely by comparing the new knowledge received through the senses for the first time with the already-possessed store of infused intelligible species.[47] Christ's new experience, then, does not really create any new knowledge; no new habit is generated. At most, the already-existing habits are "activated" or, in modern psychological terms, brought to the forefront of Christ's consciousness by sense experience received de novo. In Albert's concise locution, Christ's new sense experience "stimulates but does not create" a habit of knowledge (*non habitum quidem faciens sed excitans*).[48] Therefore, any essential progress is (as Bonaventure puts it) merely apparent (*secundum apparentiam*).[49]

In his commentary on the *Sentences*,[50] Thomas Aquinas develops a position very much like the one taken by his mendicant confreres. According to Thomas in the *Scriptum*, Christ "knew all things from the first instant of his conception."[51] Thomas does concede that his sensible experience adds an "experiential certitude" (*certitudo experimentalis*) to the store of knowledge Christ receives by miraculous infusion,[52] and he states that Christ "everyday saw things *sensibiliter* which he had not previously seen."[53] Indeed, Ambrose intended no more than this when he stated that Christ progressed in wisdom.[54] What Thomas will not admit is that Christ grew in "essential" knowledge.[55] "No other species," Thomas declares, "was freshly (*de nova*) received into the passive intellect."[56] When Luke reported that Jesus progressed in knowledge, therefore, he meant only that Christ received sensible corroboration of his infinite but incorporeal store of knowledge.

Clearly, each of the *Sentence* commentators here was trying, in classic scholastic fashion, to chart a via media between the opposed positions of Ambrose and John of Damascus, the *auctoritates* with whom each begins his discussion. Just as clearly, each is anxious to move away somewhat from the position represented by the Lombard and to give some more satisfactory account of the human dimension of Christ's created knowledge. Yet, with the Lombard, none will admit that Christ's new experience actually created novel, "essential," or "habitual" forms of knowledge. Speaking specifically of Albert and Bonaventure, Torrell has concluded: "Even these two are rather far from a true experiential knowledge."[57] Indeed, all of the commentators under consideration here argue that the progress Luke describes was merely the experiential certification and confirmation of the already-known. Even the early Thomas will go only this far. Twenty years later, as he wrote the *Tertia Pars* of the *Summa*, Thomas would stake out a much different position, one self-consciously defining itself over and against his earlier opinion and that of his mendicant contemporaries and teachers.

The Interpretation of the *Summa*

In the *Summa*, Thomas begins by agreeing with his contemporaries that Christ's habit of infused knowledge could not increase, since it had been given fully from the beginning.[58] But now he moves to criticize the argument that Christ's acquired knowledge could not increase in essence:

> Therefore, if beyond the infused habit of knowledge, there were not as well a habit of acquired knowledge in the soul of Christ (which is what some people think and what I myself once thought), none of Christ's knowledge would have increased in essence [secundum suam essentiam] but only by experience [sed solum per experientiam], that is, by comparing the infused intelligible species to sensible images [phantasmata]. In this sense they [i.e., Thomas's mendicant contemporaries] say that the knowledge of Christ grew by experience, namely by relating infused intelligible species to that which was freshly received through the senses.[59]

Appealing to the theological principle of "fittingness," Thomas proceeds to declare that it is not right that Christ should lack what is a natural activity of the intelligence. Since it is the natural function of the active intellect to abstract species from sensible images (phantasmata), it seems altogether proper (conveniens) to attribute that function to the soul of Christ.[60] Thus:

> Although elsewhere I have written otherwise, it must be said that Christ had acquired knowledge—which really is a human knowledge.... From this it follows that there was in the soul of Christ a habit of knowledge that could increase as a result of this abstracting of the species. In other words, the active intellect, having abstracted a first set of intelligible species from sensible images, could then go on to abstract others.[61]

In high-scholastic context, this is a vigorous affirmation of real progress on the level of acquired knowledge in Christ's soul. That strong affirmation is, however, almost immediately complicated by Thomas's further remarks. In the following article, Thomas considers the question, how did Christ acquire this new knowledge? Did he, in particular, learn anything from other men and women? The answer is that he did not: It was not, Thomas declares, "in keeping with his dignity" to learn anything from others.[62] Perhaps even more remarkably, Thomas argues that from the knowledge of things that Christ did experience, he was able to deduce a complex pattern of causes, and from those causes a pyramid of subsequent effects, so that, finally, Christ "was able to come to know everything as a result of what he did experience."[63] (When? Thomas does not say.) Note, then, that Thomas is not merely asserting an acquired knowledge in Christ. He is, in effect, insisting upon an acquired *omniscience*. And with the affirmation of real progress in knowledge and with the assertion of acquired omniscience, Thomas passes on to other issues.

Thomas in Ancient and Medieval Context: Some Conclusions

The mature Thomas advanced a reading of this text which represents a real departure from that proposed by his patristic predecessors and mendicant contemporaries, not to mention his own earlier position. Let us compare Thomas first with his patristic sources and then with his scholastic contemporaries. Then we will offer some brief reflections on why he differed from them.

Clearly, Thomas was attempting, *modo scholastico*, to chart a middle path between the polar positions of John of Damascus, who categorically denied that Christ progressed in knowledge, and Ambrose, who affirmed that the human soul of Christ *did* progress in human knowledge and human wisdom. In acknowledging that Christ acquired new knowledge, Thomas seems at first blush closest to the Ambrosian position. Nonetheless, despite the superficial similarity between the two, significant differences remain between the Ambrosian position and the mature Thomistic one. For that matter, despite the obvious differences from the Damascene's position, there are significant similarities between John and Thomas. Finally, we must conclude that Thomas's mature position borrows elements from both Ambrose and John of Damascus without reconciling them to his own position or to one another.

Although Thomas does declare that Christ progressed in human knowledge, his position still differs from Ambrose's in several significant ways. By the time Thomas stated that Christ progressed at the level of acquired knowledge, he had already guaranteed the omniscience of Christ's humanity by asserting that his infused knowledge was, as a result of the hypostatic union, perfect and incapable of augmentation. This high-scholastic distinction between infused and acquired knowledge was, of course, utterly unknown to Ambrose. Ambrose naturally assumed that Christ's *divine* knowledge was perfect. Indeed, *this* was the real issue for opponents of the Arians: Ambrose had to protect the perfection of Christ's *divine* knowledge against the Arian charge that it was imperfect. But he feels absolutely no need to secure the omniscience of Christ's humanity. And he never states or implies, as Thomas does, that Christ ultimately acquired perfection in human knowledge. In fact, the clear implication of Ambrose's *De Sacramento* is that, at the level of his human knowledge, Christ died in ignorance of many things. This is a concession to the humanity of Christ that Thomas could not bring himself to make. Finally, Thomas cannot fully embrace the Ambrosian position, even if Thomas does imply that his position and Ambrose's are identical.

John of Damascus, on the other hand, had denied that Christ could progress in human wisdom. For John, the human soul of Christ was omniscient from the first moment of its conception. Thomas's objection to John's position, understood in this way, is that it makes Christ less than fully human by robbing his intellect of the very capacity which would separate it from non-human creaturely perception, namely the ability to abstract ideas from empirical experience. He concludes (anachronistically, it might be observed) that John's denunciation of those who affirmed progress in human knowledge was aimed only at those who argued for augmentation of *all* his forms of knowledge and particularly those who affirmed that his infused knowledge increased. John did not, Thomas asserts, intend to deny that Christ's knowledge increased as a result of the exercise of his agent intellect.[64] This, of course, is not at all what the Damascene meant to say; John wanted to rule out progress in knowledge *tout court*. Clearly, Thomas here is attempting to smooth over the unquestionable differences between them by introducing distinctions which have no basis at all in the Damascene's thought—distinctions that would not appear in Christian thought until almost 500 years after John's death.

Nonetheless, it is curious that Thomas, who differs from John on the question of whether Christ acquired new knowledge, agrees with him that Christ ended up with perfect human knowledge. The difference—and it is a crucial one—is over the issue of *when* Christ became omniscient (for Thomas at the level of acquired knowledge). To assert, as Thomas does, that Christ acquired omniscience is still to allow that he progressed in human knowledge. This position implies that at least for *some* time in his human life Christ was not omniscient at the level of acquired knowledge. Here Thomas parts company with John, though he does not tell us this explicitly either.

This is also the point at which Thomas parts company with his contemporaries. Thomas rejects his contemporaries' position late in his career because, as he explicitly says, to deny the activity of the agent intellect to Christ would be to imply that Christ lacked an essentially human quality, the ability to abstract ideas from sense experience. Far from making Christ super-human, this would, in Thomas's eyes, make Christ less than perfectly human, since Christ would experience sensory data in the way in which non-human creatures do—that is, idly or passively, without abstracting ideas from it. Thomas saw, quite clearly I think, that his earlier position and those of his mendicant contemporaries implied that Christ was less than fully human, insofar as it suggested that Christ lacked or failed to exercise a natural and universal human capacity.

Another way of stating the same point is to say that the strongly Aristotelian quality of Thomas's epistemology encouraged him to insist that Christ
did progress in human knowledge by the exercise of his active intellect. Now,
it is, of course, perfectly well-established that there are "Platonist" elements in
parts of Thomas's corpus (where "Platonist" refers to the writings not just of
Plato but of the *Platonici*, as Thomas calls them at *Summa* 1.89.1, i.e., Plotinus, Proclus and others),[65] and more than one scholar has usefully complicated Thomas's putatively simple preference for Aristotle.[66] To be sure, one
should certainly avoid the simplistic conclusion that Thomas was a servile or
uncritical follower of Aristotle and utterly untouched by Platonic thought.
Perhaps Patrick Quinn has not have gone too far in maintaining that there
has been something like a "selective inattention to what is Platonic...in
Aquinas's thought," even "considerable resistance to the notion [based on
Thomas's own explicitly-stated preference for Aristotle] that there is a very
definite influence from the Platonic tradition" in Aquinas's writings.[67]

These remarks are well-taken. Thomas's debt to Plato—in places—is clear
and well-established. Having acknowledged Thomas's general debt to Plato,
however, we hasten to emphasize that Plato and "Platonic" epistemology made
no impact whatsoever on Thomas's discussion in the *Summa* of Christ's acquired knowledge. On *this* christological issue, at least, Thomas *was* a thor-
oughgoing Aristotelian. Whatever his reservations about the human mind's
ability to know God's essence based on sensory experience, Thomas basically
accepted the Aristotelian account of human cognition, which assumes that
humans acquire knowledge from sense experience.[68] In addition, he supposed
that Christ in the hypostatic union took on all that was human.[69] It followed
logically that Christ must also have taken on human modes of knowing. From
this it also followed with remorseless logic (*Et ex hoc sequitur...*)[70] that Christ
took on the agent intellect, the faculty which creates new knowledge out of the
raw data furnished by the senses. If he had an agent intellect, and unless it
remained latent or inert, he *must* have progressed in knowledge.[71]

Of course, it would be possible to argue that Christ's active intellect *did*
remain latent or inert. In fact, by so arguing one could safeguard the idea that
the Word did, in fact, *assume* in the hypostatic union all that was human. One
would simply quietly imply that Christ did not *use* all that he had assumed. At
the same time, this would enable one to protect Christ from the potentiality,
imperfection, error, and ignorance which Albert, Bonaventure, and the early
Thomas were so reluctant to impute to Christ. Indeed, this seems to be precisely how these commentators were trying, at least implicitly, to proceed.
After all, each of these commentators supposed that Christ *assumed* an active intellect. But none would concede that Christ could, or would, use it in

abstracting new ideas from the data given in sensory experience, linked as that abstraction necessarily is with the defect of partial ignorance.[72]

Thomas sees the possibility of arguing this way and takes pains to neutralize the argument. Relying on Aristotle's dictum that God and nature create nothing futile,[73] Thomas concludes that even less is it conceivable that any faculty in the soul of Christ could have been created *frustra*. The proper operation of the active intellect is to make intelligible species by abstracting them from the *phantasmata* encountered in everyday empirical experience. Thus, it is a matter of logical necessity to say that, if Christ assumed an agent intellect, intelligible species were received into the possible intellect through its operation—*ne eius actio*, Thomas concludes, *sit otiosa*.[74] For Thomas, Christ's progress in acquired knowledge is, in the first instance, then, a matter of philosophical necessity and an appeal to the perfection of natural and divine creation.

Lurking behind Thomas's insistence on Christ's progress in knowledge is, in addition, an important point of soteriological necessity. Had Christ really not progressed in knowledge, it would have been impossible for Thomas to maintain the central Christian conviction that Christ's humanity was consubstantial with ours. For Thomas, to state that Christ progressed in knowledge is to affirm that the Word in the hypostatic union took on *all* that was human; it is to affirm that Christ's humanity was indeed complete and utterly consubstantial with ours:

> Nothing God planted in our nature is lacking in the human nature
> assumed by the Word of God. It is clear that God planted in human
> nature not only a passive intellect but also an active intellect. Thus
> it is necessary to say that in the soul of Christ there was not only a
> passive intellect, but also an active intellect.[75]

Thomas's remarks about Christ's human knowledge are, then, also soteriological in motive and import. They are a celebration of the central Christian conviction that in the incarnation, the Word assumed *and* utilized all the faculties and powers that are constitutively human.

Equally clearly, those remarks constitute a critical verdict on the christology of his peers. To abstract *species* from the *phantasmata* given by the senses is, Thomas declares, a "natural activity of the human being" (*naturalis actio hominis*).[76] With that declaration, at least, many of his most celebrated contemporaries, including Albert and Bonaventure, would have agreed. Yet it is precisely this "natural" activity which they explicitly denied to the humanity of Christ. This denial Thomas stigmatizes with the tactful but nonetheless critical adjective *inconveniens*—not "heretical," to be sure, but decidedly less than robustly orthodox: "unfitting."[77] Torrell correctly concludes, "Thomas wrote here against the totality of theologians of his times."[78]

But should Torrell draw his contrast that sharply? What about Thomas's insistence on the acquired omniscience of Christ? It is true that Thomas says that Christ progressed to perfectly complete knowledge. And here he appears to come back round to his contemporaries' position by a different route. Are Thomas and his contemporaries actually reconcilable here?

No. The agreement is merely apparent. Thomas's contemporaries were convinced that Christ's *infused* knowledge was perfect. Thomas agreed with that proposition but also insisted on the reality (and, finally, the perfection) of Christ's *acquired* knowledge. Therein lies a major difference. In this context, Thomas's emphasis on the complete humanity of Christ, and its identity with our humanity, appears to be far more vigorous than that of his peers. Among other things, to *acquire* omniscience implies that Christ *for some time* in his life (though how long Thomas leaves discreetly unspecified) lacked perfect knowledge, a notion that Bonaventure, among others, finds quite dangerous. Because imperfect knowledge can lead to error and sin, Bonaventure cannot allow that Christ at any time in his life was ignorant of anything: "Christ," he concludes in his commentary on the *Sentences,* "by no means had the defect of ignorance (*defectum ignorantiae*) in him."[79]

In fairness to Thomas' contemporaries, it is essential to note that it was not simply their understandable reluctance to impute ignorance, error, or imperfection to the humanity of Christ which prevented Albert and Bonaventure (not to mention the early Thomas) from denying that Christ really acquired new knowledge by exercising his active intellect. There were powerful philosophical and epistemological objections to doing so as well. The first has to do with what both Bonaventure and Albert considered to be the superfluity and, indeed, the impossibility of creating new habits of knowledge at the level of acquired knowledge when Christ's infused knowledge, perfect as it was, already contained all the habits and species. It would have been utterly superfluous, each assumed, to have created new habits of knowledge by the exercise of the active intellect.[80] Perhaps even more problematically, the "storage" of a fresh but identical habit of knowledge in the passive intellect would have struck most, if not all, of Thomas's contemporaries as philosophically impossible. Indeed, one of Albert's cited "objections" to the possibility of real progress is that:

> Two forms of the same species cannot be in the same subject: the habit of cognition of all things was in Christ from the instant of his conception: therefore he was not susceptible [*non fuit susceptibilis*] of any habit through experiential cognition.[81]

Thomas did not acknowledge this problem. Or perhaps he felt unwilling to deal with it or incapable of doing so. It is a very difficult question.

In addition to these problems, perhaps nothing so discouraged Bonaventure from affirming that Christ progressed in knowledge than the idea, inherited ultimately from Augustine and mediated through influential contemporaries like Alexander of Hales, that our dependence on sensory experience was in some sense a punishment for sin and, in addition, far less reliable than forms of knowledge not reliant on sense experience. These ideas naturally rendered Aristotle's epistemology more problematic for thinkers like Bonaventure, and, indeed, it is well-established that Bonaventure's attitude toward Aristotle's epistemology was far more cautious, and even suspicious, than was Thomas's.[82]

In the final analysis, then, the differences between Thomas and contemporaries like Bonaventure on the issue of Christ's human knowledge can be explained, in part, by reference to their prior epistemological assumptions. Bonaventure's more complex and more suspicious appropriation of the Aristotelian position and his enthusiasm for Platonic-Augustinian epistemological assumptions, as well as his fear that progress would involve Christ in error, ignorance, and sin, discouraged him from believing that Christ could, or did, acquire new human knowledge as a result of his human empirical experience. On the other hand, Thomas's relatively enthusiastic acceptance of the Aristotelian epistemological position, at least so far as it related to the issue of experientially-acquired and sensory-based knowledge, allowed him, perhaps even compelled him, to affirm that Christ progressed in human knowledge and augmented the store of *habitus* in his passive intellect. However complex and nuanced his appropriation of Aristotle's thought generally speaking, Thomas's epistemological Aristotelianism and his allied commitment to all of the philosophical and soteriological implications of the hypostatic union profoundly, even decisively, influenced his mature and final judgment on the issue of Christ's progress in human knowledge. Indeed, it seems clear that it was his adhesion to the epistemology of the great Greek philosopher which alerted him to some of the implications of the hypostatic union and which drove him to his mature position on an issue of historic importance in Christian theology.

4

Christus Nesciens?

Was Christ Ignorant of the Day of Judgment?

De die autem illo vel hora nemo scit neque angeli in caelo neque
Filius nisi Pater.

—Mark 13:32

The Arian writers made much of the blunt admission by Jesus that he
was ignorant of the Day of Judgment. In this chapter, we examine
orthodox responses to the charge that this was proof of the inferiority
of the Incarnate Word's nature.[1]

Hilary of Poitiers

At the beginning of *De Trinitate*, Hilary is very clear about the way in
which the Arians interpret (or, as he puts it, "misrepresent" and
"distort") Mark 13:32.[2] Since the Son does not know what the Father
alone knows, the Arians argue, the one who does not know (*nesciens*)
must be very different (*longe alienus*) from the one who knows (*sciens*).
A nature liable to ignorance, like the creaturely nature of the Son,
does not have the strength (*virtutis*) or power (*potestatis*) of the one who
is free from the "domination of ignorance" (*dominatu ignorationis*).[3]
Lack of knowledge necessarily implies an ontological distinction between Father and Son, and the Son's not knowing the time demonstrates a "difference in divinity" (*dissimilitudinem diuinitatis*) between

the two.[4] Not surprisingly, Hilary denounces this way of interpreting the Markan text as "most impious" (inpissime).[5]

Hilary's basic response to the Arian exegesis of Mark 13:32 is to observe that there are many scriptural texts that prove the Son's full equality of essence with the Father; he cites John 10:30 ("I and the Father are one") as well as several other Johannine texts.[6] The contradictory quality of such texts, Hilary argues, requires a subtle hermeneutic. One must distinguish between the partial, concealed, or gradual revelation of the divine plan of salvation and the full expression of divine power and purposes. Some texts contain one kind of revelation, some another. Once we understand and apply this hermeneutical distinction, all the texts can be interpreted in such a way as to preclude the Son from suffering insult.[7] Clearly, Jesus' explicit acknowledgment of ignorance is not an indication of divine inferiority; it is simply an instance of revelation being withheld or concealed.

Subtle, clever, and even promising as this hermeneutic is, Hilary never exploits in the few times in De Trinitate he explicitly treats the Markan text. Instead, he bases his remarks on an a priori conception of the Son's full divinity and on the logical possibilities implied by that conception. Accordingly, Hilary concludes that it is simply not imaginable that the text could mean, or Jesus could mean, what the text states and Jesus explicitly declares. On the presumption that Christ is the origin and author (auctor) of all that is, and if "all things are through Christ and in Christ," it simply is not conceivable that the Son could be ignorant of anything. The Day of Judgment depends on him. Is he ignorant of the day of his own coming? Even human natures know beforehand what they are to do. Surely one begotten of God is aware of the dispensation of things that are to take place through his agency. And so Hilary inquires: "Is he ignorant of this day, when its time depends on him?"[8]

Ambrose of Milan

Ambrose's Commentary on Luke is his only extant exegetical work on the New Testament (he commented voluminously on the Hebrew Scriptures). The "commentary" probably originated as a series of homilies delivered in a liturgical context. Much of the text reflects contemporary theological and ecclesiastical politics—not least of all the "Arian controversy." Ambrose's debt to Greek predecessors (including Origen and Eusebius) and Latin contemporaries (including Hilary of Poitiers) is quite marked.[9] In the Luke commentary, he develops several interpretations of Mark 13:32 on which he will expand at much greater length in later dogmatic writings, especially De Fide. Ambrose may have completed this work, in fact, shortly before he finished *De Fide*, perhaps in the years 377–78. Eventually, Ambrose revised and edited the whole for "publication" sometime during or before the year 389. The text would later influence Augustine, among others.[10]

Ambrose begins by arguing that the crucial words *neque filius* are ambiguous. That is, the text does not specify whether Christ is here speaking as Son of Man or Son of God. Nonetheless, it is certain (Ambrose argues) that he knew by his divine nature when the end of days would be. If the Father had given the Son the power of judgment—a point which, of course, the Arians doubted—it follows that he surely would not have refused to disclose the time.[11] The Father and Son have one and the same knowledge, as they have one and the same power (*unum sunt cognitionis, quia unius sunt potestatis*).[12] Relying on an argument upon which he would expand in *De Fide*, Ambrose concludes that, as the Son knew the *signs* of future judgment, it follows that he must also have known the time of the end.[13] Therefore, he knew the day. But he knew it "for himself—not for me."[14] However, Ambrose is clear that he knew the day according to his divine, not his human knowledge (*non per naturam hominis, sed per naturam Dei*).[15] Here, then, Ambrose seems to imply that Christ *was* partially ignorant, according to his human nature. This is an example of the dualism that would permeate his remaining writing on christological questions.

In *De Fide*, Ambrose begins his treatment of this verse by arguing that "today" the Arians deny that Christ could have had all knowledge (*scientiam omnem*). They base their argument on Mark 13:32, wherein Jesus "himself professed that he was ignorant of the day and hour" of eschatological judgment. Naturally, they do not believe that he acquired his divine knowledge through unity with the divine nature. Rather, they insist that such knowledge as he acquired came, as it does with all creatures, via sense experience alone—by hearing, by seeing, and so forth.[16] Naturally, this is entirely consistent with their view of the Son of God as a creature who lacks knowledge that would be given to a being who was identical in substance to deity.

Against this "sacrilegious interpretation," Ambrose replies with a series of arguments. The first is based on what we might call primitive textual criticism. Ambrose argues that some ancient Greek manuscripts do not contain the disputed clause "nor the Son," an argument which would prove popular in the West.[17] The second is founded on what an unsympathetic contemporary postmodern student might call a paranoid hermeneutics of suspicion, as Ambrose gravely suggests that the Arians, who of course are not reluctant to doctor the meaning of the Scriptures, may just as easily and deviously interpolated the embarrassing phrase *neque filius*.[18]

Ambrose then turns to a christologically dualistic approach to the problem. The word "Son," he argues, refers to both of his natures, divine and human. The verse does not suggest he was ignorant in his divine nature; it is not, after all, appropriate for the Wisdom of God to know in part and in part to be ignorant.[19] But Ambrose will admit he seems *not* to have known "in the ignorance (*inprudentiam*) attached to the assumption of our nature."[20] If the Son knew not, it was human, not divine ignorance. As we have seen, the Arians, with their doctrine of *soma apsychon*, favored an anthropology of an incomplete human nature in the Incarnate Word. In their eyes, then, such a distinction would not have been acceptable and, without such an anthropological distinction in place, such an interpretation would be unimaginable. Nonetheless, Ambrose does seem to concede here that he was partially ignorant or nescient in his human nature.

Ambrose's fourth approach to the problem is based on a theology of creation that would again prove popular among other Western pro-Nicene writers. Since the Word is precisely that divine person through whom creation occurred, "the Creator of all things could not be ignorant of what he did, including number our days."[21] Beyond that, the Incarnate Son predicted all sorts of things about the eschatological day: the Temple would be destroyed, many impostors would come in his name, great earthquakes, famines, and pestilence and wars would come. Ignoring the one thing that Jesus does not predict—the time—Ambrose simply concludes, based on the Son's knowledge of all the other elements of the apocalyptic scenario: "Therefore he knew all things," including of course the "day and time."[22]

Beyond that, Ambrose proceeds, it was not to our advantage to know. It is economically better that we be ignorant of the precise moment of judgment. Thus we shall stand on guard, "set on the watchtower of virtue" (*in quadam virtutis specula conlocati*), and anxious always to avoid sin. It is better for us to fear the future rather than to know it.[23] And so Ambrose concludes rhetorically, "How was he ignorant, who knows all?" How could the Son of God be ignorant of the day, as (invoking Col 2:3) the treasures of the wisdom and knowledge of God are hidden in him?[24] When asked after his resurrection by the disciples (who, unlike Arius, understood that the Son knew) when he would restore the kingdom of Israel, he responded that it was not for the disciples to know (again a reference to Acts 1:7). From this, Ambrose concludes, "He said 'for you' not 'for me.'"[25] Jesus does not say it was not "for me" to know; he says it was not for the disciples to know. That is, the Son had esoteric knowledge of the end that he refused to disclose to the disciples when asked.

In 381, again in response to a request from the Emperor Gratian, Ambrose composed a tract, *De Spiritu*. It was meant to complement the already-completed

De Fide. While the text in general is intended to demonstrate the divinity of the Holy Spirit, Ambrose also again takes on Mark 13:32. Ambrose acknowledges again that the Arians had used the text to suggest that the Son, lacking knowledge that the Father possessed, was to be enumerated among the creatures, as one who was created.[26]

Ambrose's lengthy response would seem to vindicate Jerome's harsh judgment of *De Spiritu*, which he reprehended because of its flawed logic, not to mention for "putting bad things in Latin taken from good things in Greek," for being "flabby and soft, sleek and pretty," and replete with purple prose— an opinion for which erstwhile friend and fellow monk, Rufinus of Aquileia (345–410), now a bitter rival in the Origenist controversy, vigorously reprimanded him in 401.[27]

Upon inspection, it becomes obvious that Ambrose's strategy is, not so much to confront the challenge of the Arian argument, as to assume precisely that which the Markan text seems *not* to prove, or even explicitly to contradict. In fact, Ambrose argues for a replete, exclusive knowledge based apparently solely on an antecedently-held conception of the coequality of Father, Son, and Spirit.[28] He simply states that the Son has foreknowledge of all things, "that he is not mistaken ever, that the Son of God is not deceived, that he is not ignorant of the future."[29] Again, Ambrose declares that the Son knows all, has knowledge of the future and has knowledge of the very things of which the Arians believe are unknown to him.[30] Treating the crucial clause "nor the Son" (*neque filius*), Ambrose states that the Holy Spirit was not mentioned in this biblical verse and thus "excepted from ignorance." How, then, he goes on to ask, "if the Holy Spirit was excepted from ignorance was the Son of God not excepted?"[31] He concludes by commanding his reader, with something of the aristocratic imperiousness and inflexibility for which he was renown, "Accept, then, that the Son of God knows the Day of Judgment."[32]

Jerome

Jerome's Matthew commentary (398) was written at the request of his friend and companion from Jerusalem, Eusebius of Cremona (d. 420). Eusebius specifically requested an austerely historical and literal treatment of the Gospel, so that he could read it on his journey back to Italy from Jerusalem; it's a piece of travel reading.[33] Jerome began it at the moment he was convalescing from an illness that had laid him up for three months. Nonetheless, he managed to finish the work in two weeks in March 398. The text bears the marks of being hastily written. Interestingly, it depends heavily on Origen's Matthew commentary (though it criticizes the Alexandrian father's errors) and that of Hilary of Poitiers.[34] Jerome complied with Eusebius' request, and, given the circumstances of its composition, it is not surprising to learn that the commentary is not notable for doctrinal originality or profundity. Nonetheless, it is important for our purposes, because at one point it takes up the problem of Christ's apparent ignorance of the Day of Judgment.

Like Ambrose, Jerome observes that the disputed words *neque Filius* are added in certain Latin manuscripts, which he believes are lacking in the Greek exemplars. Naturally, this causes Arius and Eunomius, ignorant as they are, to rejoice, because they believe that one who is ignorant of the Day of Judgment cannot be equal to the one who knows (*non potest aequalis esse qui nouit et qui ignorat*).[35] He then repeats an argument often heard in the ancient West, namely, that because "Jesus made all of the times" as Word of God, including the Day of Judgment, he could not have been ignorant of the day: Does not the Johannine text say, "All things through him were made, and without him nothing was made" (John 1:3)? How is it possible for one who knows the whole to be ignorant of the part? Moreover, he asks, what is greater, knowledge of the Father, or of the Day of Judgment? Since he possessed the greater knowledge of the Father (presuming precisely what Arius and the early Arians vigorously denied), how could he be ignorant of the lesser knowledge? If all that is the Father's is the Son's (presuming, some might say, that which the Arians demanded be demonstrated), for what reason would the Father reserve for himself knowledge of a single day and not wish to communicate it to the Son? Therefore, Jerome triumphantly, if not altogether convincingly, concludes, "we have proved that the Son was not ignorant of the day of consummation."[36]

Why then is he said to be ignorant, as Jerome acknowledges he was? Christ was, as the Apostle said, the mystery of God, "in whom are hidden all the treasures of wisdom and knowledge" (Col 2:3). Why, though, are they hidden? After the resurrection, when interrogated by the apostles, concerning the day, he more fully (*manifestius*) than in Mark 13 replied, "It is not for you to know the times or the dates the Father has set by his own authority."[37] When the risen Jesus says, "it is not yours to know," Jerome says, he shows that *he* knows. But it was not expedient for the *apostles* to know, as then they would remain always uncertain about the coming of the judgment day and thus live in the expectation of being judged. Whenever the Gospel says "the Father alone knows," he concludes, the Son knows, since the Son is comprehended in the Father.[38]

Jerome wrote his *Tractates on Mark,* one of his lesser-known works, in the first decade of the fifth century.[39] It was a time of enormous exegetical fecundity for Jerome, whose commentarial work had been interrupted by the task of translation for many years; he commented on seven books of the Hebrew

Bible during this time period. Jerome was one of the few Latin fathers to give any extended attention to Mark. Most concentrated attention on Matthew or Luke, on the assumption that Mark was a mere epitome of Matthew.[40] Jerome treats the text of Mark in homilies arranged in ten "treatises" and the disputed text in Mark 13 in the last of these, where he observes that the verse deserves a "long explanation" (*magnam expositionem*).[41]

Jerome's argument here rests, first, on the presumption of ontological or essential unity he thinks believers must credit by their baptismal promises; second, on the theology of creation through the Word we have already encountered; third on the economic plan which requires, for our benefit, that we remain ignorant of the day (an argument we have previously seen); and, finally, and most originally, on the way in which the context of the disputed verse in Mark, particularly the verse immediately following it, qualifies its meaning. In baptism, he begins, we accept equally the Father, Son, and Holy Spirit. We must also believe they have one name, God. But if God is one, how can there be different degrees of knowledge (*diuersa scientia*) in one God?[42]

It is said of the Savior, Jerome observes, "Through him all things were made" (John 1:3). If all things were made through him, it follows that the Day of Judgment must have been made through him as well (*ergo et dies iudicii*). Is it possible for the artificer not to know his work?[43] Obviously not. Besides, it is better that we not know. If we knew that the Day of Judgment would not be for two-thousand years, we would be "more negligent" (*neglegentiores*) than if we remained in a state of pious ignorance.

Finally, Jerome insists that the entire pericope, and particularly the text immediately surrounding the difficult verse, be taken into consideration. In fact, he focuses his attention on the verse immediately after Mark 13:32: "Be on guard! Be alert! You do not know when that time will come" (Mark 13:33). Notice, Jerome says, that Jesus did not say *we* do not know. He said, rather, *you* do not know. Similarly, in Acts, after the resurrection, when, in response to a query from the disciples, he replies, "it is not yours to know" (Acts 1:7). Again, he did not say, *I* do not know. He said it is not *yours* to know.

Augustine

It was not until the first decade of the fifth century that Augustine directly took on the Arian problem, but it preoccupied him in the very last years of his life.[44] From ca. 410–30, he wrote three works explicitly on the problem: *Against an Arian Sermon* (418/19),[45] *Debate with Maximinus* (427/28)[46] and *Against Maximinus the Arian* (428).[47] His *Tractates on John* (413–18)[48] also deal with

Arianism. Surprisingly, *On the Trinity* (400–420) does not deal with it in detail.[49] About ten of his many sermons treat the heresy at some length as well,[50] and others touch on it. Some of his early works treat the difficulties of Arian theology and exegesis, too, though often *en passant*.

One early work which treated the Arian exegesis of Mark 13:32 is Question 60 in Augustine's *On Eighty Three Different Questions* (388–96). In his *Retractions,* Augustine tells us that his eighty-three responses were individually written in response to queries of friends who, whenever they saw him free, would interrupt his leisure. He began these responses shortly after his conversion. After becoming bishop, he had them gathered, numbered, and made up into a single book. Many of the questions have to do with difficult exegetical issues.[51]

In Question 60, he responds to a friend who had asked about the text that states that the Son of Man has not knowledge of "that day and hour." (This actually is the parallel to the Markan text in Matt 24:36.) Augustine's response rests on a distinction between two different meanings or modes of divine knowing. Thus, it could mean that God does not approve of a certain behavior (as in Matt 25:12, where Jesus declares, "I do not know you"). Or it could mean that God causes human beings not to know. In the case of this text, it is not that the Son does not know; he simply causes human beings not to know. That is, he does not reveal to them that which is not religiously useful for them to know (here echoing both Ambrose and Jerome). In either case, this way of speaking does not mean that God does not know.[52] Obviously, Augustine, like so many of his contemporaries, was assuming exactly what the Arians would have wanted him to prove: namely, that the Son of Man alluded to in the text was not a creature.

Augustine's *Sermon* 97 also deals with Mark 13:32, though the homiletical form and liturgical context of this brief work to some degree shape his treatment of the problematic text. His treatment of the text is framed by exhortatory warnings. We may suppose the last day is a long way off, but our own last day may find us napping. We should all be vigilant by leading worthy lives. Otherwise our personal last day may find us unprepared. He concludes, chillingly, that in that case, "each of our works will come to our aid, or else they will become our torment."[53]

Between the paraenetic beginning and end of the sermon, Augustine briefly treats the christological problems raised by the text. Curiously, he announces portentously that the text certainly raises "an important question" (*quidem magna quaestio*), but he provides nothing (owing, perhaps, to the liturgical context) like an analogously ample response. First, he urges his auditors not to be too literal-minded about this passage. Excessive literal-mindedness could lead us into supposing the Father knows something of which the Son is ignorant.

Then, repeating arguments by now familiar to us, he assures his audience that the Day of Judgment is itself made by the Son, and that we should not therefore suppose the Father knows something of which the Son is himself ignorant.[54]

Augustine's *Enarrationes in Psalmos,* his longest work, were given as brief exegetical comments, dictated exposition (possibly to be read in church by his priest), and in homily form. Written over a period of more than two decades, they actually exceed in number the total of psalms, as Augustine sometimes gave two sermons, or more, on a single psalm. Two of his *enarrationes* (a term given by Erasmus, meaning a "running commentary"), both written in 392, deal briefly with Mark 13:32.[55]

Neither is the center of the commentary in question, nor does either really offer anything new in Augustine's thought, though both treatments are shaped by the homiletical context and the ends for which they were presumably composed. In *Enarratio* 6.1, the discussion is framed by a rather spirited critique of those who presume to reckon the date of the last day. Augustine touches briefly on the christological problem of Mark 13 when he declares that the phrase "nor the Son" implies, not that Jesus himself is ignorant of the day but is simply an announcement of Jesus' intention not to reveal it. He is *said* to be ignorant only because he leaves in ignorance those for whom such knowledge would not be fruitful.[56] Thus we are meant to resist the urge to speculate on the date of the parousia. Similarly, in *Enarratio* 9.35, Augustine explains, in the midst of a discourse on the "secrets of the Son," that the Son is *declared* to be ignorant, not in terms of his knowledge of it, which of course he has, but in terms of his desire to reveal it.[57]

In his great dogmatic work *On the Trinity,* composed in two stages over the course of more than twenty years (ca. 399–420), Augustine is, in general, not preoccupied with the Arian view of deity.[58] He treats the disputed text in Mark only once at length, in Book 1.12. The treatment of the text accorded Augustine is shaped by the prior chapter (1.11) dedicated solely to exegetical rules treating contradictory and mutually incompatible statements about the ontological status of the Son. Augustine distinguishes scriptural texts referring to the Son "according to the form of God" (*secundum formam Dei*) and "according to the form of a servant" (*secundum formam serui*).[59] Mark 13:32 is one of those texts which falls into the latter category. It is not that the Son as God was ignorant; he was "ignorant" only in the sense that he made others—that is, the disciples—ignorant. Yet Augustine seems also to presume that Jesus is ignorant in his humanity. What he knew before the incarnation (*ante incarnationem*) he appears not to know after. What he knew among the perfect, he was ignorant of among children.[60] Augustine seems here to suggest that, as Son of God, he keeps the disciples ignorant of the Day of Judgment for their own good but that, as Son of Man, he was, in fact, truly ignorant of the day.

High-Medieval Reflection on Mark 13:32

Peter Lombard

The Lombard begins by asking whether it was fitting or appropriate for Christ to have assumed infirmities such as hunger, sadness, or fear. For several reasons, he concludes it was. First of all, the Son of God takes on a passible and mortal body and soul precisely in order to prove that he assumed a true humanity in the Incarnation. Accordingly, he took up both defects of the body (such as hunger and thirst) and defects of the soul (like sadness, fear, *dolor*) and so forth. In short, he assumed such defects in order to exhibit the genuinely human body and soul he assumed in the Incarnation.[61] Like us, Christ had a passible soul and passible and mortal flesh. Christ also took on a passible, mortal body and a passible soul, the Lombard argues, for reasons of soteriological necessity. Hearkening back to a theme that has its roots in ancient Christian thought, the Lombard argues that he took up what was ours in order to sanctify and to heal us:

> He took up what was ours, in order that he might give us what
> was his and so that he might bear our defect. He took our oldness
> in order that we might be filled with his newness.[62]

In short, Christ had indeed assumed human infirmities in order to demonstrate the reality of his "flesh" (which includes a passible soul, capable of suffering pain) and to complete his salvific work (here conceived as an exchange in which we receive what was his, while Christ bears and thus cure our defects) and, the Lombard adds, to support our hope.[63]

Nonetheless, the Lombard insists that he did not assume all of our defects, but only those it was expedient to humanity for him to assume and which did not derogate from his dignity.[64] In particular, he assumed no defects that could have led him into error or in accomplishing the good, the very defects that mark us out as human after the fall:

> [Christ] assumed no ignorance . . . it is certain that in us there is ig-
> norance and also a difficulty in wishing and doing the good, which
> pertains to our wretched condition. . . . These, however, Christ did not
> have.[65]

It follows, then, that Christ did *not* accept *all* of the defects of our infirmity, save sin.[66] In fact, the Lombard and his later commentators are all anxious to prove that he did not assume the defect of ignorance. The main principle here is that he assumed defects only which it was expedient for our salvation for him to assume. Thus it follows that there were all sorts of imperfections and illnesses of the body, for example, from which he remained entirely immune.

In the fourteenth distinction of the third book of his *Sentences*, Peter Lombard asks the question, whether the soul of Christ knew all that God knew. His response is unambiguous. While Christ could not *do* all the things that God could, he *knew* all the things which God did. He would certainly have agreed with John of Damascus that the Savior's soul was imbued with a fullness of wisdom from the moment of conception, a plenitude that, by definition, could not be augmented or perfected. True, he did not know them as "clearly and perspicuously" as did God. But it is only in this limited sense that his knowledge was unequal to the Creator's. There is a slight difference in degree, or clarity of perception, not in the quantum of knowledge. As Marcia Colish has put it, "The human Christ knows the same things, but less exhaustively and with less penetration than God knows them."[67] Or, as Peter concludes, "he knew all the things which God himself knew."[68]

Bonaventure

In his treatment of the disputed text, Bonaventure acknowledges that it seems as if the hour of judgment is known to *no* creature, including the created soul of Christ. Does not Matthew 24 state that the hour is known to no one, not even the Angels, nor even the Son? It seems obvious, then, that Christ did not know the hour of judgment.[69] Just as God had revealed to the prophets many things, even about the future, he did not reveal to them the hour of judgment. Thus it seems that God had reserved this knowledge for himself alone.[70]

On the other hand, as we have already seen, Bonaventure denied that Christ was able to progress in knowledge. If at any time he was to know this knowledge, then he knew it as a creature.[71] Therefore without doubt it must be stated that the Day of Judgment is known not only to the entire Trinity but also to the humanity assumed (*homini assumto*) by the Word.

Thomas

Like Bonaventure, Thomas too concedes that it seems as if the Son was ignorant of the day. Invoking Mark 13.32, Thomas concedes in his Sentence commentary that the text seems to imply that, at least according to his human nature, Christ did not know all that his Father knew. The soul of Christ, being finite, was not able to comprehend the infinite. Therefore it seems as if the soul of Christ did not know all that God knew.[72] Nonetheless, Thomas argues (altogether traditionally) the Son is said not to know simply because he does not cause us to know. Neither the Son nor the Holy Spirit is excluded from knowledge held by the Father. Thus the Son knew the day both as man and as God.[73]

The high-medieval tradition under examination here, then, would not allow that Christ was ignorant in any respect when it came to the facts of salvation history. Here, Peter Lombard, Bonaventure, and Thomas hew closely to the path laid out by patristic predecessors like Hilary and Jerome. Indeed, they use the very arguments formulated classically by their patristic predecessors. But none of these figures concede that which Ambrose and Augustine seem openly to acknowledge: that in his human nature, at least, Christ was ignorant of the time and day. But of course Ambrose and Augustine stopped well short of daring to imply what the Arians had stated with full confidence: that it was the *logos* itself that was the subject of such ignorance.

5

Christus Patiens?

Did Christ Suffer Pain in the Passion?

Direct your thoughts, reader, to these words [of Hilary] with pious diligence, lest they be for you vessels of death.

—Peter Lombard, *Sentences* 3.17.3

Ever since the fifth century, when Augustine respectfully acclaimed him an authoritative scriptural interpreter and theologian, Hilary of Poitiers (ca. 315–367) has been honored as a vigorous, effective, even heroic (sometimes "brilliant") champion of Nicene orthodoxy.[1] Indeed, for his role in the "Arian controversy" and for his defense of the Nicene faith, he is commonly denominated by admirers the "Athanasius of the West" (intended wholly without irony of course as a heartfelt honorific). Incomplete and even misleading as this asserted parallel may be, partisans for a millennium and a half have only multiplied its use, meaning, and implications—so much so that by the nineteenth century one commentator could appoint Hilary the "pillar" of the Western church, one who occupied the same glorious post in the Occident as Athanasius in the East.[2]

Whatever the merit of the analogy, there are certainly many superficial parallels, and some deeper ones, in their ecclesiastical careers. Like Athanasius, Hilary worked steadily for the "triumph" of the Nicene faith, and he, too, was banished for his efforts, which nonetheless were ultimately effective. Indeed, many scholars would contend that Hilary was the pivotal figure in the defeat of Western "Arianism." Thomas Torrance is only among the most recent to defend this view. "It was largely owing to [Hilary's] efforts," he asserts, "that Arianism was eventually overthrown in the West,"[3] and his student G. M. Newlands wholeheartedly concurs. Hilary was, Newlands states, "the principal architect of the victory of the Western Church over Arianism" and, he adds, "the courageous defender of the claims of the Church over Emperor."[4] So: scourge of heretics, bold leader of the homoousian party in the West, exile for the faith of Nicaea, a father of Western trinitarianism. And, as Hilary described himself, a "disciple of the truth" (*discipulus ueritatis*).[5] All of this seemed to provide sufficient grounds for Pope Pius IX to proclaim him, in 1851, a "doctor of the church." Not surprisingly, this ecclesiastical tribute has only solidified his reputation as a grand patron of orthodoxy.[6]

Precisely because of his reputation as a champion of orthodox faith, established already early in the fifth century, high-medieval readers were astonished to discover that several of his central christological opinions appeared to border on heresy. Peter Lombard (ca. 1100–1160), for example, dedicated a section of his *Sentences* just to discussion and interpretation of "several very obscure chapters of Hilary" (*De quibusdam Hilarii capitulis valde obscuris*).[7] He wrote a second chapter addressing (among other things) other problematic elements of Hilary's Christology.[8] Having assigned several chapters of the *Sentences* to the problem of Hilary, the Lombard succeeded in alerting his numerous high-medieval commentators to it as well. As a result, they too had to think through and make some sense of the difficulties in Hilary's Christology. Many of them explicitly stated, as the Lombard did not, that the problem of Hilary involved, not something so innocuous as unclarity or obscurity (the Lombard's generous euphemisms), but error. No less a figure than Bonaventure, for example, declared that several of Hilary's christological opinions appeared to be "false, doubtful and erroneous" (*falsa, et dubia et erronea*), seemed, indeed, to be "against the faith" (*contra fidem*).[9] The first, troubling impression Hilary made upon those who actually read his words, then, directly clashed with the brilliant, untarnished image of him they had inherited from the past.[10]

To this tension between inherited orthodox image and heterodox reality, Hilary's high-medieval readers responded in instructively odd ways. Despite vividly registering their initial impressions of unorthodoxy, Bonaventure and virtually all of his high-scholastic contemporaries strove to interpret and revise Hilary so as to retrieve him from suspicion of error. The result is a Hilary who, after laborious (and some would insist tortured) "explanation" (*expositio*), only *seemed* to lapse into error and who, rightly read, reemerges as a fully respectable, unimpeachably orthodox defender of the faith. In other words, christological opinions contained in part of the tradition that had been as highly prized as Hilary's anti-Arian writings could not simply be dismissed as erroneous, even if they seemed to be, or according to medieval criteria *were*, outrageously erroneous. Nor could this part of tradition simply be allowed to lapse into oblivion, nor fine distinctions made between those of Hilary's opinions which were orthodox and those which were not. No: A rescue and retrieval operation had to be undertaken. Hilary's erroneous opinions had to be revised, modernized, rectified—transformed. One who for centuries had been recognized as a pillar of orthodoxy had to remain, *regardless of his actual opinions*, a pillar of orthodoxy.

This way of treating Hilary raises a number of interesting questions about the medieval interpretation and transmission of patristic tradition. How were important opinions in the theological tradition interpreted when they appeared to be problematic or, as in this case, laden with error? What is the relationship between the received opinion and the one transmitted in cases like these? What kind of continuity, if any, is there between (in this case) the opinion of the historical Hilary and the one "processed" and handed on by the great medieval scholastics?

The argument I wish to make here is, first, that there is very little conceptual or ideational continuity. Such continuity as there is in a case like this is, in fact, largely if not entirely verbal or nominal. Medieval inheritors of deeply problematic opinions in the orthodox tradition, if they wished to preserve them somehow for subsequent use, had utterly to evacuate the intention and meaning of an author's suspicious words. Having drained the offending words of their intended meaning, high-medieval handlers of tradition then proceeded to fill the emptied verbal forms with entirely new, more satisfyingly orthodox content. In this case, there is only the most superficial, verbal continuity between the historical Hilary and the "Hilary" transmitted by his high-scholastic readers. The second part of my argument is that Hilary's high medieval readers, having completely transformed the meaning of Hilary's words, transmit the new, reinterpreted "Hilary" as if it were the unchanging transmission of the historical Hilary. In other words, the creation of an entirely new tradition of opinion is represented as if it were a pure handing-on of the old. This way of interpreting and preserving Hilary makes an instructive case study for understanding abiding features of the Christian tradition.

Hilary's Impassible Son

As we have seen, no part of Hilary's literary corpus caused more trouble for his high-medieval readers than a section of his most famous and important writing, the work traditionally entitled *De Trinitate*. This is especially true of the last five books of the work. In each of these five books, Hilary undertook a systematic refutation of the Arian arguments that attempted to establish the inferiority of the Son to the Father. In Book 10, Hilary turned to a discussion of the Arian interpretation of the passion and death of Christ; this is the part of *De Trinitate* that caused such surprise and confusion among the *Sentence* commentators of the high Middle Ages.

One of the features of Arian theology which caused all their orthodox opponents difficulty was the Arians' eagerness to comb the gospels for putative proof of the imperfection of Christ's divine nature. Nowhere did they find more copious evidence of such imperfection than in the accounts of the passion and death of Christ. To the Arians these texts made it clear that the Son of God had experienced pain (*dolor*), sorrow, fear, and other sorts of creaturely limitation and weakness. Moreover, they insisted that it was the divine *logos,* not merely the physical organism assumed by the Word, which experienced these defects. In other words, from the Arian point of view, these texts referred to the deity of the incarnate Son, not to the assumed physical organism (as, for example, Athanasius had argued).[11] For the Arians, it followed logically that the *logos,* though divine, was less than fully divine and therefore inferior to the Father. Deeply troubled at the implications of the Arian theology, Hilary set out to counter these arguments in Book 10 of *De Trinitate.*

Among the Arian arguments Hilary is most anxious to counter is the idea that the Son of God experienced pain (*dolor*) in the passion. Hilary responds to this argument *not* by maintaining that the Son of God did not suffer. Hilary declares that he did: "The Lord Jesus Christ truly suffered when he is struck, suspended, crucified and died."[12] But Hilary goes on to distinguish between the suffering that occurred, as it were objectively, and pain which the Son of God might have experienced subjectively. Though the Son of God truly suffered, in the sense that he was visibly scourged and crucified, this suffering caused him no pain.[13] In short, the Son of God truly suffered, but impassibly and painlessly; neither his divine person nor his human soul was affected by suffering. It is as if he were both an actor in and dispassionate spectator of his own passion.

According to Hilary, the Son of God "suffered" in this way because he had a unique body, owing to the unusual circumstances of its conception.[14] Because the body of the Son of God had its origins in a spiritual conception (*ex conceptu Spiritus*), it had a different nature that did not and could not experience the weakness of ordinary human bodies. In particular, it had a nature that made it incapable of feeling pain (*non tamen naturam dolendi*).[15] Again, Hilary recognizes that harsh blows really struck Christ and wounds really pierced his flesh. Nonetheless, because of the unique quality of that flesh, Christ felt only the force of the suffering (*inpetus passionis*) but not the pain of the passion (*non tamen dolorem passionis*).[16] If one were to pass a dagger through water or air or fire, Hilary argues, one would not say that the air was wounded or the fire pierced. Neither element has the kind of nature which would allow it to experience pain. Analogously, Christ could not have suffered pain in the passion because he simply did not have a nature that could experience it.[17] Hilary, therefore, had not (he thought) denied the reality of the passion and the suffering of Christ; he had merely denied its power to cause Christ pain. Christ's flesh was really mutilated and his body really expired as a result of a bloody crucifixion. But Christ felt none of the sting of the corporal punishment inflicted by his tormentors. Arguing against the Arians, therefore, Hilary insists not only that the Word of God remained sovereignly immune to physical passion. He also asserts that the human flesh of Christ remained free of pain, even if that flesh was grievously wounded.

One of the reasons that Hilary is so anxious to emphasize Christ's insusceptibility to physical pain is that it allows him to argue that Christ felt none of the *psychological* passions, especially fear and sorrow, normally caused by the prospect of crucifixion and death.[18] Apparently, the Arians took Jesus' prayer in Gethsemane for direct evidence that the Son of God was overcome with fear and that he did not possess the nature of impassible deity.[19] They also apparently concluded that his nature was weak because he confessed that he was "sorrowful unto death" (Matt 26:38). That they did so Hilary takes as further evidence of the "godless perversity" of the Arians.[20] Nevertheless, the Arians concentrated heavily on the Gethsemane narrative,[21] and Hilary was forced to dedicate much of Book 10 of *De Trinitate* to refuting their exegesis of it.

Hilary responds to the Arians by categorically denying that the prospect of suffering and death caused Christ to experience fear or sorrow. "Where, I ask," Hilary inquires, "is there fear in the passion?"[22] To this rhetorical question, Hilary responds that Christ felt no fear at the prospect of death because he died of his own volition and because he knew he would rise again:

> There is no fear of death in one who dies willingly and who will not remain dead for long... death cannot be feared where there is the willingness to die and the power to live.[23]

Thus when Christ prayed for the cup to pass away from him, he did not pray for himself, nor was he sad for himself. In fact, he was praying for his disciples in the hope that the cup of passion might pass from them.[24] Jesus' confession that he was sorrowful unto death meant that death was the end, not the cause, of sorrow (*mors non iam tristitiae est causa sed finis*).[25] In short, Christ experienced none of the physical or psychological passions that the Arians claimed he suffered in his crucifixion and death.

Hilary in the High Middle Ages

Many of these christological opinions of Hilary were collected in the twelfth century by Peter Lombard and excerpted in his *Book of Sentences*. [26] As a result, the great Franciscan and Dominican Sentence commentators of the high Middle Ages were compelled to come to terms with, understand, and interpret them. Their response to Hilary is exceptional both for its length and, in some cases, its intensity. High-scholastic commentators are not, to say the least, known for the expression of colorful or emphatic feeling. But some of these Sentence commentaries, at least the parts dealing with Hilary, are vehement in their repudiation of Hilary's apparent meaning.

This is probably nowhere more clearly illustrated than in Bonaventure's treatment of Hilary's insistence that Christ remained serenely immune to suffering in his passion. It is this opinion that Bonaventure stigmatizes as "false, doubtful, and erroneous."[27] To say what Hilary appeared to say is, Bonaventure declares, to contradict the gospel and the Catholic faith, both of which expressly declare that Christ truly experienced the passion of pain (*doloris passio*).[28] Christ had passible and "pierceable" flesh (*caro perforabilis*). Moreover, he had the power of feeling (*virtus sentiendi*), and he had a soul that suffered when his body was wounded.[29] Given all this, it must undoubtedly be held that in Christ there was "the real feeling of pain" (*vera doloris passio*).[30]

If anyone were to pronounce otherwise (*aliter dicat*) on this issue, Bonaventure states, he would be expressing an heretical opinion. Indeed, one who maintained that Christ did not truly have pain, even though he seemed to suffer and feel it, would be recapitulating ancient error.[31] But the consequences of uttering such an opinion are even more dire than that. Anyone who truly maintained that Christ felt no pain in the passion "not only evacuates the faith of Christ and the gospel of Christ but also evacuates our redemption. He says that Christ is not the Christ."[32] In Bonaventure's mind, then, Hilary had jeopardized the reality of Christian salvation. The stakes were that high. If Hilary were correct, then no satisfaction occurred as a result of the passion. And, as a result: "the human race has not been redeemed."[33] If one were to say he only feigned to suffer, one calls Christ a liar, not the Son of God, nor the messenger or mediator of God, but a deceiver; and to say this is, of course, to blaspheme Christ quite impiously.[34]

But this, all the high-medieval commentators agreed, is not what Hilary really could have meant. Accordingly, they offered three possible interpretations to account for his true intentions. First of all, Albertus Magnus, Bonaventure, and Thomas Aquinas all suggest that Hilary may have retracted this opinion in a letter or book of retraction.[35] In fact, Bonaventure states that William, bishop of Paris, had actually seen and read the book or letter.[36] What is interesting about this remark is that all three commentators seem implicitly to grant here that Hilary had once made statements that were erroneous or heretical. In any case, both Albert and Bonaventure observe that, because they have not seen the mysterious book of retraction, it is fitting to try and (in Albert's words) "make sense" (*vim facere*) of the problematic words of Hilary,[37] and all three commentators proceed to do just that.

The next explanation the commentators furnish is that Hilary may have intended only to suggest that Christ did not experience infirmity and pain in his divine nature; he felt it only in his human nature.[38] When Hilary insists that Christ was free from the experience of *dolor,* he was speaking (as Thomas put it) "with respect to the Deity" (*quantum ad Deitatem*) of the Incarnate Word.[39] Hilary was, after all, arguing against the Arians, who had maintained that the Son of God was a creature. In the disputed passages, therefore, he was merely trying to exclude the error of Arius, who said that Christ suffered absolutely (*secundum se*), both in his divine as well as his human nature.[40]

A third explanation offered by these high-medieval commentators is that Hilary was attempting to argue against those who said that Christ completely succumbed to the passions and was overcome by them. When Hilary said that Christ did not feel pain, he merely meant that Christ did not utterly surrender to it.[41] As Bonaventure puts it: "Hilary says that, although Christ truly suffered, nevertheless he did not feel pain—that is, he did not succumb to the passions."[42] Thus Hilary did not wish to deny the sense and experience (*sensum et experimentum*) of the passion; he wished only to delimit its force (*vim*) and to deny that it had dominated the soul of Christ.[43] Thomas follows a similar line of argumentation, maintaining that Hilary meant only to suggest that the pain and suffering Christ experienced did not affect his sense of reason (*sensum rationis*), which never deviated from its state of equanimity (*a sua aequalitate*) during the period of suffering. "Therefore," Thomas concludes, "pain did not have dominion over him."[44]

Our high-medieval commentators give much the same sort of response when it comes to the question whether Christ experienced sorrow or fear in the passion, as Hilary had categorically denied. All affirm that Christ experienced fear and sorrow in his human nature. However, Christ experienced them differently than we do.[45] Appealing to a distinction first developed by Jerome, they argue that Christ experienced a sort of "half-passion" (*propassio*) of fear and sorrow rather than a full-blown passion (*passio*).[46] Fear and sorrow of this variety never threatened to swamp the capacities of Christ's reason and to throw his soul into disorder and confusion.[47] When Hilary asserted that Christ did not experience fear or sorrow, therefore, he meant only that he did not experience a full-blown *passio*, which would have overcome reason's capacities to control them.[48]

Conclusions

The story of the interpretation and transformation of Hilary could go on. The attempt to improve Hilary, to explain his words away and to remove him from suspicion of error consumed enormous dogmatic and scholarly energy long after the close of the Middle Ages. Between the seventeenth and twentieth centuries, many scholars tortured themselves to show that Hilary did not in fact say what he clearly did and emphatically meant to say.[49] These efforts have continued right down to our own day.[50] One would think that the spectacle of scores of commentators over the course of centuries laboring to vindicate the orthodoxy of Hilary would have troubled these modern commentators or at least have struck them as ironic. But none seems to have regarded (or to have been willing to regard) the sheer volume of commentary on *De Trinitate* as a sign of possible defects in Hilary's Christology. Very few have been able to bring themselves to agree with the recently promulgated verdict of Hanson, who pronounces Hilary's Christology, not without justice, "nakedly Docetic."[51]

The point is not, however, to decide the issue of Hilary's doctrinal purity here, even if such a question, which presumes the existence of transhistorical criteria of orthodoxy, could profitably be addressed. The point is that Hilary's medieval readers felt quite able to define the borders of orthodoxy, and virtually all felt that, in the apparent and simple meaning of his words, he had strayed over them. He appeared to have denied that the Son of God had truly suffered pain in the passion, that his flesh was like ordinary human flesh, and that he experienced any of the psychological anguish commonly associated with the expectation of suffering and death. As the high-medieval commentators themselves recognized, and explicitly stated, all of these opinions were stigmata of ancient heresy, hopelessly inconsistent with the meaning of the historic conciliarly defined faith and even, if true, catastrophic for the hope of salvation.

Yet none could admit, finally, that these opinions of Hilary were heretical— or even that these *were* the opinions of Hilary. The most they could concede was that Hilary's language *appeared* to be erroneous and to contradict the articles of the Catholic faith. They could admit only that *if* Hilary said what he seemed to say, *then* he was in error. But all finally assert that Hilary did not in fact say what he appeared to say. Having diagnosed a serious problem with his work, they then proceed to declare the problem merely apparent and to furnish his apparently heterodox words with their "true" and benign meaning.

They must do this, however, by introducing distinctions which have no basis at all in Hilary's thought. When Hilary declared that Christ did not experience *dolor* in the passion, he meant that neither his human soul nor his divine person experienced *dolor*. But the medieval commentators insist that Hilary was speaking only *quantum ad Deitatem* and that Hilary meant that Christ experienced *dolor* in his human soul. As we have seen, he meant no such thing. Again, when Hilary says that Christ experienced neither fear nor sorrow, he meant that Christ did not experience these passions *at all*. But the medieval commentators argue that Hilary only meant to deny that Christ experienced them as full-blown *passiones*, not that he was utterly invulnerable to them or incapable of experiencing them as *propassiones*. Again, Hilary meant precisely that he was utterly immune to passion of any sort.

What is going on here? It might be argued that the medieval commentators are merely clarifying the implicit or immanent meaning of Hilary's language. Indeed, the medieval commentators imply by their practice that that is precisely what they are doing. In fact, they are not clarifying Hilary's meaning: They are *changing* it—and changing that meaning in what fairness itself could recognize as only the grossest, most drastic fashion imaginable. Meanings utterly alien to Hilary's intentions are being attached to his words. The medieval commentators cling tenaciously to the name and the words of Hilary, but they utterly repudiate his purpose and meaning. They conserve the form of his words but empty the form of its original substance. When we compare the opinions of the real Hilary to the interpreted Hilary, it can be said (and said without exaggeration) that there is absolutely *no* substantial or essential continuity between the two. The continuity between the two is purely verbal or nominal.

Now, it is of course true that theologians and exegetes in a later age must explain the past (or at least they have explained the past) in terms of new knowledge and new terminology. In that sense, it is also of course true that later theologians and exegetes must always create *something* new, at least at the linguistic level, when they interpret ancient texts. After all, absolutely perfect or exact continuity could only occur if medieval thinkers preserved ancient opinion in exactly the same linguistic form in which they received it. But perfect linguistic continuity of this sort certainly can not function as a normative criterion of continuity for thinkers anxious to interpret ancient wisdom in their own terms and for their own age. For then *any* change in language or terminology would necessarily involve the charge of discontinuity or infidelity to the received tradition. Indeed, it would paralyze thinkers who treasure past knowledge and who wish to interpret and transmit it for a new age. Ancient insight and truth, if it is to be preserved and transmitted for use in religious communities, must of course be adapted to new knowledge, new terminology and new habits of thought.

Yet it would be patently absurd to suggest that new knowledge and new terminology must involve radical or even significant change in meaning. Indeed, it is always possible to distinguish novelty in form or expression from novelty in meaning or content, and the former does not *require* the latter. Of course, one might argue that form affects content, and that may be true. But novel linguistic terms and expressions need not necessarily change or alter the meaning of an ancient texts in fundamental or important ways. Indeed, there can be nothing theoretically objectionable about asserting the possibility of a new linguistic expression conveying ancient opinion with essentially unchanged meaning. Thus the true criterion of continuity must be, not whether exactly the same linguistic expressions are used by a later thinker but *whether the essential meaning of an ancient author has been preserved.* Even where new terminology and expressions are used, it is possible to ask, and often to answer, whether the essential meaning of an ancient author has been upheld.

Not *always,* naturally, but *often.* It is true that ancient texts *can* be ambiguous, and the question of an author's intention *can* also be a difficult one. Yet, it is also true, though not as often argued, that some ancient texts are not really all that ambiguous, nor are all authorial intentions opaque. In this case, Hilary's opinions are so clear, his intentions so explicit, and his ideas on Christ's body and soul so monotonously repeated, that his meaning and purposes cannot honestly be said to be unclear or ambiguous at all. In fact, one might argue that the problem for the high-medieval theologians under consideration here was precisely the alarming clarity of Hilary's positions. Hilary's christological opinions were problematic and required laborious "re-interpretation" precisely because they *lacked* ambiguity. Indeed, the problem was, as Bonaventure explicitly and candidly acknowledged, the transparent error of the plain and apparent meaning of his words. It was thus the task of his medieval interpreters to *introduce* ambiguity where there had been shining, if discomfiting, clarity.[52]

This they achieved by smuggling in new readings under the guise of an unchanging transmission of the old tradition. The medieval guardians of tradition made the true opinions of Hilary disappear. But they did so under the guise of simply explaining or clarifying the old tradition and re-presenting it in more intelligible but essentially unchanged form (*"Hilarius dicit..."*). Radical discontinuity in tradition was presented as if it were perfect continuity. The new was passed on as if it were the established. The hope seems to have been that radical discontinuity would be interpreted as identity and verbal manipulation unperceived or overlooked in the name of protecting the reputation and opinions of a putative saint and patron of orthodoxy.

It would be wrong to characterize this sort of handling of tradition and attitude toward authority as "premodern" pure and simple. In a limited but real sense, the high-medieval attitude toward what has been handed down (*traditum*) is rather "modern." There is real discontent and dissatisfaction with what has been received; the past is experienced as burden. There is a perception that the *auctoritates* that have been inherited are not adequate as they stand. There is an incipient but very "modern" spirit of criticism of received opinion, a willingness to question and to challenge authority and to subject it to rational criticism and clarification. The past is untenable; it needs to be changed. There is at least an initial announcement of gross defects in the tradition. There is in fact a willingness to jettison the received and, ironically, ample evidence to suggest that received opinions *have* in fact been repudiated. The medieval commentators' first impulse is to criticize and even reject and abandon a part of the tradition experienced as unsatisfactory.

But the impulse toward the modern—by which I mean here simply the impulse to criticize the inherited and to challenge the authority of the accepted— is quickly suppressed. What we see here are medieval figures caught between the spirit of rational criticism and the spirit of authority. Along with the willingness to criticize and even jettison the tradition, there is an unwillingness to *state* that the established has been rejected, even though it is perfectly clear that that is what has happened. The past cannot be consciously or explicitly rejected; it must be done tacitly. Perhaps these commentators could not acknowledge, even to themselves, that the past had in fact been repudiated. After all, for these medieval commentators, the anti-Arian tradition of Hilarian opinion in *De Trinitate* was an "object of reverence" with enormous normative power. As Edward Shils has observed, "sheer pastness may commend the performance of an action or the acceptance of a belief."[53] In this case, the pastness of so venerable a defender of Nicene orthodoxy as Hilary, and the cultural and religious status he had achieved within a tradition so reverent and protective of its theological saints, compelled the acceptance of his words—at least in some sense. In a real sense, for Hilary's medieval inheritors, the issue was not what Hilary really meant by those words; the only issue was what opinions those weighty words could be made to express. Given the medieval piety of the past,[54] it may have been difficult, perhaps unthinkable, to admit that *some* of Hilary's words were, in fact, unworthy of the normative power that they had acquired.

Those words and Hilary's name had—somehow—to be conserved. Hilary's words, as the Lombard admonished his readers, had to be understood "piously." Yet in order for this part of the tradition to be made useable, the "pious" reading of Hilary required that the accident of his words be totally—*totally*—transformed by the interpretive ministrations of his medieval inheritors. Only then was their substance thought ready for consumption.

6

Christus Passibilis?

Did Christ Experience Fear and Sorrow in Gethsemane?

Coepit Iesus pavere et taedere

—Mark 14:33

Powerful and even inexpressibly poignant though it might be to modern readers, Jesus' Agony in the Garden (Matt 26:36–46; Mark 14:32–42; Luke 22:40–46) was a plague and embarrassment to patristic and medieval interpreters.[1] Few narratives in the New Testament were so inimical to received christological assumptions. Ancient and medieval interpreters, at least those judged, ultimately, to be "orthodox," ascribed to the Incarnate Word the qualities of divine consubstantiality, omnipotence, omniscience, obedience, and impassibility. However, the pericope, at least in its Markan and Matthean versions,[2] presents them with a figure who appears in all-too-human form, that is, powerless, ignorant, recalcitrant, and passible.

In large part because of these narrative qualities, the Markan and Matthean narratives generated an enormous explanatory literature over the course of the first thirteen centuries of Christian history. The purpose of this chapter is to analyze, in the high-medieval interpretation of these narratives, a portion of that literature which again sharply focuses some fundamental questions on the use of patristic tradition in Christian thought, in particular on the perennial issue of continuity and change.

Gethsemane: The Christological Problems

Premodern interpreters, at least those with "orthodox" christological sympathies, found it awkward that, among other things, Jesus appears in Gethsemane in a pose of weakness and reliance upon his Father's powers. Few ancient exegetes expressed the disturbing implications of this feature of the narrative more memorably than Ambrose of Milan: "Do not open your ears," the archbishop admonishes his readers, "to those treacherous people [Ambrose is thinking of the homoian "Arians"] who suggest that it was out of infirmity that the Son of God prayed, as though he had to ask for something which he was powerless to achieve himself."[3] Almost a thousand years later, Thomas Aquinas would observe, no less anxiously, that, "since Christ could do all things, it does not appear that there should be any need for him to petition anything from another."[4] Given the assumption of omnipotence, though, why *does* the Son of God pray to his Father here?

Even if ancient and medieval readers could overcome the problem of Jesus' apparent weakness by arguing that the Son of God was simply harnessing his own divine power here, or furnishing his followers an example of filial prayer,[5] problems remained. One involved the apparent doubt and ignorance of Jesus. How could Jesus ask his Father for deliverance from the cross? Was he in doubt about his salvific role or about his Father's chosen means of salvation? And what about the beginning of Jesus' prayer? "My Father, *if* it is possible... (Matt 26:39; emphasis mine). Do these words imply that he was in doubt about his Father's power to answer his prayer? This possibility was so problematic that it generated in high-medieval *Sentence* commentaries the production of a new theological *quaestio: Utrum Christus dubitavit quando dixit, Si possibile est, etc.* (Whether Christ doubted when he said, "If it is possible...").[6] For medieval commentators, responding to this question would be made no easier by Ambrose's blunt admission that "as a man he doubted (*Ut homo ergo dubitat*)."[7] As if to make their task more challenging, Bonaventure and Thomas Aquinas would later problematize the verse even further by noting that doubt implies the existence of other defects in the doubter, namely fear, ignorance and error.[8]

Still more difficult questions are raised by Jesus' importunity. In the Matthean version of the pericope, Jesus prays to his Father three times about the possibility of deliverance from the cup of his passion (Matt 26:39, 42, 44). Many premodern interpreters, pondering the meaning of this thrice-repeated prayer, found themselves wondering whether Christ had submitted to death involuntarily and asking whether Jesus' resistance to his Father's will, or his submission to it, was finally stronger.

Perhaps the most remarkable feature of the pericope, in light of Helle-nistic reflection on the role of the passions in the life of the good or ideal man, are the depth and power of the παθή Jesus appears to experience in the Garden. Particularly important in this connection is the intensity of Jesus' grief and fear. At the beginning of the pericope in Matthew, the narrator announces that Jesus is "grieved and anxious" (λυπεῖσθαι καὶ ἀδημονεῖν; Matt 26:37). Jesus himself tells Peter, James and John that his "soul is deeply sorrowful" (περίλυπος; Matt 26:38) and then collapses under the heavy weight of his grief (Matt 26:39). Equally problematic are the fervor of his anguished pleas for deliverance (Matt 26:39, 42, 44) and the depth of his exasperation with the failure of his disciples (Matt 26:40, 43). One need only think of Athanasius's *Life* of Antony to realize how important the ideal of *apatheia* became in the life of the church by the beginning of the fourth century.[9] Looking back at the Gethsemane story, could Athanasius have concluded that Jesus had achieved the summit of Christian perfection?

Again, to many modern readers, there is hardly a more moving spectacle in the New Testament than Jesus collapsing in the Garden and praying, in fear and trembling, to his Father. But the features which make the narrative so attractive to moderns are precisely those which so troubled the ancients. Jesus almost nowhere else in the Gospels appears so impressively "human" as he does here. To ancient and medieval exegetes, few narrative features could be more distressing than these, almost none as potentially adverse to received christological assumptions.

The first literary evidence of embarrassment with so weak and passible a figure appears, however, not in second- and third-century patristic commen-taries but as early as the Gospel of Luke. Luke begins his version of the pe-ricope, we recall, by transferring the sorrow present in the Markan narrative from Jesus to the disciples. The disciples, Luke tells us, are sleeping "because of their grief" (ἀπὸ τῆς λύπης; Luke 22:45). And their Lord? Luke says nothing explicit about his psychic state. However, his redaction of the Markan original is quite telling. Not only does Luke purge the Markan reference to Jesus' grief. He also has Jesus pray not, as in Mark, three times but only once. In the hands of Luke, the grieving and fearful Jesus is transformed into a Socratic figure of equanimity and poise in the face of death, one whose soul not even the most appalling suffering can vex.[10]

The author of the Fourth Gospel has, of course, no precise equivalent to the Gethsemane pericope. But in the passion prediction found in John 12, we do hear an echo of the pericope, leading one to believe that the evangelist was responding to the Markan version of the story (or to something very like it). Following the "Markan" tradition, the author of the Fourth Gospel allows Jesus to admit that his "soul is troubled" (ἡ ψυχή μου τετάρακται; John 12:27). But he permits this, it seems, only to ridicule the weakness of the "Markan" Jesus and to assert the sovereignty, obedience and serenity of his: "And what shall I say?" Jesus asks (sarcastically?). " 'Father, save me from this hour'?" (the Markan Jesus' prayer). And he answers, with unswerving resolve: "No, for this purpose I have come to this hour" (John 12:27).

Thus Luke and John, taming the wilder elements of the text, inaugurate the dominant trend in the history of the interpretation of the earliest version of the pericope. That is, the domestication of the text begins almost immediately, within the canonical period, or (speaking from a *post* sixth-century perspective) within the covers of the New Testament codex itself. It is a trend that only a few would resist over the course of the next thirteen centuries.

Patristic Loci

Analysis of high-medieval exegesis of Jesus in Gethsemane must begin with the patristic *sententiae* extracted from the writings of the fathers by Peter Lombard. Not only was Peter's *Sentences* the standard textbook of theology in the Middle Ages, but all of the major high-scholastic thinkers commented on the text, and the interpretation of each follows the general lines set down in it. Biblical commentaries and *summae* written in the period were also influenced by it. Thus, virtually all high-medieval reflection on the Gethsemane pericope at least begins with the *auctoritates* and *sententiae* selected by the Lombard and with his own creative resolution (*determinatio auctoritatum*).

In this case, Peter gathers the opinions of four major patristic thinkers: Ambrose, Hilary, Augustine, and Jerome. He finds that the authors not only appear to contradict one another but themselves. Indeed, he locates no fewer than three different opinions of Jerome. He begins, however, with Ambrose.

Much of Ambrose's christological thought was directed, more or less explicitly, against the Arians. As we have seen, the Arians, in an effort to prove that the *logos* was an inferior deity, attributed the *pathē* experienced by Jesus in the Gospels to the divine Word. To overcome this exegetical maneuver, Ambrose assigned the *passiones* to the humanity of the Incarnate Word. When he comes to consider Gethsemane, therefore, Ambrose bluntly admits that, "Christ feared . . . as a man [*ut homo*] he is troubled, as a man he weeps . . . as a man he had sadness" and as a man doubted the power of his Father.[11] That is, in order to screen the *Verbum* from mutability, Ambrose siphons the passions of fear and sorrow, assigned by the Arians to the *logos*, to the humanity assumed by God the Word.

Like Ambrose, Hilary of Poitiers was a vigorous opponent of the Arians. Like Ambrose, too, much of his exegetical writings became problematic in high-medieval reflection. However, Ambrose became a problem because he appeared to emphasize too much the reality of Christ's *passiones*, Hilary for appearing to deemphasize them out of existence. Throughout Book 10 of *De Trinitate*, Hilary insists, over and over again, that Christ had a body but one which, because of its origin, was unique.[12] Indeed, Hilary suggests that the nature of this body prevented him from not only feeling sadness or fear but even, as we have seen, physical pain (*dolor*).[13] When he comes to those texts which suggest that Jesus *did* feel doubt or fear or grief, he characteristically replies that it does not "stand to reason" (*[non] ratione subsistat*)[14] that Jesus felt these passions, and he then presents his own proof-texts that demonstrate his courage and his freedom from grief (e.g., rebuking Peter for not recognizing the necessity of the passion).[15] So apparently unorthodox and so voluminous were these texts that the Lombard was forced to dedicate a separate theological *quaestio* concerning "several unintelligible chapters of Hilary" (*de quibusdam capitulis Hilarii obscuris*),[16] and all of the major mendicant commentators committed several *quaestiones* to interpreting them as well.[17]

Hilary became a problem because he appeared to be unorthodox, not because he was inconsistent. On the other hand, both Jerome and Augustine said self-contradictory things about the passage. At one point in his writings, Jerome, like Hilary, colorfully denies that Christ felt fear in the Garden: "Let those who think that the Savior feared death and in fear of his passion said, 'Let this cup pass from me'—let them turn pink with shame."[18] In his *Enarrationes* on the Psalms, Augustine appears to agree, denying that Christ felt true sadness and alleging, by appeal to the Tyconian head-members exegetical technique enshrined in *De Doctrina Christiana*, that when Jesus prays, "*Transeat a me calix iste*," he is praying, not for himself, but for his mystical body—i.e., for the church.[19] At another point both Jerome and Augustine seem simply to agree with Ambrose: Christ suffered, but only in the humanity he assumed, leaving the divine Word free of suffering and change.[20] At yet another point, Jerome qualifies the nature of Christ's sufferings significantly by distinguishing them from ordinary human afflictions. According to Jerome, we suffer passions that "dominate the soul." But Christ experienced only "half-passions," or *propassiones*, which did not overcome his human soul. Jerome then cleverly suggests that this is why the evangelist specifies that Jesus "*began* to be sorrowful and troubled" (Matt 26:38). "It is one thing to be saddened," Jerome concludes, "another *to begin* to be saddened."[21]

High-medieval thinkers would find this explanation extremely appealing. Indeed, the category of *propassio*, refined, clarified, and embellished by

thirteenth-century thinkers, would influence the terms of the scholastic discussion more than any other. If high-medieval discussion was in continuity
with any strand of patristic interpretation, it was with this third explanation of
Jerome.

High-Medieval Interpretations

The Lombard's own creative interpretation depends to a great extent on Jerome's. According to Peter, Christ did not suffer fear and sorrow in their full-
blown form (*secundum passionem*) but only in diminished form (*secundum propassionem*).[22] But what do Jerome's terms really mean? Peter elaborates. One
who voluntarily endures fear and sorrow so that the mind is moved neither
from virtue nor from the contemplation of God experiences a *propassio*. One
who involuntarily experiences these passions as a result of sin suffers a complete *passio* because the mind is truly moved and troubled.[23] Christ assumed
these passions voluntarily, not *causa peccati*, as we did.[24] Thus, in Gethsemane
Christ "was not so troubled in his soul by fear or sadness that he deviated in
any way from virtue or the contemplation of God."[25]

The same distinction allows Peter to reconcile apparently contradictory
patristic opinion. The Lombard explicitly recognized that the fathers not only
appeared to contradict one another but themselves as well. Speaking of Augustine's exegesis of Gethsemane, for example, Peter will admit that, unless
the proper way (*intelligentiae causa*) to interpret his words is found, "you will
clearly observe that the same thinker contradicts himself."[26] But Jerome's interpretive key allows Augustine truly to say *both* that Jesus did not truly fear *and*
that he truly did feel fear.[27] One need only distinguish in what sense—*secundum propassionem* or *secundum passionem*—Augustine was speaking at the
moment. When one knows and applies this sense, "then," the Lombard concludes, "there is no contradiction."[28] Augustine meant only to suggest that
Christ experienced fear and sorrow voluntarily and *secundum propassionem*, not,
as we would, necessarily and *secundum passionem*. We ought to accept this
distinction, Peter insists, precisely because, if we do not, "some unfavorable
diversity [could] be imputed to the sacred literature"—that is, to the writings of
the fathers.[29]

All of the mendicant *Sentence* commentators here take the Lombard's
interpretation as their basic point of departure. But all also elaborate greatly
on the terms of his exegesis. All furnish a much richer, more detailed and (to
them) more precise description of exactly what was happening in Jesus' soul
in Gethsemane. Indeed, so much more sophisticated and technical is their

exegesis than the Lombard's that it represents a new development in the interpretation of Jesus' Agony in the Garden, though one linked at least formally with Peter's. It is also an interpretation that makes one wonder if high-medieval commentators believed that it was indeed something like that normally implied in our word "agony" that Jesus experienced in the Garden.

Each of the high-scholastic commentators under consideration here begins his analysis of Christ's *passiones* in the Garden by stating that Christ did experience "real sorrow" (*vera tristitia*). Bonaventure emphatically declares that "without doubt, as the Master [i.e., the Lombard] says and as the gospel text also confirms, there was real sorrow in Christ."[30] Bonaventure even allows that he appears to experience sorrow "truly and intensely" (*veraciter et intense*).[31] Each medieval commentator hastens to add, however, that Christ did not experience sorrow precisely as we do.[32] In order to describe Christ's experience of sorrow, each distinguishes that kind of sorrow which is against the judgment of reason from that sorrow which is subject to its command and sovereignty. The first category of sorrow arises from the sensitive part of the soul (*pars sensitiva*) and throws the soul into complete disorder and confusion (*perturbatio*). The second arises when reason stimulates the sensitive power of the soul to be sorrowful about something and contains it within the sensitive appetite, so that reason is not overcome.[33] While we routinely experience that first variety of sorrow, which throws the soul into turmoil, Jesus experienced sorrow only of the second variety. Christ "was made sorrowful," Bonaventure declares, "by nothing except what reason told him to be."[34]

Our medieval exegetes proceed in similar fashion when it comes to the question of whether Christ experienced fear at the prospect of his imminent death. Bonaventure admits that Mark 14:33 certainly makes it appear as if he did: "*Coepit Iesus pavere et taedere.*" He then begins by distinguishing three kinds of fear: that fear in which the sensitive part of the soul overcomes reason, that fear which is subject to reason, and that fear which is experienced by the rational part of the soul itself. The first and third are part of our corrupt nature and throw the soul into disorder. The second form of fear (which is also part of our corrupt nature) does not overcome the soul's rationality. According to Bonaventure, it is this kind of fear which Christ experienced in Gethsemane.[35] Many of his contemporaries agreed with him.[36]

Once again, it is reason which stimulates the lower regions of the soul to act, rather than the other way around. Christ's reason first perceives that he is about to die. It then transmits this information by producing an image of death in the sensitive part of the soul. Only then does the sensitive part of the soul experience the horror of death.[37] Because reason is in control of this entire order of experience, Bonaventure can even conclude that Christ "was most secure [*securissima*] and knew very well that nothing could happen to him which it [i.e., reason] did not first desire or wish."[38] Thomas also adds that Christ did not experience the kind of fear that would imply ignorance or uncertainty in the one who feared.[39]

Interestingly enough, Bonaventure anticipates what seems to be the natural objection to this argument, namely, that it inverts the familiar order of human experience. He first grants the objection some force:

> So if you say that this is not the sequence in which we experience things, namely that fear is given by reason to the sensitive part of the soul, I would answer that it is true for us, because we acquire knowledge from the lower parts of the soul.[40]

But, he goes on, "it could be different in Christ" because in him there was a "perfect obedience of the lower powers of his soul to the higher."[41] That is, where in our unruly and disordered spirits, the fear of death springs from the sensitive region of the soul and overcomes the power of reason to curb it, the rational part of Christ's soul first perceives the threat and can then dictate to its sensitive power that, and to what proportionate degree, it should feel fear.

Notice that both Thomas and Bonaventure go well beyond most classical Greek thinking in their depiction of the man perfectly guided by reason. Neither medieval exegete, after all, is asserting that reason bridled the passions that percolated up involuntarily from the depths of Jesus' soul. That would be to state the case entirely too weakly and indeed falsely. For Bonaventure and Thomas, reason is so thoroughly in control of Jesus' soul that it does not "bridle" or restrain his emotions but actually dictates to its lower powers under what conditions and to what extent it should emote. In Jesus' soul, reason is never a reactor; it is always a dictator.

Having offered this interpretation of the biblical text, our medieval commentators then turn to an analysis of the patristic opinions that they began by citing. The bulk of their attention here is given to Ambrose and Hilary, whose opinions were the most dichotomous of those gathered by the Lombard. All agree that Ambrose seemed quite categorically to ascribe sorrow, fear, and doubt to Jesus in Gethsemane. Despite appearances, however, that was *not* what Ambrose meant. Appealing to the distinctions just developed, all insist that Ambrose meant to assign a *certain kind* of passion to Christ. While it seemed to observers that Christ's reason was overcome by fear, for example, Christ experienced fear only within the sensitive realm of his soul. *This* is what Ambrose meant to imply.[42] All agree, also, that the doubt that Ambrose assigned to Christ was not noetic: Christ was not in doubt about his Father's design nor was he ignorant of his role in salvation history and the necessity of his death. No,

Ambrose meant to assign to Christ doubt of another sort altogether, where doubt signifies a certain hesitation (*indifferentia*) of the sensitive power of the soul to follow the command of reason and to obey instead the natural desire to avoid death.[43] In short, as Albert puts it, Ambrose puts nothing blameworthy (*vituperabile*) in the soul of Christ.[44]

Our commentators then turn to Hilary, who seemed no less categorical than Ambrose, though at the opposite, docetic end of the christological spectrum. Again, all of the medieval commentators agree that Hilary did not intend to imply that Christ experienced *no* fear or doubt or sorrow in Gethsemane, only that he did not experience a certain, incriminating kind of fear. As Bonaventure puts it:

> Hilary does not intend to remove fear from Christ in the way that Scripture and the Saints attribute it to him but in the way that the heretics [Bonaventure has the "Arians" in mind] do, who say that he feared from a lack of security (*defectus securitatis*).[45]

This, Bonaventure concludes, is a pusillanimous fear (*timor pusillanimitatis*)—and "it is undoubtedly true that Christ did not experience this."[46] Those, like Hilary, who say that Christ did not fear meant only that his fear did not overcome the power of reason to constrain it.[47] Hilary, like Ambrose, meant only to assign to Christ's human soul passions which were assumed voluntarily rather than necessarily, dictated by reason rather than spontaneously felt, weak in breadth and ephemeral in effect.

So apparently irreconcilable at the outset, Ambrose and Hilary turn out, on deeper examination, to have intended precisely the same interpretation of the psychology of Jesus' soul in Gethsemane. Put another way, Bonaventure and Thomas bring Ambrose and Hilary together by invoking the Hieronymian concept of *propassio*. This concept is certainly used and extended by the high-medieval scholastics under consideration here. Indeed, this is one of the few instances in the study in which a patristic idea—the idea of a "half-passion"—can be said to be basically continuous with high-medieval notions of how Christ experienced the passions. However, it does do great violence to the thought of Ambrose and Hilary, neither of whom would have been comfortable with Jerome's notion of *propassio*.

7

Christus Orans?

A Praying God?

In the tenth book of *De Trinitate,* Hilary of Poitiers gave extended
consideration to the motive and meaning of three prayers from the
passion narrative: "My Father, if it is possible, let this cup pass from
me" (Matt 26:39); "My God, My God, why have you forsaken me?"
(Matt 27:46; Mark 15:34); and "Father, into your hands I commend my
spirit" (Luke 23:46). All three prayers were used by the Arians in an
attempt to establish the ontological inferiority of the Son to the Father.
In fact, Hilary states (as we saw in the second chapter) that the latter
two prayers comprise, together, the "chief weapons" in the Arian
campaign to deny the divinity of the Son.[1] In this chapter, we focus
upon key ancient and medieval inquiries into the question, why did
the Incarnate Son pray?

Hilary of Poitiers

Given the anti-Arian aim of *De Trinitate,* it is not surprising that
Hilary argues vigorously that the Son's prayers in the passion narratives do not prove that he is a reduced divinity or a creature. Why,
then, did he pray? Was he powerless to effect what only High Divinity
could achieve? And did he pray for himself, as certainly appears to
be the case in the biblical narrative? These sorts of questions put
Hilary in a very awkward position, and his responses seem close to

justifying Hanson's observation, recorded below, that Hilary's exegesis could be quite tortured.[2]

Beginning with Jesus' prayer that the chalice of passion might pass from him, Hilary observes that Jesus was obviously not genuinely praying that he might avoid the cup of passion. After all, that cup was "already before him," the pouring out of his blood even then being enacted. What effect would it have to pray for the removal of the cup then? Hilary goes on to argue that the Son prayed, not that the cup would not be with him, but that it would pass away from him. (This seems to be a distinction without a meaningful difference.) Far from praying for something contrary to the wishes and even the salvific plan of the Father, the Son prays in fact that his will *not* be done. He prays rather to demonstrate his solidarity with the anxiety of the human condition; he utters his prayer conditionally rather than absolutely. So far from requesting something contrary to the will of the Father, the Son's will is in perfect union with the Father's effective will. Accordingly, Jesus prefaces his plea with the condition, "if it be possible."

Of course, this clause raises the possibility that Jesus harbored doubt about the Father's power in general and of his ability to deliver his son from this situation of agony in particular. Hilary quickly dismisses this possibility by declaring that such a possibility is irrelevant to the point of absurdity because, as is axiomatic, "nothing is impossible for the Father." Moving thus over these problematic implications of Jesus' prayer, Hilary finally concludes that it was not for himself that Jesus was sorrowful or prayed, nor was his prayer in tension with the will of the Father. Instead, he was sorrowful for the disciples; it was for them he prayed. Jesus implored God not that the cup pass away from him, but that it not abide with *them*. Knowing that they (particularly Peter) would face similar tribulation, he prays that their faith not fail in the moment of trial.[3]

The Arian exegesis of scripture is once again in the background when Hilary turns to Jesus' prayer of dereliction on the cross and the commending of his Spirit to the Father. For Arian interpreters, both prayers were essentially confessions of weakness and inferiority, definitive proof that the Son of God was incapable of delivering himself from the agony of passion and death. The Arians also apparently read Jesus' prayer of dereliction as a sign of his doubt about his own role in salvation history. Naturally, they also made much of his passibility in the account of his suffering.

Hilary sees none of this. Far from an expression of the doubts of the Son, or a confession of weakness, Jesus prayed to the Father to scatter *our* doubts, to insure that we were certain he had died and therefore had truly assumed human form. When he addresses God as Father, it is for our instruction; thus it is that we know he is the Son. Since his prayer was of no avail to him, it is obvious that it was intended to cure our ignorance of his identity and role. Again, the Son prays not from weakness and certainly not as a complaint for suffering. Indeed, "he found his greatest joy in suffering," and, though it appears as if he despaired, he actually "rejoiced upon the cross." "Ever secure of his identity," he was indifferent, Hilary assures his readers, to suffering and death.[4] Hilary observes that the Arians die in a state of "godless unbelief" because they infer he prayed out of weakness and powerlessness, that he accepted passion and death involuntarily and because he doubted the Father's sovereign power. But that, Hilary concludes, is all too typical of these "idiotic and terribly impious men" (*stultissimi atque impiissimi homines*).[5]

Ambrose of Milan

As with Hilary, the Arian context shapes Ambrose's treatment of the problem of Jesus' prayers. One of Ambrose's briefest and earliest treatments comes in his *Commentary on Luke*, where he treats Jesus' prayer, "let this cup pass from me" (Luke 22:42). Ambrose is very much aware of the Arian view of this text, which underlined the Son's creaturely weakness, and so he exhorts his reader to refuse to open his ears to those theological traitors who imagine that "the very source of power prays because he could not fulfill his own wishes."[6] Unlike Hilary, who assumed the human nature had been unconditionally transformed by proximity to and union with the divine, Ambrose here assumes a strict division between the human and divine natures of the Incarnate Son. Accordingly, he interprets the prayer in Gethsemane as a kind of internal disputation between two plaintiffs, one fleshly and one spiritual, each making its case before the Supreme Judge. Thus it is the plea of the flesh that implores God to let the cup pass; it is the voice of the spirit that trumps the former by qualifying the prayer with the addition, "not what I will, but you." It is the former that takes on wretchedness and infirmity; but God's nature "could not feel" (*natura Dei sentire non potuit*) these.[7]

This dualistic explanation is altogether typical of Ambrose. It can almost be regarded as the key to his Christology. In order to protect the full divinity of the Son, Ambrose channeled all infirmity and passion to the human nature of the Incarnate Word, thus screening the Father from passibility and—crucially important—securing the integrity of human salvation. What Ambrose (again characteristically) seems not to have perceived is that this christological dualism seems to leave the humanity hermetically sealed, so to speak, from the divine nature and thus untouched by it. It would not be before that a similarly dualistic christological position would be condemned in the East. Perhaps Ambrose succeeded in preserving the integrity of the divine nature; but later thinkers, including high scholastic Latin commentators on his work, would find he paid too dear a theological price.

Turning to the same prayers in *De Fide*, Ambrose focuses intently on the Arian taunt that the conditional *if it be possible* proves that the Son of God was ignorant of the role of the cross in salvation history or was doubtful of his Father's capacity to deliver him from the cup of passion. Again, his strictly dualistic christological assumptions profoundly shape his handling of these problems. For Ambrose, the hermeneutical key is to be found in establishing "in what character" Christ speaks when he prays. Not surprisingly, he concludes that it is not as God but as a man (*quasi homo*) that he prays for the passing of the cup. It is as a man that Christ doubts and fears (and here Ambrose concedes much more than Hilary). Like Hilary, though, Ambrose asserts (and here "gnostic" Docetism—Valentinus, Marcion, and Mani's followers are all explicitly mentioned—is in the background), that the man exhibits the weakness of the flesh in order that "the wickedness of those who deny the mystery of the Incarnation have no excuse."[8]

Ambrose takes advantage of a similar strategy when treating the possibility that Jesus experienced doubt in Gethsemane. Again, he strictly segregates experiences the Son has *ut homo*–an expression used scores of times in *De Fide*—from those he has as God: "the will of God is one, the human will another."[9] Ambrose assigns to the human will Jesus' grief, his sorrow and weeping, and finally—and with surprising bluntness—his doubt: "As a human being, he doubts and is troubled."[10] His Godhead, again, is utterly unaffected. "He endured the passion," Ambrose concludes, "in his humanity" (*in natura hominis subiit passionem*).[11] But since he took on a soul (Ambrose's concession of this is likely a result of the Apollinarian controversy),[12] he took on its affections. He could not have doubted or been distressed, much less died, insofar as he was God. It is as a man that he begs God to know why he had been forsaken. It is as a man that he bore our terrors, is distressed, doubts, weeps, and is crucified.[13]

This straightforward, even slightly crude concession that the Son doubted the Father *ut homo* would become highly problematic in the Middle Ages. Peter Lombard would record—and attempt to rectify—Ambrose's remark in his *Sentences*, alerting scores of later medieval commentators on the *Sentences* to the problem—and generating thus hundreds of pages of commentary on an apparently erroneous opinion expressed by a Doctor of the Latin church. High-medieval commentators would find not only the specific comment, then de-contextualized, problematic but the dualistic christological assumptions that made it possible. If Hilary were regarded with alarm for his quasi-docetic christological remarks, Ambrose became a difficulty for too radically divorcing the human soul of Jesus from the eternal Word and leaving the former apparently untouched and untransformed by the latter. To medieval readers, it would seem as if the human and divine wills were simply not in communication with one another.[14] In fact, it appeared as if a somewhat recalcitrant human will were acting with utter sovereignty—"free-lancing," to put it in the vernacular—and even in defiance of the will of the divine word which apparently resided in such intimate proximity to it. Ambrose's words make it easy to believe that, in his view, the divinity and humanity were merely juxtaposed in (to use the Greek term) a loose "association" (συνάφεια). Many Greek writers in the Cyrillian tradition (and later Latin writers who absorbed that tradition through acceptance of the Chalcedonian definition) would find the ascription of sayings, titles or saving actions to two different natures, two kinds of scriptures, or two "characters" false and even heretical. Looking back from the vantage of Chalcedon, could it be said that, for Ambrose, the humanity and divinity existed "without division and without separation"? If we are speaking with respect to Jesus' human actions, will and "consciousness," we would almost certainly be forced to conclude that Ambrose would have been found gravely wanting by the Chalcedonian canon. Be that as it may, it is clear that, on first blush, his medieval readers certainly found him lacking not only for his christological dualism but for anthropological crudity as well.

John of Damascus

The experience of the passions, recoiling from pain, Jesus' prayer that he might be spared the cup of his passion—these were all, John begins, "in conformity with his nature," by which, of course, John meant his human nature. But, unlike Ambrose, John will not allow that these experiences or impulses sprang independently or in defiance of the divine nature with which it was in relation. Rather, the Word economically willed and allowed Christ to suffer and to "perform things proper to him."[15] His human will was ever subordinate and obedient to his divine will. Never governed by its own inclinations, it willed only what the divine will willed, because it was only with the permission and oversight, so to speak, of the divine will that he suffered what was proper to his nature. His prayer to escape death, therefore, was not a spontaneous outcry of agony and fear; it was with his divine will willing and permitting it that he so prayed. Indeed, the passion became voluntary for him, and it was voluntarily that he surrendered himself to death; he even "grew bold in the face of death."

Pedagogically, this obedience to God in subjecting his human nature to the Father, or having it so bent, was intended for us as a type and example.[16]

So for John it is entirely fitting and appropriate that God the Word should raise his voice in prayer to God the Father. Given John's definition of prayer, however, it is slightly awkward to explain how this could be the case. "Prayer," he states, in a formula that would be accepted and quoted time and again by high-medieval thinkers, "is the raising of the mind to God or a petitioning of God for what is fitting."[17] For Ambrose, it was enough to say simply that Christ had prayed *ut homo* or *quasi homo* or *secundum humanitatem*—"as a man." But John was writing well after such dualistic christological assumptions could have been regarded as compatible with the orthodox theology of the hypostatic union. Thus it is that he concedes Christ's holy mind was in no need of uprising, nor of any petition of God precisely because "Christ was one" and his humanity united with God.

The solution for John is again related to divine *paideia:* Christ "became an example for us and taught us to ask of God and strain toward him." When he prays that the cup may pass, he does not show himself to be "an enemy of God"—that is, in disharmony with the Father's will. Nor does the conditional clause "if it be possible" mean that he was in ignorance; for what, John asks rhetorically, is impossible to God? Only that which is impossible is against the will of God. Thus, Christ is teaching us to prefer God's will to our own.

Christ also made this prayer to prove that he possessed two wills (here the Monothelite controversy is again in the background) and to show that he had assumed the natural will of humanity, which seeks to escape death. But we are by no means to believe that these two wills were opposed to one another. When he utters words of dereliction on the cross, it is not because he was forsaken by his divinity. It was *we* who were forsaken. When he addresses God as "Father," he proves, somehow, that he is of the same essence, and thus capable of whatever the Father is. He says this prayer of dereliction for us, kenotically ranking himself among us and appropriating our curse and our desertion on our behalf.[18]

The opinions of all three of these writers would find their way into the scholastic literature of the high Middle Ages. Those of Hilary and Ambrose were found to be particularly problematic. Different as they are, it could be said that, viewed from one perspective, they shared the same christological flaw. For both, there seems to be no mutual "exchange of attributes," no *communicatio idiomatum.* For Hilary, the human nature of the Incarnate Son is so utterly transformed by union with divinity that it ceases to be truly human, while the human experiences to which Christ is subject most emphatically do not touch or change his divine nature. There is no exchange: all the change occurs, so to speak, in one direction.

Ambrose protects the impassibility of the divine in a different way, by radically splitting the two natures from one another. This move, however, would leave the impulsive, irrational human nature of Christ untouched by the divine in ways that later thinkers would find troubling and even (as they put it) "erroneous." The high-medieval task could be described as an attempt to reconcile Ambrose and Hilary by use of extremely fine and sophisticated anthropological distinctions, so as to make compatible their apparently radically opposed vision of the meaning and christological implications of Christ's prayer.

Peter Lombard

When one turns from the patristic to the scholastic discussion, one is struck immediately by the highly-developed anthropology of the medieval figures. In their discussion of the motive, meaning and implications of Jesus' prayer (the prayer for the removal of the cup is always assumed or stated to be the prayer in need of explication), high-medieval thinkers without exception begin by introducing sophisticated, fine distinctions between different human sources of, or different human impulses for, Jesus' plea to be spared the cup of crucifixion.

The literary source for this new anthropology was without doubt (high scholastic writers cite it explicitly) Hugh of St. Victor's very influential book On the Four Wills of Christ, certainly one of the least well known of the Victorine's influential works, though very important in the realm of medieval Christology.[19] Hugh fundamentally distinguished between Christ's divine and human wills. His human will he further distinguished into three operations or moments: the will of reason, the will of piety, and the will of the flesh.[20] These wills are organized hierarchically, and each will seeks something different and unique as its primary end: the divine will justice; the rational human will obedience to the divine will, the pious will mercy. The fleshly will—often called by later commentators the "sensitive" or "sensual" will—follows the desires of nature, for example, the desire not to die.[21] This four-fold distinction would exercise an enormous influence on contemporary and subsequent christological discussion. No thirteenth-century mendicant commentator on the Sentences would fail to exploit it.

Even before he takes on the fundamental question of why Christ prayed, Peter Lombard attempts to clarify the patristic discussion by introducing voluntary distinctions nowhere stated or even implied in the ancient writings. The Lombard's essential point is that Christ's prayer in Gethsemane reveals that his human will had two moments or even (it would not be incorrect to say) two components, each of which inclined Christ to desire something different.

Christ's rational will wished to suffer and die in Gethsemane; his sensitive will fled death. Thus Christ had a rational will, which wills as the divine will wishes, and a sensitive will.[22]

All human beings have a sensitive or sensual will, as did the Incarnate Christ. Because of its affinity with and connection to the flesh, it naturally flees death. It is this will, or in this moment of willing, that Christ prays for removal of the cup; this prayer that goes unheard or unanswered by God. But Christ also has a rational will. Unlike the sensitive will, this will or moment of willing is informed by charity. In this moment of willing, Christ, far from fleeing death, wished to die in accordance with the will of God. According to this will, he never asked for that which he knew God would not do, nor did he wish such a thing to be done by his rational or divine will.[23] Later medieval thinkers, including all of those under consideration in this study, would accept, and further refine, this binary view of Christ's human will.

Having established this view of Christ's will, the Lombard then poses the question, why, then, did Christ pray? The response he furnishes seems oddly to overlook the distinction he has just made and to focus on the prayer of the rational will. That prayer was intended to show his "members" (i.e., the church) the appropriate form of calling upon God and of subjecting one's will to the divine will when trouble is imminent. If burdened by anxiety, then, they might pray for its removal, as Christ had. If unable to avoid difficulty, they might bend themselves to the example of Christ, who himself was unable to avoid suffering. Nowhere here does the Lombard suggest that Christ prayed because overwhelmed by fear or powerlessness. Even less does he propose that Christ's prayer was informed by doubt. Rather, he prayed as a moral pedagogue.[24]

It is not surprising, then, to find the Lombard confessing, on the following page, that the words of Ambrose regarding Christ's prayer disturb him "not a little" (non parum). Indeed, they seem to suggest that Christ, at least according to his human affect, doubted the power of his Father when praying in Gethsemane, "Father, if it be possible. . . ." But, the Lombard argues, what Ambrose appeared to suggest has to be distinguished from that which he intended to say. He was not suggesting that, insofar as he was God or rather Son of God, he doubted; only that he doubted according to his human affect. (It might be observed here that Ambrose himself never suggested that Christ doubted as Son of God.) It is only in this sense that Ambrose meant that Christ doubted the power of his father. It was not that the Son of God qua Son doubted. Rather, in the union of human and divine, he assumed and bore the human mode of doubting (modum dubitantis). Thus, it appeared to those observing him (hominibus dubitare videbatur) that he, as Son of God, doubted the power of God the Father to remove from him the cup of the passion.[25]

This is a curious explanation, more elusive than appears on first viewing. First, Peter, like Ambrose, seems only to want to distinguish activities proper to each nature, human and divine, and to insist, as had Ambrose, that such doubting as may have occurred took place only within the human. What Hanson said about Ambrose seems, at first, to apply with equal force to the Lombard: He "establishes an exact division between what Christ says as a man and what he says as God."[26] Because the divine nature assumed a soul in the incarnation, he assumed its powers and passions. But the distinction between human weakness and the power of God is so absolute that it cannot be maintained that doubt in any way affected the Son of God. Only did it affect the Incarnate Word *ut homo,* as a man, and, more precisely, in the realm of human affect.

All of this the Lombard seems prepared initially to accept and, to this point, his explanation seems perfectly consistent with Ambrose's. However, at the end of his comment, he seems to back away subtly from Ambrose's blunt *ut homo* concessions. For to say that he bore the mode of doubting is to say something rather different than that he doubted. For it is possible to bear all sorts of capacities and qualities without exercising them, and this comment leaves open the possibility that Christ bore the capacity to doubt without actually doubting.

The Lombard's final comment leaves us even more in the dark about how he wants us to interpret the words of Ambrose. To say that it "appeared to men" that Christ was experiencing doubt is, after all, to suggest that those observing him had been deceived, had mistaken appearance for reality. And here the Lombard appears subtly to be suggesting that Christ had not, in fact, not even as a human being, experienced doubt about the Father's power. Here he really does distinguish himself from Ambrose or—not to put too fine a point on it—he puts words in Ambrose's mouth. In fact, he seems to suggest that such doubt as was present in Gethsemane was experienced in the perceptions of Christ's observers (who are not mentioned, by the way, in the biblical text) rather than in the soul of Christ. And that is a very different thing than to say bluntly, and with Ambrose, that, as a man, Christ doubted.

Peter concludes this chapter with a very enigmatic mention—*discussion* would be the wrong word—of Hilary's problematic comments on the prayer in Gethsemane. The Lombard is somewhat startled to report that Hilary "seems to assert" that Christ prayed, not for himself, but for others when he said, *Transeat a me calix iste.* This suggests that he feared for his disciples, not for himself. Hilary seems to be suggesting (the Lombard understood him quite correctly) that he was praying that the cup of passion might pass from *them.* He then quotes Hilary very extensively to prove that Hilary not only seemed to assert, but did assert, precisely what the Lombard feared he stated. In this most rare of cases, the Lombard in effect throws up his hands and simply warns his readers to take Hilary's words with a "pious diligence," lest they become for them "vessels of death."[27] Here, seemingly, there is no interpretation that can be put on Hilary's words that are compatible with his original intention, the biblical text, or orthodox Christology. It is the rare case that a remark by a father of the church is so beyond the pale that it defeats the Lombard's capacity to rescue it for future, orthodox use.

Thomas and Bonaventure

In their reflections on Christ's prayer, Thomas and Bonaventure organize their comments around five questions, as follows.

Was It Fitting for Christ to Pray at All?

Thomas and Bonaventure would conclude that it was quite appropriate and even essential for Christ to pray. Thomas declares that, insofar as he was God, it was not fitting for Christ to pray nor to obey or submit to another. Nor should he do anything (lest he give support and comfort to the Arians, one presumes) that expresses reduction or that pertains to a will in conflict with the Father's. But insofar as he was man, it was fitting for him to pray for three reasons, as John of Damascus said:[28] first to establish the truth of the assumed human nature, according to which he is less than the Father, and, being obedient, prays to him; second, as an example given us of how to pray, since every action of his is for our instruction; third, so as to honor God as his own cause and beginning (*principium*) and to demonstrate that he was not adverse to him.[29]

In the *Summa*, Thomas would argue that, if there had been only one will in Christ (namely, the Divine), it would be otiose to pray, since the divine will of itself effects whatever Christ wished by it. But because the divine and the human wills are distinct in Christ, and the human will of itself is not efficacious to do what it wishes, except by Divine power, to pray belongs to Christ "as man and as having a human will."[30] Bonaventure would agree with all of this and add that it is the role of a priest to offer prayers on behalf of sin and sinners, and thus it was most appropriate for Christ to pray.[31] Here Bonaventure does not seem to perceive, or to acknowledge that Christ, when imploring his Father to let the cup of passion and death pass, appears not to be praying for sinners.

As usual, some of the most interesting argumentation comes in the friars' replies to the objections of the proposition under consideration. Both concede that there are strong arguments for the proposition that it was *in*appropriate for him to pray. Both observe (invoking John of Damascus) that prayer is the ascent of the intellect to God. But if, as both maintain, the intellect of Christ was always united to God, it was clearly not fitting that Christ pray.[32] Second (again invoking the Damascene), if prayer is the petitioning of fitting things from God, and if Christ is (as both of course assumed) divine, then it would be pointless to pray: no one petitions something from himself.[33] Third, Christ would never entreat God except for that which he knew the Father also desired; and whatever Christ desired was clearly foreknown by God.[34] Bonaventure adds three additional reasons for why it seems inappropriate for Christ to pray (the Arian controversy is clearly, if distantly, in the background). First, no one seeks from another what he can do for himself (begging the question, of course, of whether Christ *could* indeed have delivered himself from his agony).[35] As Augustine put it, what would be more foolish than to pray for something which one has the power to effect oneself?[36] Second, prayer is the act of a person inferior to the one to whom he prays. But, as Christ was equal (this time begging the question of whether he was unequal to the Father), it was not fitting.[37] Finally, it was not fitting for Christ to pray for anything in vain; yet he petitioned for something—deliverance from suffering—in vain.[38] All three of these latter arguments could have been (and were) made by Latin Arian writers of the fourth and fifth centuries.

In the *Summa*, Thomas compiles a similar list of objections. For three reasons, he acknowledges, it seems quite inappropriate for Christ to pray. First of all, omnipotent beings should not need prayer. On the understanding that prayer is the supplicating of suitable things of the Deity, and on the assumption that Christ could do all things, "it does not seem becoming" that Christ should ask for anything from anyone.[39]

Second, omniscient beings should not need prayer. Even finite human beings do not ask in prayer for that which they know for certain will be given. We, for example, know that the sun will rise tomorrow, Thomas observes, and so we never ask God for it to do so. How much more absurd would it seem, then, for Christ, "who [as Thomas declares] knew all things that were going to happen," to ask for anything in prayer.[40] Naturally, the Arian, or neo-Arian objection to this observation would have been to question whether Christ were in fact omniscient or nescient and if, in the latter case, less than the Father.

Third, a being wholly united to the divine should not need prayer. If John of Damascus—one of the Eastern fathers Thomas is extremely fond of citing in the christological part of *Scriptum* and the *Summa*—were correct that prayer involves "the raising of the mind to God," and on the assumption that Christ, his mind always united to God by virtue of the hypostatic union, needed no uplifting, then it seems unfitting that Christ should pray at all. And yet, as Scripture everywhere attests, Christ did pray and could be even be found, as in Luke 6, spending entire nights in prayer.[41]

This brief catalogue of objections is quite interesting. It reads as if lifted straight out of a fourth or fifth century Arian compendium of arguments against the divinity of the logos. Notice how the first of the objections suggests that Christ is physically, the second that he is intellectually and the third that he is spiritually or metaphysically finite, incompetent, and creaturely. The Arians themselves could hardly have been more satisfied with so compact a barrage of theses, so lucid and taut a synopsis of their own theology of subordination.

In his *Scriptum*, Thomas first tackles the objection that, because Christ's intellect was always joined to God, it was unfitting for him to pray. His reply there contains an extremely fine distinction, so fine as to be weak and possibly nugatory. Thomas concedes that in the act of prayer, Christ's intellect did not have to rise. But while praying, the divine power he implored was "above" him (*supra ipsum*); it is in this sense that he ascended to God.[42] It is very difficult to know what Thomas meant by the divine power being "above" Christ when he says his intellect did not have to rise. Since that power is not ontologically or essentially superior, could he have been thinking in crude cosmological terms? In any case, his reply in the *Scriptum* leaves much to be desired.

His reply in the *Summa*, relying on the fine distinctions of Aristotelian physics, is slightly more satisfying. Distinguishing two senses of movement expressed by Aristotle in *De Anima* 3.7.431a6, Thomas argues that Christ did not move from potentiality to act, as that would imply the act of an imperfect being. But in the sense that "movement" connotes the act of something perfect ("existing in act")—in the way that understanding and feeling are called "movements"—he "moved" to what was "above him" only in the sense that he was *always* raised up to God in contemplation.[43] Readers may differ as to whether this response meets the objection.

To the objection that prayer is an act of a person inferior to the one to whom he prays, Bonaventure replies that this is true with respect to the person of Christ but not according to Christ's humanity, according to which he was, in fact, inferior to the Father.[44] In response to the argument that no one asks something of himself that he can himself effect, Bonaventure replies that to petition and pray was fitting for Christ according to the nature assumed; to be able to fulfill the prayer's desire belongs to him according to the nature assuming (i.e., the divine).[45]

Against the objection that it was unfitting for Christ to pray for that which he knew God desired, Thomas replies that Christ prayed because he knew God wished some things to be fulfilled through his prayer; just as God wishes to save someone by the prayers of another saint, in which case it is by no means superfluous for that saint to pray.[46] Bonaventure provides a very similar reply.[47] A potential difficulty with this answer is precisely that there was something for which Christ prayed—that the cup might pass—not fulfilled by his prayer.

Turning in the *Summa* to the objection that, given his ability to do all things, Christ should not have prayed, Thomas replies, first, that Christ as a man was not able to accomplish all that he wished.[48] Nor did he offer prayers because he was powerless to achieve something he wished (as the Arians argued). Here he invokes Ambrose's warning that we not think the Son of God prays as a weakling in order to implore God for that which he cannot himself effect. Rather, he did so for our instruction. Observing, with Augustine, that Christ could have prayed in silence, Thomas notes that he did not and thus wished to furnish us with an example of filial piety.[49]

Was Christ's Will in Conformity with the Paternal Divine Will?

Bonaventure begins his response to this question, *modo scholastico*, by distinguishing two senses of "conformity" (*conformitas*). Conformity of will to will consists, Bonaventure says, in two things: in that which is wished for (*in volito*); and in the manner of wishing (*in ratione volendi*). Conformity in the thing wished for occurs when two different wills want one and the same thing.[50] Conformity in the manner of wishing is when the two wills wish for the same thing in the same way, or when one of them (i.e., the "inferior" or subordinate will) wishes for something in the way in which the superior will wishes it to will. It is indeed possible for Christ's "different" human wills and his human and divine will to be in conformity *in ratione volendi* but for them not to wish for the same thing. And this, Bonaventure argues, is because the superior will does not want the inferior will to want what it itself wills but rather to wish for the contrary thing. Not only is it possible for Christ's wills to be in conformity in this sense; it is in fact in this sense that they *were* in harmony. Each of the subordinate wills wished as the superior will wished. Thus the sensual will wished as the rational will wished it to will; and the rational will of Christ wishes as the divine will wished it to will. Therefore in Christ, there was "harmony" (*concordia*), although there was not identity in the thing desired (*ex parte voliti non esset identitas*).[51]

Bonaventure then addresses an impressive barrage of objections to the affirmative answer to this question. First, the dominical prayer, in which Christ says, *not as I wish but you* (Matt 26.39) indicates he wished for something according to his humanity but, according to his divinity, wished for the opposite. Therefore, his human will was not in conformity with the divine.[52] Here

Bonaventure replies by, again, distinguishing two kinds of conformity: conformity of assimilation (*conformitas assimilationis*) and conformity of subjection (*conformitas subiectionis*). God did not require conformity of assimilation from the sensitive will of Christ, so that it would wish for the same thing for which he wished. Instead, he demanded conformity of subjection, so that the sensitive will would want that for which God had ordained it to wish. When Christ prays *not as I wish,* he demonstrates his conformity of subjection, because he shows he wishes to be subordinate to the divine will. In short, there was a twofold will in Christ, a rational will that was similar–and wished to be subject to–the divine and a sensitive will (which reason subjected to the divine will), even if the sensitive appetite itself wished for the contrary. But because it was subject, there was not a mutual contradiction of wills.[53]

Second, as Augustine says (and as the Lombard quoted him), the distance of the will of God from the human will is as far as God is from humanity.[54] Thus, bearing humanity, Christ had a certain will repugnant to the divine will. Accordingly, it seems as if his will was not in conformity with the divine will. But, Bonaventure responds, Augustine meant this distance to pertain to the diversity of wills and to the distance of things wished for, not however to the order of subjection (*subiectionis ordinem*) in the act of wishing. Therefore, the distance of which he spoke is not a controversial matter.[55]

Third, Christ wept over the destruction of Jerusalem (Luke 19.41); therefore, he wished Jerusalem not to be destroyed. But according to divine justice, he wished for it to be destroyed; therefore he seems again to have been opposed to the divine will.[56] Actually, however (thus Bonaventure invoking Hugh of St. Victor), Christ wept with the will of piety, which aspires to mercy. God wished it—the will of piety—to will this way and so it was not repugnant to the divine will. Indeed, it was in conformity in the fashion of wanting, although not in the object desired.[57]

Fourth, Augustine says that wills are contrary which desire different things.[58] The rational will wanted to die, the sensitive will to live. Therefore, the rational and sensitive wills were contrary.[59] Basically, the same distinction applies. Only if we define conformity as identity in the thing desired (*identitatem ex parte voliti*) is it possible to maintain there was contrariety.[60]

Fifth, panic and security are contrary affections. But in the rational will, there was security; in the sensitive will there was timidity. But such wills are contrary to one another.[61] Here Bonaventure replies again according to his anthropology of subjection. Each of Christ's affections was subject to another. Thus his fear was subject to security, sorrow to joy, and so forth. In fact, there was no sadness in Christ for this reason and, even more (Bonaventure implausibly suggests), he gloried in sadness and pain.[62]

In his *Scriptum,* Thomas also considers the question, was Christ's human will conformed to the divine in the thing desired? Thomas argues that the human will, considered as nature (i.e., in view of what it desires instinctively, so to speak) only imperfectly willed what the divine will willed. In this sense, Christ most assuredly did not wish to die. Death, considered absolutely (*secundum se*) was evil and contrary to nature. Only considered in relation to a certain end (in this case human salvation) could it have been considered good. Neither the sensitive nor the natural will unmodified by reason conforms perfectly to what the divine will wishes; they conform *sub conditione*—that is, under the condition that the rational will should not desire something opposite to what they desire. This sort of conditional wish Thomas calls "velleity" (*velleitas*)—an anemic wish that barely counts as volitional. Nonetheless, both conformed to the divine will *in modo volendi* and in view of the final end of death (i.e., human salvation). The natural and sensitive will recoiled from death, which it perceives as harmful to its nature. Only when the natural will is modified by reason (which conforms to the divine in the thing desired) is there something like conformity of human and divine willing.[63]

Thomas also tackles a most interesting objection in this question. It is certainly the case that we ordinary human beings do not know what God wishes in every respect. But it would really seem as if Christ, who was a "true comprehender" (*verus comprehensor*)[64] of all the intentions of God, should have been conformed to the divine will in all of the things for which God wished— including, presumably, the means by which God intended to save humanity (i.e., by the death of his Son).[65] Remarkably, Thomas replies by acknowledging that Christ did not know what God wished in every case by every power of his soul. Nor did he always know the reason for which God wished something in view of the achievement of some end. Nonetheless, Thomas insists that Christ (presumably with his other powers) "knew what God wished in all things."[66] Again, we see evidence of the bifurcated consciousness about which we have already spoken at length. At one level of consciousness Christ knows things about which, at other levels, he is utterly ignorant and by which he is even surprised; and this includes such things as how humanity is to be saved and his role in the saving acts of God.

Was His Prayer Answered?

Bonaventure and Thomas argue that prayer proceeding from the rational will of Christ was in every case heard, because this will was in all things conformed to the divine will. Prayer proceeding from the pious or fleshly wills were not heard in every case because *not* conformed to the divine will and also because those prayers were ordered for our instruction more than to be answered by God. In short, Christ's prayer was answered in every case in which he genuinely prayed so that his prayer might be answered. When he prayed the cup be removed from, it was for our instruction and to show the reality of his assumed nature. He did not pray, really, to have this wish granted.[67]

Did He Pray for Himself When He Asked the Cup to Pass?

In his commentary on the Lombard's *Sentences,* Thomas argues that any prayer Christ made for spiritual goods was not for himself but for others. He suffered no defect in these because, at one level of consciousness, he enjoyed beatitude (*beatus erat*). Any prayer he prayed regarding spiritual goods was not for himself but for others. However, he did suffer defects or infirmities insofar as he was passible in the body and soul. Thus any prayer he prayed pertained only to his body.[68]

In the *Summa,* Thomas provides a rather different answer. There Thomas openly acknowledges that when he prayed that the cup of passion might pass from him, he was simply expressing the desire of his sensitive or simple will. Second he also expressed the desire of his rational will and in this gave us an example "that we might give thanks for blessing received and ask in prayer for those we have not as yet received."

Thomas and Bonaventure then proceed to inquire whether his prayer was irrationally driven or reasonable? Bonaventure acknowledges that Christ's prayer that the cup might pass certainly seemed to originate from the sensitive will. No one, after all, petitions for that which is contrary to what he wills. Since Christ's rational will wished to die, the petition for avoiding death seems to have sprung from the sensual will.[69]

Bonaventure responds to these challenges by arguing that prayer can be spoken of *dupliciter,* according to its matter or according to its form. If we speak about prayer according to its matter, Christ's prayer in Gethsemane was the petition of the sensitive will. This is because the matter of the prayer regarded the desire of the one praying, which was not to die.[70] According to its form, however, the prayer regards the discretion or discernment (*discretio*) of the one praying, and this mode of prayer occurs in the discernment of the reason of the one praying. In this respect, the prayer was a product of the rational will.[71] It cannot be concluded, therefore, that the question can be answered simply.[72] It depends on the perspective from which the question is being posed.

Like Bonaventure, Thomas concludes that the prayer in which he petitions that he be spared by death was an act of Jesus' sensitive will.[73] Here reason acts as the "advocate" (*advocatus*) of the sensitive will by proposing to God the appetite of the sensitive will. But reason does this for pedagogical reasons only, to teach us to subject our will to the will of God and to place ourselves before God in every situation of need.[74]

Did Christ Doubt the Father's Power?

According to Bonaventure, Ambrose's statement that "as a man" Christ doubted seems to be false. Because Christ had knowledge of all future things *sub certitudine*, it seems as if he could not have doubted. Only one who lacks knowledge of future contingents could have so doubted. Again, whoever experiences doubt can fall into ignorance and error. But "Christ could have fallen into neither of these."[75]

The answer lies in distinguishing two senses of doubt. Properly speaking, doubt signifies the hesitation of the reason to make a judgment with respect to two sides of an argument. In this sense, there was no doubt in Christ. In another sense, doubt is the hesitation of the sensitive will to obey the commands of reason (such as to accept the necessity of painful death for a greater cause). Doubt of this kind could be in Christ. Indeed, Bonaventure claims, this is the sort of doubt Ambrose wished to ascribe to Christ.[76] In Bonaventure's mind, doubt could reside in Christ's human, sensitive faculties but not in his intellective ones. Doubt could not be noetic, nor imply a defect of knowledge or ignorance. A wise man could experience an ephemeral hesitation to follow reason; he could not lack knowledge.

For Thomas, too, the answer lies in distinguishing two meanings of doubt. First and principally, doubt signifies the movement of reason over two parts of an argument when experiencing difficulty in judging which is correct. This kind of doubt occurs because of a lack of "sufficient means" (*ex defectu medii sufficientis*) to determine the truth. Put another way, this sort of doubt occurs as a result of lack of knowledge (*ex defectu scientiae*). Because this sort of doubt involves some sort of noetic defect, Thomas can conclude that "this was not in Christ."[77]

The second meaning of doubt implies the fear of the affect in approaching or sustaining "something terrible" (*aliquod terribile*). This sort of doubt occurs because one cannot perceive a way to avoid imminent danger. Because Christ had infirmity of flesh, and because the sensitive faculty feared the pain of death, doubt could occur in Christ *quantum ad sensualitatem*, although there was great freedom from anxiety *quantum ad rationem*. Unlike the sensitive faculty, which could not apprehend such a thing, the rational faculty saw that divine aid was coming (though Thomas does not specify in what form it would come).[78]

Reflections

All of the authors considered in this chapter, patristic and medieval, agreed that it was appropriate and right for the Incarnate Son to pray to his Father. Most emphasized that he did so not out of necessity or anxiety, but pedagogically, to supply his followers an appropriate example of how to pray and how, in troubles, to bend one's will to the divine will. All also generally agreed that Christ prayed to show the reality of the flesh he had assumed, though few successfully reconcile this idea with the assertion (held by all but Ambrose) that even the assumed flesh felt overwhelmed by sorrow or fear to such a degree that it needed prayer for assurance or to petition the divine.

Only Ambrose declares categorically that "as a man" Christ prayed and it was only to the Archbishop of Milan that it seemed obvious that Christ prayed for himself. For Hilary, this would have sounded like a dangerous concession to "Arianism," and he went so far as to assert that the desire of his human will *not* be effected.

The Victorine anthropology developed by Hugh in his *On the Four Wills*, not to mention other, non-Victorine (and non-Aristotelian) distinctions, profoundly reshaped the medieval discussion and the ways in which patristic authorities like Ambrose and Hilary were managed, interpreted, and transmitted. Essentially, Peter Lombard, Thomas, and Bonaventure all agree that Christ did not doubt, did not fear, did not ask for the removal of the cup with his rational will but, rather, with some inferior "natural" human will which could contain, discipline, and finally reorder the anxieties that were brewing in the nether regions of Christ's will. In this sense, if only in this sense, there was a perfect "concord" of wills. Christ's will is not in utter conformity with the Father's will from the point of view of *what* is willed (*in volito*) but *in ratione volendi*—that is, in *how* Christ willed. If there is no identity in the thing desired, there is an ordered concord of wills. Needless to say, Hilary and Ambrose both would have been surprised to learn that this is what they meant to say.

8

Conclusion: The Passions of Christ in Ancient and Medieval Thought

Continuities and Discontinuities

The major focus of this study, around which other themes have revolved, has been what Cardinal Newman, thinking of the difference between the earliest expression of a dogma and its developed form, called a *"prima facie* dissimilitude" between the two.[1] In Newman's mind, the truth of the developed form of an idea stood or fell on whether it could be proven that the ultimate shape of the idea could be tied—"really belong[ed]"[2]—to the idea from which it took its origin and whose characteristics, however embellished, it never failed to maintain. This is not to say that an idea and its development had to be verbally, formulaically indistinguishable. Newman explicitly says that, usually, they are *not.*[3] Still, the developed or even final form of an ideal should, in order to be judged an authentic, faithful development, contain within it the rudiments of the original; the latter likewise should be visible "in miniature" in the former.[4] In this way, the later idea can be said to complete what was inchoate, immanent, or implicit in the earlier.

For Newman, of course, the "prima facie dissimilitude" was, in many cases in the history of dogma, quite misleading. In fact, on further inspection, the dissimilitude often concealed the deeper fact of *development:*[5] the drawing out of implications and consequences; the making explicit of the implicit; the complication and enrichment of the simple; the making known or clarifying of the mysterious, dim, and confused; the expansion of the laconic; the completion of the rudimentary, the slow bringing to maturity of the embryonic; and so forth. In this sense, the early and the late are, or can be separated by centuries of development yet still be "identical"—which is to say, the earlier is preserved, though not always in the same verbal formulae, in the latter. A doctrine can and often will, in this sense, grow and develop and be modified but yet be one and the same with itself.[6]

Whatever one might think of the great Cardinal Newman's theory of dogmatic development (reduced to its essentials here), and whatever of the history of Christian thought it might be believed to elucidate, it simply cannot begin to do justice to the evidence considered in this study. Time and again, we have seen "prima facie" dissimilitudes between an ancient christological doctrine and its medieval development. However, closer inspection and analysis have revealed, in virtually all these cases, that the "dissimilitude" was very far from superficial. Indeed, by Cardinal Newman's criteria, the conceptual differences between the early and late are, almost invariably, profound and unbridgeable. It is not simply that the later is not linguistically or formulaically identical with the former; as we have already argued, that could never be a meaningful way to consider continuity and development. The deeper problem is that high-medieval christological thought regarding the passions of Christ is usually discontinuous, often radically so, with the ancient thought explicitly invoked as its authoritative source. Far from completing what was contained within patristic thought, high-medieval christological thought is often concerned to *correct* it, to bring what had slipped the channels back within the borders of orthodoxy. In no way is the early visible in inchoate or implicit form in the latter; and in this sense, the history of relations between ancient and medieval thought on the passions of Christ is a history of correction and improvement. It is therefore, remorselessly, a history of fissure and discontinuity. We should be thinking, when we think of high medieval thought on the passions of Christ, therefore, not in the categories of growth, development, and modification. We should be thinking in terms of invention, novelty, and innovation. Finally, we should also observe that this whole process occurs is anchored by the assumption that what is transmitted is preserved *essentially* unchanged.

The scholastic strategy we have been analyzing was to take two (or more) categorical, conflicting, and heterodox patristic opinions and, by exploiting sophisticated anthropological distinctions, to render them conditional, compatible, and orthodox. That such an exegetical maneuver requires a modification, and a rather drastic one at that, of the meaning intended by the fathers will by now require little emphasis. The high-scholastic figures under consideration here actually contributed to the substantial erasure of the ancient, authoritative sources they were ostensibly attempting to rehabilitate. If this is true,

though, we are led to ask this question: In what sense are the patristic authorities whom our medieval exegetes invoke truly authoritative for their exegesis? In what sense, more generally speaking, is medieval exegesis and
theology in meaningful continuity with patristic exegesis and theology?

I take these questions to be worth asking for a number of reasons. First,
scholasticism is a form of exegesis and theology which, as we have seen, begins
interpretation by reflection upon patristic exegesis. In scholastic exegesis, the
sacred text is always refracted—at least so it appears—through the prism of
patristic thought. Second, a casual inspection of scholastic exegetical practice
appears to show that medieval interpreters regularly invoke the authority of the
ancients in support of their own exegesis, and they seem to think it important
to bring their opinions in line with the established *sententiae* of the fathers.
Third, we medievalists have not spent much time analyzing whether patristic
and medieval exegetical opinion *is*, in fact, in essential agreement. Our largely
unquestioned assumption has been that the *substance* of medieval exegesis was
more or less identical with that of patristic exegesis, and that it was only in its
accidents—its technical language and formal structure—that it differed. That
is, we have assumed that vintage wine was simply being transferred into new
and better skins. At most scholastic manipulation of the tradition is usually
said to consist in the resolution of ambiguities in patristic language and the
organization of patristic disorder.

There are a number of problems with this popular description of the
high-scholastic enterprise. First, in the cases examined in this study at least,
the language and meaning of the fathers in not, I think, all that ambiguous.
Indeed, the problem is the blinding clarity with which they stated their positions. If anything, it is the scholastics who render the clear patristic opinion
ambiguous. It is *they* who bring complexity and nuance where there was once
stark, if (as they might see it) clumsy, simplicity.

Second, the scholastics in this case do not really bring their own positions
in line with the established *sententiae* of the fathers. They try, instead, to bring
the fathers in line with *their* opinions. To put the matter plainly, they put their
opinions on the lips of the patristic authorities and present them as the intended meanings of the fathers. Medieval scholastics were in search of a "usable past," but the past became usable, in cases like this, only when grossly
garbled or strained.

If this is true, then the third problem with our inherited conception of
high-scholasticism is that medieval schoolmen are furnishing us not simply
with a deeper or better or more "scientific" understanding of the established
positions of Latin exegesis but with a *different* understanding of the scriptures. When we examine the actual exegetical practice of high-medieval

scholastics, it seems quite clear that they are not just "modernizing" or streamlining in the formal sense but innovating in the material sense. Nor are the scholastics simply making explicit what had been implicit in patristic thought. They are *transforming* the meaning of patristic thought, at least of much of it. That is, the substance as well as the accidents of exegesis changes in the high-scholastic period. There may be new skins; but they contain new wine, too.

Is there any sense, then, in which patristic exegesis *is* truly authoritative for medieval exegesis and theology? The answer is that of course there is, though in exactly what sense needs to be carefully analyzed and defined. In any case, we have to discern when patristic opinion is problematic or heterodox, as in the cases considered here, and when it is not. In cases like this, the past become authoritative only when misrepresented. In such cases, there is a theoretical deference to the opinions of the fathers but a practical reliance only on the authority of their names. In these difficult cases, the authority of tradition for later Christian thought must be considered (if I may be permitted one final medieval analogy) more nominal than real.

Notes

CHAPTER I

1. I agree with the most widely (if not unanimously) accepted version of the literary relationship between Mark, on the one hand, and Matthew and Luke on the other, which posits, essentially, that Mark was a major source for Matthew and Luke. Recently, other theories have been put forward. See, e.g., D. J. Neville, *Mark's Gospel—Prior or Posterior? A Reappraisal of the Phenomenon of Order* (London: Sheffield Academic Press, 2002).

2. The crucial clause οὐδὲ ὁ υἱός is missing in many Matthean mss. As Bruce Metzger has observed, "The omission of the words because of the doctrinal difficulty they present is more probable than their addition by assimilation to Mark. 13:32" (*A Textual Commentary on the Greek New Testament*, 2nd ed. [Stuttgart: Deutsche Bibelgesellschaft; United Bible Societies, 1994]), 51–52.

3. For discussion of the problematic implications of this category, see discussion in chapter 2, xx–xx.

4. Ed. Irena Backus, 2 vols. (Leiden: Brill, 1997).

5. See, e.g., Leo Elders, "Thomas Aquinas and the Fathers of the Church," *Reception of the Fathers*, 337–366, esp. 341. Elders's 1997 essay reflects almost all of the views regarding Thomas's use of patristic authorities that have dominated the field for more than a century. Like many of Thomas's commentators, Elders asserts that Thomas is capable of "bridging the gap" (337) between patristic and medieval thought. What "bridging the gap" might entail Elders did not attempt to define with any philosophical rigor. He goes on to say that Thomas realizes that the fathers had different opinions on matters not *de fide*. Yet he does not seem to perceive that these opinions often touched on matters central to the faith, such as the Trinity

and Incarnation. Again, Thomas recognizes, Elder argues, that some of the statements of the fathers are "doubtful" but can be "explained." But what does *doubtful*
mean? Obscure? Heretical? We don't know. And "explained" is even more problematic. Explicated? Improved? Changed? Elders argues that Thomas believes that certain
errors could be corrected "reverently." But, again, what does *that* mean? Quite clearly,
Elders does not make the sort of argument I want to make here, namely that "explanation" or "interpretation" involved quite radical distortion of patristic opinion. The
intellectual (and religious?) assumptions underlying virtually all of this century's work
on high-medieval scholasticism, particularly that undertaken by French and German
Catholics, have not only precluded such a conclusion. They have forestalled interpreters from taking seriously, or even perceiving, the data on which it is based.

6. First edition, *An Essay on the Development of Christian Doctrine* (London: J.
Toovey, 1845). I use here the 1878 edition. See conclusion for a brief discussion of
Newman's *Essay* and its relevance for this study.

7. P. Gondreau, *The Passions of Christ's Soul in the Theology of St. Thomas Aquinas*
(Münster: Ashendorf, 2002).

8. See J.G. Bougerol, *Introduction á Saint Bonaventure* (Paris: J. Vrin, 1988),
113–118. In another study, Bougerol sums up the consensus of scholarship by de-
claring, "it is common knowledge that St. Thomas had read the 'lectura' of the *Sen-
tences* of Bonaventure when he, in turn, lectured on Lombard's *Sentences*"
("*Auctoritates* in Scholastic Theology to Bonaventure," in *The Reception of the Church
Fathers in the West*, 2:289–336, citing 305). In a very fine revised dissertation, Gilles
Emery (*La Trinité Créatrice: Trinité Et Création dans Les Commentaires Aux Sentences de
Thomas D'Aquin et de Ses Précurseurs Albert Le Grand et Bonaventure* [Bibliothèque
Thomiste. Paris: J. Vrin, 1995]) proved that Thomas often went beyond his immediate
literary sources on a variety of theological issues. Bonaventure also likely relied on the
commentary of Albert. See E.-H Wéber, *Dialogue Et Dissensions entre Saint Bonaventure
et Saint Thomas d'Aquin à Paris*, 1252–1273 (Bibliothèque Thomiste. [Paris: J. Vrin,
1974]).

9. Russell L. Friedman, "The *Sentences* Commentary, 1250–1320," in G. R.
Evans, *Mediaeval Commentaries on the Sentences of Peter Lombard* (Leiden ; Boston:
Brill, 2002), 47.

10. I am thus expanding in some ways the argument made by P. Worrall in
"St. Thomas and Arianism," *Récherches de Théologie Ancienne et Mediévales*23 (1956):
208–259; and 24 (1957): 45–99.

CHAPTER 2

1. In the past two decades, scholars have identified many difficulties with the
term "Arian Controversy"; thus the quotation marks. In 1988 R. P. C. Hanson called
the term a "serious misnomer" (*The Search for the Christian Doctrine of God* [Edin-
burgh: T. & T. Clark, 1988], xvii). Thus Hanson's main title, notable for the con-
spicuous absence of the words "Arian" and "Controversy," though it concentrates on
the same figures and issues formerly indicated by them. Finding themselves in

agreement with Hanson's observation that Arius neither was, nor was regarded in his day or after his death a significant writer, Michael H. Barnes and Daniel H. Williams have nicely summarized the findings of recent scholarship: "Perhaps the most central finding in the last fifteen years...has been to show how peripheral the person of Arius was to the actual debates which occupied the Church for most of the [fourth] century." See Barnes and Williams, *Arianism after Arius: Essays on the Development of the Fourth Century Trinitarian Conflicts* (Edinburgh: T & T Clark, 1993), xiv. Likewise the term "controversy" has been forsaken by many, in part because it clouds the complexity of the theological and political issues and groups involved and in part because the period to which it usually refers is sometimes largely absent of contro- versy. Rowan Williams has suggestively argued that the Lucianists were, in large measure, the theological precursors of the sundry fourth century groups catego- rized as "Arian." See *Arius: A Heresy and Tradition* (London: Darton, Longman, and Todd, 1987), 162–167 and 246–247. For more useful discussion of the inherited terminology, see the introductory essay in Daniel H. Williams, *Ambrose of Milan and the End of the Nicene-Arian Conflict* (Oxford: Clarendon Press, 1995), esp. 1–2. I use the terms "Arian" and "Arianism" in this study in the absence of a better term and as a shorthand way of referring to the Latin theological opponents of the Nicene party.

2. *Christ in Christian Tradition: From the Apostolic Age to Chalcedon* (New York: Sheed and Ward, 1965), 7.

3. *PG* 56:612–946.

4. This has led Robert C. Gregg and Dennis E. Groh to suggest that the Arians were the source of the veneration and cult of Job (*Early Arianism: A View of Salvation* [Philadelphia: Fortress, 1981]), 394–398.

5. See, e.g., Anonymous, *Commentary on Job*, in *PG* 17:371–522; Anonymous, *Commentary on Luke*, in A. Mai, *Scriptorum Veterum Nova Collectio*, 10 vols. (Rome: Burliaeum, 1825–1838), 3: 191–207; *Apostolic Constitutions*, in *Didascalia et Con- stitutiones Apostolorum*, ed. F.X. Funk (Paderborn: Schönig, 1905), vol. 1; R. Gryson, *Scolies Ariennes sur le Concile d'Aquilée*, in *SC* 267 (Paris: Éditions du Cerf, 1980); R. Gryson, *Scripta Arriana Latina*, *CCL* 87 (Turnhout: Brepols, 1982), an invaluable collection of Latin Arian writings that includes the *Collectio Veronensis*, an edition of an ms. from Verona containing various small tracts, virtually all of them Arian, brief commentaries or *scoliae* on the Council of Aquileia; fragments from an Arian com- mentary on Luke and a variety of theological fragments; and Julianus, *Commentary on Job*, ed. D. Hagedorn, *Der Hiobkommentar des Arianers Julian* (Berlin: de Gruyter, 1973).

6. E.g., E. Boularand, *L'Hérésie d'Arius et la "foi" de Nicée* (Paris, Letouzey & Ané, 1972).

7. E.g, H.M. Gwatkin, *Studies in Arianism*, 2, 16, 17–18, 20, 26, and passim. "Arian" was sometimes used as an term of derogation in Enlightenment England to denounce Deist and other anti-Trinitarian thinkers. In the early eighteenth century, for example, Thomas Bishop preached eight sermons at St. Paul in London. They were collected and entitled, *The Error and Absurdities of the Arian and semi-Arian schemes: and Especially the Polytheism and Idolatry by which They Have Corrupted the*

Christian Faith (London: Bernard Lintot), 1726. Bishop, of course, is not referring to fourth- or fifth-century Arianism but to the "neo-Arianism" he sees reemerging in his own day. For stimulating discussion of British "Arianism," see Wiles, *Archetypal Heresy: Arianism through the Centuries,* esp. chapter four.

8. See, e.g., *History of Dogma* 4.7 and 4.39.

9. "The Logic of Arianism," *Journal of Theological Studies* n.s. 34 (1983): 356–381, particularly at 57 and 80.

10. As Hanson observes in *Search,* 96.

11. *Search,* 97.

12. *Search,* 96.

13. *Search,* 96.

14. *Early Arianism,* 16.

15. *Early Arianism,* 113.

16. *Search,* 97–98.

17. While Hanson is surely correct that the notion of a suffering God is all-important for the Arians, I am not quite convinced that the idea of the Son as an exemplar of moral progress is utterly absent in their writings. In this sense, I side with Gregg and Groh. I would simply disengage this soteriological emphasis (as Hanson also has done) from the language and thought-world of late Stoicism and tether it more firmly to the language and narrative of the Bible.

18. *Search,* 112.

19. Of course, these are precisely the conditions which, in the eyes of Athanasius and the pro-Nicenes would have nullified human salvation. See Gregg and Groh: "As [Bishop] Alexander of [Alexandria] and Athanasius understood the gulf between divine and creaturely natures, the Arian Christology made salvation impossible" (*Early Arianism,* 58).

20. Hanson, *Search,* 122.

21. *PG* 56: 853

22. *Early Arianism,* 3.

23. *Search,* 8, 422.

24. M. Meslin observes that, for both the Arians and their opponents, "c'est la même conception d'une Écriture, domain exclusif de l'autorité cléricale et considérée comme critère de ségrégation (*Les Ariens,* 229). Hanson makes a similar point in *Search,* 848–849. Hanson shrewdly observes that it has been asserted that "the pro-Nicenes were ready to accept Scripture within the context of tradition and a broad philosophical outlook ... But the pro-Nicene writers are equally insistent upon the unique position of Scripture as a norm of faith ... a number of passages from pro-Nicene writers can be produced which make them seem as devout observers of the text of the Bible as any Arian" (*Search,* 827–829).

25. "The Exegesis of Scripture and the Arian Controversy," *Bulletin of the John Rylands Library* 41 (1959): 414–429, at 415. Pollard could hardly be further from the mark, or more self-contradictory, when he states, "Athanasius was able to expose the unscriptural nature of Arian doctrine" ("The Exegesis of Scriptures," 428). Pollard

also observes, this time correctly, that Athanasius frequently emphasizes, as a principle of his exegesis, the "sufficiency" of scripture ("Exegesis of Scripture," 419).

26. "The Exegesis of Scripture," 416.

27. *Search,* 26 Hanson seems almost angrily critical of orthodox or Nicene exegesis; adjectives like "grotesque," "contorted," "perverted," or "tortuous" seem to appear whenever he discusses it. (*Search,* 826) Athanasius' interpretation of Proverbs 8:22 (a crucial text in the controversy) he finds "ridiculously far-fetched." Athanasius "labors to show" that Mark 13:32, in which Jesus acknowledges ignorance of the Judgment Day, "that the text does not mean what it quite obviously does mean." Hilary of Poitiers' account of the passion he finds (perhaps not without justice) "amazing." Ambrose's interpretations are, in general, "fantastic nonsense woven into purely delusive harmony." When treating texts that exhibit Jesus as weak, fearful, or ignorant, Athanasius and Hilary led themselves into impossible "exegetical mazes." If the Arian exegesis of the first three Gospels is "confident" and "embarrassing" to their opponents, the pro-Nicenes treat the Synoptics in "uncertain" and "strained" ways (*Search,* 424, 454, 499, 673, 830, 834, 840, 847 and passim).

28. "In nostrum magisterium devenit divina Scriptura, ut a nobis emendationem accipiat" (*Collatio Augustini cum Maximino,* PL 42: 736). Quoted in Hanson, *Search,* 736. Hanson translates *emendatio* "improvement."

29. *Search,* 824.

30. "The Exegesis of Scripture and the Arian Controversy," 415.

31. *Search,* 453.

32. *Early Arianism,* 1. See also, 8: "the Arians instinctively gravitated to those scriptural texts which emphasized the empirical commonality of the redeemer's characteristics."

33. *Orationes* 3.26 in *The Orations of St. Athanasius against the Arians,* ed. W. Bright (Oxford: Clarendon Press, 1873), 180–181.

34. *Orations,* 3.24, p. 178.

35. *Athanasius Werke,* 3 vols., ed. Hans-Georg Opitz (Berlin: W. de Gruyter & Co., 1934), 3.1.14.37.

36. "Namque his sibi dictis, ut religiose inpii sint, blandiuntur: Tristis est anima mea usque ad mortem, ut longe a beatitudine adque incorruptione Dei sit, in cuius animam dominans metus tristitiae inminentis inciderit; qui etiam usque ad hanc praecem consternatus fuerit passionis necessitate: *Pater, si possibile est, transeat calix iste a me,* et sine dubio timere uideretur perpeti quod ne pateretur orauerit: quia patiendi trepidatio causam adtulerit depraecandi; in tantum uero infirmitatem eius obtinuerit uis doloris, ut in ipso crucis tempore diceret: *Deus Deus meus, quare me dereliquisti?*" (*Sancti Hilarii Pictaviensis Episcopi De Trinitate,* ed. P. Smulders, CCL 62–62a. (Turnhout: Brepols, 1979–80; 2.31, 1: 29).

37. *Orations,* 3.26., p. 180.

38. For a magisterial analysis of Stoic thought in ancient and medieval thought, see Marcia L. Colish, *The Stoic Tradition from Antiquity to the Early Middle Ages,* 2 vols. (Leiden: Brill, 1985).

39. *Early Arianism*, 16.

40. "Erubescant qui putant Salvatorem timuisse mortem, et passionis pavore dixisse: 'Transeat a me calix iste'" (*Commentariorum in Matheum Libri IV, CCL* 77, ed. D. Hurst and M. Adriaen [Turnhout: Brepols, 1969], 244). See also Pseudo-Vigilius Thapsensis, *Opus contra Varimadum Arianum* 1.33, who later gives precise instructions on how to respond to the Arians who invoke this text:

> Si tibi opposuerint quod ipse Filius dixerit: Quid me dicis bonum? non est bonus, nisi unus Deus. *Responsio*. Quis malum judicet, qui se ipsum past-orem bonum pronuntiet? Aut quis inaequalem Patri affirmet, qui se unum cum Patre esse demonstrat. Ego sum, ait, pastor bonus. Et David in persona Patris Filium intimantis, in psalmo quadragesimo quarto dicit: Eructavit cor meum verbum bonum. Et Jeremias: Bonus est Dominus eis qui sustinent eum, et in die tribulationis agnoscet eos qui timent eum. Et ipse Dominus: An oculus tuus nequam est, quia ego bonus sum? Et in psalmo centesimo octavo decimo: Bonus es, Domine, et in bonitate tua doce me justificationes tuas. Et Apostolus: Quoniam bonus odor Christi sumus, in his qui salvi fiunt, et in his qui pereunt. Vides quia non caret bonitate, qui omnem in se divi-nitatis continet plenitudinem. (*CCL* 90, ed. B. Schwank [Turnhout: Brepols, 1961], 44)

41. "Aut fatere igitur potiorem esse spiritum dei filio, ut iam non solum quasi Arrianus, sed etiam quasi Fotinianus loquaris, aut agnosce, quo referre debeas, quod nescire filium dei dixit" (*De Spiritu Sancto* 2.11, *CSEL*, ed. O. Faller [Vienna: Hoelder-Pichler-Tempsky, 1964]), 132).

42. "Illud itaque quod saepius dictum est: ego in patre et pater in me, non unam substantiam, sed duo significat, patris ingenitam et fili unigenitam. Et ideo intellegitur filius in sinu patris, quod sentitur in caritate adque in potestate illius qui omnia tenet, ipse autem est infinitus. Hic et illum circu(m)tenet, filius uero omnium quae post illum et per ipsum facta sunt a patre accipiens potestate circu(m)tenet uniuersa. Non est igitur unus et ipse pater et filius, qui circumtenet et qui circumtenetur, ingenitus et unigenitus, genitor et qui genitus est, qui mandat et qui mandatum accipit et ob-temperat, qui dat et qui datum suscipit, qui iubet et qui iussionem obte(m)perat, qui mittit et qui mittitur, qui uisus est et quem nemo uidit hominum nec uidere potest, qui inpassibilis est et qui pro nobis passus est, qui resurrexit a mortuis et qui eum re-suscitauit pater, qui ascendit super caelos filius et qui numquam desce(n)dit pater, qui sedet in dextera d(e)i et qui iussit eum in dextera sua sedere pater" (*Fragmenta Theo-logica*, in *CCL* 87, ed. R. Gryson [Turnhout: Brepols, 1982], 255).

43. "...filius qui negauit se scire diem illam et pater qui in sua posuit potestate, qui iudicaturus est filius et qui neminem iudicat pater, sed omnem iudicium dedit filio" (*Fragmenta Theologica* 17, p. 255).

44. *Orations* 3.27, p. 182.

45. *Early Arianism*, 16.

46. *Orations*, 3.26.

47. Legimus quidem quod iesus proficiebat aetate et sapientia, et gratia dei erat in illo: sed secundum formam hominis quam pro nobis accepit ex nobis, non secundum formam dei, in qua non alienum arbitratus est esse aequalis deo (*Contra Maximinum, PL* 42: 802).

Brian Daley has argued that Augustine's "public controversy with Arian Christians may have begun as early as 406, in a discussion held by the bishop and his friend Alypius with Count Pascentius who was also an enthusiastic but somewhat confused Arian" ("The Giant's Twin Substances: Ambrose and the Christology of Augustine's *Contra sermonem Arianorum,*" in *Augustine: Presbyter Factus Sum,* ed. Joseph Lienhard, Earl C. Muller, and Roland J. Teske [New York: Peter Lang, 1993)], 477–495, at 477–478).

48. See, e.g., *De Fide* 5.18 (*De Fide libri V ad Gratianum Augustum, CSEL* 78, ed. O.Faller [Vienna: Hoelder-Pichler-Tempsky, 1962]), 300–301; and the more extensive (and later controversial) discussion in *De incarnationis* 7 (*De incarnationis dominicae sacramento, CSEL* 79, ed. O.Faller [Vienna: Hoelder-Pichler-Tempsky, 1962]), 256–264.

49. See Jerome's commentary on Psalm 15 in *Tractatum in Psalmos Series Altera, CCL* 78 , ed. G. Morin (Turnhout: Brepols, 1958), 375.

50. *Orations,* 3.26, p. 181.

51. *Orations* 2.27, p. 5–97.

52. *Orations* 2.26, 31, pp. 80–81, 185–186.

53. *The Five Theological Orations of Gregory of Nazianzus,* ed. by Arthur J. Mason (Cambridge: Cambridge University Press, 1899), 3.29.18; 4.30. 6, 12. See also *PG* 35–36.

54. See, e.g., Epiphanius, *Ancoratus und Panarion,* 3 vols., ed. K. Holl. *GCS* 25, 31, 37 (Leipzig: J. C. Hinrichs, 1915–1933). For the *Ancoratus,* see especially 17.2–6 (1:25, 26); 20.1–10 (1:28); 37.1–7 (1:46–47); 38.1–8 (1:47–49); for the *Panarion,* see especially 66.35 (2:75). Basil of Caesarea, *Letter* 236. 1, in *Lettres: Texte établi et traduit,* 2 vols., ed. by Y. Courtonne (Paris: Société d'édition "Les Belles Lettres," 1956–66), 2:876–877.

55. "Feruntur contra hunc asterii et apollinaris libri, sabellianae eum haereseos arguentes, sed et hilarius in septimo 'aduersus arianos' libro nominis eius quasi haeretici meminit" (*De viris illustribus* 86, *PL* 23:693).

56. Hilary refers explicitly to his exile late in the work: "per hoc exilii nostri tempus" (*De Trinitate* 10.4, 2: 461). Some scholars have argued that at least the first three books of this work, which they believe was entitled by Hilary *De Fide,* were finished before Hilary was exiled. See J. Doignon, *Hilaire de Poitiers avant l'exil* (Paris: Études Augustiniennes, 1971), 82–83; and C.F.A. Borchardt, *Hilary of Poitiers' Role in the Arian Struggle* (The Hague: Martinus Nijhoff, 1966), 40–43.

57. This notion that the Scriptures are properly and legally possessed by the church and misappropriated by its unorthodox enemies is reminiscent of the

arguments against the heretics of his day by Tertullian, by whom Hilary was certainly influenced. See Tertullian, *De Praescriptione Haereticorum* 15. For Tertullian's influence on Hilary, see Hanson, *Search*, 471–477, 480–487, and 493–494.

58.

> Has enim omnes piae fidei nostrae professiones ad inpietatis suae rapiunt usurpationem: ut timuerit, qui tristis est, qui et transferri a se calicem depraecatus sit; ut doluerit, qui derelictum se a Deo in passione conquaestus sit; ut infirmus quoque fuerit, qui Spiritum suum Patri commendaverit. (*De Trinitate* 10.9, in *De Trinitate*, 2:466)

The *fidei nostrae professiones* that Hilary alludes to are scriptural passages.

59. "Respondentes quoque stultissimis eorum professionibus, usque ad ignoratae horae descendimus demonstrationem: quae etiamsi secundum illos a Filio adpraehensa non esset, tamen id ad contumeliam diuinitatis unigenitae non pertineret: quia natura non ferret ut eum natiuitas retroageret ad innascibilitatis ininitiabilem substitutionem, potestati suae Patre momentum definiendi adhuc diei ad demonstrationem auctoritatis innascibilis reseruante. Neque in eo infirmam intellegi posse naturam, in qua tantum inesset ex natiuitate naturae, quantum inplere posset perfecta natiuitas; neque ad differentiam diuinitatis unigenito Deo ignorationem diei et horae deputandam, cum ad demonstrandam aduersum hereticos sabellianos innascibilem in Patre adque ininitiabilem potestatem, innascibilis haec in eo sit potestatis exceptio. Sed quia hanc nescitae diei professionem non ignorationis esse infirmitatem, sed tacendi dispensationem docuimus, expurganda etiam nunc est omnis inpiae adsertionis occasio, et omnes hereticae blasfemiae transcurrendae sunt praedicationes, ut ueritas euangelii per ea ipsa quibus obscurari uidetur eluceat" (*De Trinitate* 10.8, pp. 464–465).

60. See *De Trinitate* 1.31–32, 6.25, 10.9, 10.31, 10.49, 10.51 and 10.60.

61. "Et cum nobis haec sola sit proprietas ad salutem, ut Dei Filium confiteamur ex mortuis, cur, rogo, in hac inreligiositate moriamur, ut cum Christus intra fiduciam diuinitatis suae manens, mori se per significationem adsumpti hominis cum securitate morientis ostenderit hoc maxime ad abnegandum eum Deum proficiat, quod se nobis Dei Filius et hominis filium est professus et mortuum?" (*De Trinitate* 10.71, 2:528).

62. On the passion of fear, see Gregg and Groh: "the suffering (τὸ πάθος) of Jesus, as well as his ignorance, would have indicated to Arius that his redeemer was not considered to be *sophos*. Since no πάθη was considered more problematic than fear (φόβος), Christ's expressions of agitation and fear would further remove him from the corridors of wisdom" (*Early Arianism*, 16).

63. "Volunt enim plerique eorum ex passionis metu et ex infirmitate patiendi non in natura eum inpassibilis Dei fuisse: ut qui timuit et doluit, non fuerit uel in ea potestatis securitate quae non timet, uel in ea Spiritus incorruptione quae non dolet; sed inferioris a Deo Patre naturae, et humanae passionis trepidauerit metu, et ad corporalis poenae congemuerit atrocitatem. Adque hac inpietatis suae adsertione nitantur, quia scribtum sit: Tristis est anima mea usque ad mortem, et rursum: Pater, si

possibile est, transeat calix iste a me, sed et illud: deus Deus meus, quare me dereliquisti? Hoc quoque adiciant: Pater, commendo in manus tuas Spiritum meum. Has
enim omnes piae fidei nostrae professiones ad inpietatis suae rapiunt usurpationem:
ut timuerit, qui tristis est, qui et transferri a se calicem depraecatus sit; ut doluerit, qui
derelictum se a Deo in passione conquaestus sit; ut infirmus quoque fuerit, qui
Spiritum suum Patri commendauerit. Nec anxietas admittat similitudinem ex-
aequatae ad Deum in unigeniti natiuitate naturae: quae infirmitatem diuersitatem
que suam et depraecatione calicis et desolationis quaerella et commendationis con-
fessione testetur" (De Trinitate 10.9, pp. 465–466).

64. "Deinde conmendat suum spiritum patri ut se ostenderet patri semper esse
subiectum ut bonum a bono genitum piu(m) a pio benignum a benigno" (Collectio
Veronensis 3.4 (48r) in Scripta Arriana Latina, p. 58).

65. See Ambrose's very lengthy response in De Fide 5.5, pp. 238–241; and
Pseudo-Vigilius, Opus contra Uarimadum Arianum 1.14:

> Si autem dixerint tibi, quod Filius duobus discipulis dixerit: Calicem quidem
> meum bibetis, sedere autem ad dexteram meam, vel ad sinistram non est
> meum dare vobis. Responsio. Propriae potestatis Filium esse, et praecedenti
> jam disputatione docuimus, et nunc ipso opitulante docebimus, Evangelio
> protestante: Vocatis duodecim discipulis suis dedit, eis potestatem spir-
> ituum immundorum, ut ejicerent eos, et curarent omnem languorem, et
> omnem infirmitatem in populo. Et iterum: Amen dico vobis quod vos qui
> secuti estis me, in regeneratione, cum Filius hominis sederit in sede ma-
> jestatis suae, sedebitis et vos cum eo super duodecim sedes, judicantes
> duodecim tribus Israel. Et iterum: Ecce dedi vobis potestatem ut calcetis
> super serpentes, et scorpiones, et super omnem virtutem inimici, et si quod
> venenum biberitis, nihil vobis nocebit. Et iterum: Quotquot autem receper-
> unt eum, dedit eis potestatem filios Dei fieri, iis qui credunt in nomine ejus.
> Et in Apocalypsi: Qui vicerit, dabo illi sedere mecum in sede mea, sicut et ego
> vici, et sedi cum Patre in sede ipsius. Item ibi: Qui vicerit dabo illi manducare
> de ligno vitae, quod est in paradiso Dei mei. Qui omnibus discipulis, duo-
> decim tribus judicandi potestatem dedit, et secum sedere permisit, duobus
> tantum discipulis, ut ad dexteram vel ad sinistram ejus sederent, licentiam
> dare non habuit? (Opus, in CCL 90, ed. B. Schwank [Turnhout: Brepols,
> 1961], 28–29)

66. See C.H. Turner, "An Arian Sermon from a MS in the Chapter Library of
Verona," Journal of Theological Studies 13, o.s. (1912): 19–28.

67. "Deum igitur Dominum nostrum Iesum Christum ex eo negandum per
naturam heretici existimant, quia dixerit: Quid me dicis bonum?" (De Trinitate 9.2,
p. 466).

68. "Et homo bonus de bono thensauro cordis sui profert bona sed non conparatur ei per quem factus est bonus. Ita nec filius connumeratur ei a quo bonitatem
cum uitam accepit et ideo ait Quid me dicis bonum" (Scolia 22 in Concilium Aqvi-
leiense, in Scripta Arriana Latina, p. 159).

69. "Nemo bonus nisi unus d(eu)s. Nam et omnis creatura d(e)I bona valde, [ut] arbitro, nec ipsa creatura lumini quo repleta est conparatur, nec homo Cr(ist)o, nec Cr(istu)s patri. Hoc secundum diuinum magisterium Arii cr(ist)iana professio, hoc et The[o]gnius ep(iscopus), hoc et Eusebius storiografus et ceteri conplurimi ep(isco)p(I) quorum professiones et nomina in sequentibus dicenda sunt" (*Scolia 22*, pp. 159–160).

70. See *Gesta Concilii Aquileiensis* 36, *CSEL* 82/3, ed. M. Zelzer (Vienna: Hoelder-Pichler-Tempsky, 1982), 347–48.

71. *Early Arianism*, 3.

CHAPTER 3

1. The essay, originally Froehlich's inaugural lecture as Warfield Professor of Ecclesiastical History at Princeton Theological Seminary, was first published in *Princeton Seminary Bulletin*, n.s., 1 (1978): 213–224. It has been reprinted in *Biblical Hermeneutics in Historical Perspective: Studies in Honor of Karlfried Froehlich on His Sixtieth Birthday*, ed. Mark S. Burrows and Paul Rorem (Grand Rapids, Mich.: Eerdman's, 1991), 1–15, citing 10. I use this version of the essay. An earlier version of this essay was published as, "Did Jesus 'Progress in Wisdom'? Thomas Aquinas on Luke 2:52 in Ancient and High-Medieval Context," *Traditio* 52 (1997): 179–200. Reprinted with permission.

2. *Saint Bonaventure's Disputed Questions on the Knowledge of Christ*, trans. Zachary Hayes (St. Bonaventure, NY: Franciscan Institute, 1996, p. 30).

3. Note that the Greek text says that Jesus increased in σοφία, while the Vulgate tells us that Jesus progressed in *sapientia*. However, Western medieval theological and exegetical discussion of this text usually centers on the question of whether Jesus progressed in knowledge (*scientia* or sometimes *cognitio*).

4. See A. Claverie, "La Science du Christ," *Revue Thomiste* 18 (1910): 766–779; P. Vigué, "Quelques Précisions concernant L'Objet de la Science Acquise du Christ," *Récherches de Science Religieuse* 10 (1920): 1–27. For the fifty years after the publication of Vigué's article, there was virtually no scholarly study of this subject. For more recent scholarship, see Jan Th. Ernst, *Die Lehre der hochmittelalterlichen Theologen von der volLukeommenen Erkenntnis Christi* (Freiburg:Herder, 1971), esp. 170–203; Philipp Kaiser, *Das Wissen Jesu Christi in der lateinischen (westlichen) Theologie* (Regensburg: Friedrich Pustet 1981), esp. 150–167; and J.-P. Torrell, "S. Thomas d'Aquin et la science du Christ: Une Relecture des Questions 9–12 de la 'Tertia Pars' de La Somme de Théologie," in *Saint Thomas au XXe Siècle* (Paris: Saint-Paul 1994), 394–409. See Torrell's succinct summary of this scholarship: "Thomas a été le premier des médiévaux à admettre pleinement cette science acquise chez le Christ," "Une Relecture," 398.

5. As is well-known, Thomas (and many other high-scholastic thinkers, including Bonaventure) distinguished two faculties or powers of the intellect. Relying upon Aristotle's famous distinction in *De Anima* 3.5, the high-scholastic thinkers distinguished between the active intellect (*intellectus agens*) and the receptive or passive intellect (*intellectus possibilis*). Basically, the active intellect has the capacity to abstract

universal ideas from the data of sense experience (*phantasmata*), while the passive intellect serves as the "storehouse" of these abstract ideas.

6. In this section, I will concentrate on Arius, Athanasius, Ambrose, and John of Damascus. Ambrose and John are of particular interest because Thomas explicitly invokes them in his discussion of the question in the *Summa*. I summarize the Athanasian position briefly. However, it must be stressed that Thomas did *not* know Athanasius directly, nor does he refer to him explicitly in his discussion of acquired knowledge in the *Summa*. I summarize Athanasius for two reasons. First, I wish to provide a rich exegetical context for understanding Thomas. Second, and more importantly, because the position that Athanasius develops in *Orationes contra Arianos* remained influential throughout the patristic and medieval period, even if unattributed or mediated indirectly through other writers (like Peter Lombard). I also briefly summarize the Arian exegesis of Luke 2:52 in order to understand the context of Athanasius's exegesis. We will not consider in detail in this chapter the fifth major interpretation of the text in the early church, which ascribed progress in wisdom to the mystical body of Christ. Thus, Augustine, for example, will ascribe progress in wisdom to the church in *De diversis quaestionibus octoginta tribus*, ed. A. Mutzenbecher, (*CCL* 44A [Turnhout: Brepols, 1975], q. 75, 216–217).

7. The word πάθος in ancient trinitarian and christological discussion generally refers to that which is involved in change or becoming and, more specifically, to experiences of limitation, finitude, and passion.

8. We know of the Arian interpretation of the text from Athanasius's *Contra Arianos* 3.51–53. See *Orationes*, pp. 203–206, as well as from other sources considered in the previous chapter.

9. This is now generally-accepted. See A. Grillmeier, *Christ in Christian Tradition*, 308–28; and Hanson, *Search*, 451–452, where the author points out that only after the year 362 did Athanasius realize "the necessity of allowing a human soul to Jesus." The *Orationes* were probably written between 339 and 345.

10. *Orations* 3.52–3, pp. 205–206.

11. Though see *Orations* 3.53, p. 206. At one point in this paragraph, Athanasius says τὸ ἀνθρώπινον ἐν τῇ Σοφίᾳ προέκοπτεν. That is, he ascribes progress in wisdom to the soulless "human part."

12. Where Athanasius also tackles another favorite proof-text of the Arians, Mark 13:32: "But of that Day or that hour no one knows, not even the angels in heaven, nor the Son, but only the Father." These two difficult texts pertaining to Christ's human knowledge were often dealt with together in the history of Christian thought, and the exegetical strategies used to interpret both are not dissimilar.

13. *Orations* 3.52, p. 205.

14. *Orations* 3.52, p. 205.

15. *Orations* 3.51, p. 204.

16. "...ἐπεὶ προκόπτειν οὐκεῖχε" (*Orations* 3.52, p. 205).

17. *Orations* 3.51, p. 204.

18. *Orations* 3.53, p. 206.

19. Though Williams has argued that the work had a broader intention than merely providing the emperor with an orthodox Christology. He also argues that it was undertaken in order to defend the church from the Arian charge that Catholic Christianity was tritheistic (*Ambrose of Milan and the End of the Arian-Nicene Conflicts,* 128–153.) Other important studies of the work include L. Hermann, "Ambrosius von Mailand als Trinitätstheologie,"in *Zeitschrift für Kirchengeschichte* (1958): 197–218; and A. Pertusi, "Le antiche traduzioni greche delle opere di s. Ambrogio," *Aevum* 18 (1944): 184–207.

20. For solid review of the scholarship and stimulating analysis of the Council, see Williams, *Ambrose of Milan and the End of the Arian-Nicene Conflicts,* chapter 6.

21. See Hanson, *Search,* 667, for a brief introduction to Ambrose's anti-Arian activity.

22. See *De Fide* 2.7.56, p. 75.

23. "Et ideo quia suscepit animam, suscepit et animae passiones" (*De Fide* 2.7.56, p. 75).

24. "Nisi forte debilitatem illam impii putabatis, quando vulnera videbatis. Erant quidem illa corporis vulnera, sed non erat vulneris illius ulla debilitas, ex quo vita omnium profluebat (*De Fide* 4.5.54, pp. 175–176). See also 2.7.56, p. 75: "Non turbatur ut virtus, non turbatur eius divinitas, sed 'turbatur *anima*,' turbatur secundum humanae fragilitatis adsumptionem."

25. See, e.g., *De Fide* 2.5.44, p. 71; and 2.9.77–78, pp. 84–85: "Servemus distinctionem divinitatis et carnis...Quasi deus loquitur quae sunt divina, quia verbum est, quasi homo dicit quae sunt humana, quia in mea substantia loquebatur."

26. "Disce distantiam: rogat quasi filius hominis, imperat quasi dei filius" (*De Fide* 3.4.32, p. 119).

27. See *De Fide* 5.16.193–197, pp. 289–291.

28. "ut quasi hominis filius secundum susceptionem nostrae inprudentiae vel perfectus non plene adhuc scisse omnia crederetur" (*De Fide* 5.18.222, p. 301).

29. On *De Incarnationis,* see E. Bellini, "Per una lettura globale del 'De Incarnationis Dominicae sacramento," in *La Scuola Cattolica* 102 (1974): 389–402.

30. See *De Sacramento* 7.72, p. 261.

31. For a fine study of the Damascene's Christology, see K. Rozemond, *La christologie de Saint Jean Damascène* (Ettal: Buch-Kunstverlag Ettal, 1959).

32. See Frances Young's stimulating discussion of the *status quaestionis* in *From Nicaea to Chalcedon* (London, 1983), 229–239.

33. *De Fide Orthodoxa* 3.22, PG 94: 1088.

34. John seems to be relying upon, without specifically invoking, the notion of *communicatio idiomatum,* the doctrine that because of the personal unity of the Incarnate Word, qualities that are properly divine may be predicated of the human nature (and vice versa).

35. John's position, notice, seems to be significantly different than that of Athanasius. Athanasius maintains that the wisdom of the *logos* is progressively revealed through the human instrument. John seems to have meant that the wisdom of the transformed σάρξ is revealed.

36. "Ad quod sane dici potest ipsum, secundum hominem, tantam a conceptione acccpisse sapientiae et gratiae plenitudinem, ut Deus ei plenius conferre non potuerit" (*Sent.* 3.13.5, p. 85).

37. "Si enim proficiebat sapientia et gratia, non videtur a conceptione habuisse plenitudinem gratiae sine mensura" (*Sent.* 3.13.4, p. 85).

38. "Aperte enim videtur Ambrosius innuere, quod Christus secundum humanum sensum profecerit, et quod infantia eius expers cognitionis, et patrem et matrem ignoraverit" (*Sent.* 3.13.9, pp. 88–89).

39. "quod nec Ecclesia recipit, nec praemissae auctoritates patiuntur sic intelligi" (*Sent.* 3.13.9, pp. 88–89).

40. "Proficiebat ergo humanus sensus in eo secundum ostensionem, et aliorum hominum opinionem" (*Sent.* 3., 13.9, pp. 88–89). Can the Lombard's position on Christ's human knowledge be tied to his understanding of the hypostatic union? It is tempting to appeal to the Lombard's famous report of three contemporary opinions on the hypostatic union in *Sent.* 3.6, pp. 49–59 and to tie him to the *habitus* theory that he explains there. There are at least two problems with this. First, it is still not at all certain which, if any, of these three christological opinions Peter favors. To assume that he preferred the *habitus* theory is to fall into the error of Peter's contemporaries, who, basing their verdicts on the earlier works of the Lombard, criticized him for sympathy with the *habitus* theory. See, e.g., Gerhoch of Reichersberg, *Libellus de ordine donorum Sancti Spiritus,* in *Opera inedita,* eds. D. and O. Van den Eynde and A. Rijmersdael, with P. Classen, 2 vols. in 3 (Rome: Pontificium Athenaeum Antonianum, 1955–56), 1: 71; and Walter of St. Victor, *Contra quatuor labyrinthos* 3: 1–2, ed. P. Glorieux, in *Archives d'histoire doctrinale et littéraire du moyen âge* 19 (1952): 246–249. Of course, one cannot accept Gerhoch's criticism as an accurate report of Peter's mature christological opinions. Second, Peter is vigorously critical of the *habitus* theory on several grounds, one of which is that it regards the humanity of Christ as quite accidental. Thus one should hesitate before recommending that Peter's views on the hypostatic union or his putative preference for the *habitus* theory be invoked to explain his reluctance to affirm real growth in Christ's human knowledge.

41. "Dicendum sine praejudicio, quod plus veritatis est in verbis Ambrosii quam Magister eliciat ex eis" (*Sent.* 3. 3.10. Sol., p. 249).

42. The term *habitus* in the medieval discussion of Luke 2:52 really has two meanings. At the most basic philosophical level it is virtually synonymous with "concepts" or "ideas," i.e., intellectual understanding of the *data* given to humanity through sense experience by exercise of its active intellect (and to Christ through "infusion"). Second, it refers to the mind's readiness to know and recognize again what it has been previously given through sense experience. For a discussion of the meaning of *habitus* in high-medieval Christology, see Zachary Hayes, *The Hidden Center: Spirituality and Speculative Christology in St. Bonaventure* (Ramsey, N.J.: Paulist Press, 1981), 106–107.

43. Bonaventure furnishes us with this definition: "Cognitio simplicis notitiae consistebat in habitibus et speciebus ipsi animae Christi inditis a primordio suae conditionis ex beneficio Conditoris" (*Sent.* 3.14.3.2. resp., p. 322).

44. See Albert, *Sent.* 3.13.10. Sol., pp. 249–251; Thomas, *Sent.* 3.14.3, Quaestiuncula 5, p. 461; Bonaventure, *Sent.* 3. 4.3.2., p. 322.

45. "Quoniam ergo habitus et species impressae fuerunt ipsi animae Christi in omnimoda plenitudine, hinc est quod Christus proficere non potuit cognitione simplicis notitiae" [(*Sent.* 3.14.3.2. Resp., p. 322) emphasis mine]. See also Bonaventure's discussion in *Sent.* 3. 15.2.1, Resp., p. 337: " . . . anima eius debuit esse deiformis, ac per hoc repleta luce sapientiae et rectitudine iustitiae; ignorantia autem privatio est scientiae et potest esse via in errorem et obliquationem a rectitudine iustitiae, ac per hoc Christo non competebat." Here we see another reason, aside from that of divine goodness and omnipotence, that medieval exegetes stress Christ's omniscience: namely, that ignorance could lead to error and sin.

46. "Christus non proficiebat veniendo in notitiam rei prius incognitae" (*Sent.* 3. 14.3.2. Resp., p. 322). See also the extended discussion in *Sent.* 3. 15.2.1., p. 337, which concludes: "Concedendum est igitur Christum defectum ignorantiae nequaquam in se habuisse."

47. As Bonaventure puts it: "Quia vero sensus exterior ad aliquid convertabatur de novo ad quod prius conversus non fuerat, hinc est quod cognitione experientiae proficiebat" (*Sent.* 3. 14.3.2. Resp., p. 322).

48. *Sent.* 3.13.10. Sol., p. 249.

49. *Sent.* 3.14.3.2. Resp., p. 322.

50. Again, Thomas lectured for four years on the *Sentences* (1252–1256) while *sententiarius* in Paris. As will be evident in a moment, Thomas's early opinion on the possibility of acquired knowledge is highly dependent on previously written commentaries. Indeed, his position is much like the one developed by Albert the Great and Bonaventure.

Note that I am *not* arguing that the *whole* of the *Scriptum* is derivative or dependent on contemporary opinion. But there is no doubt that *this* opinion was highly derivative. This is provable not only by comparing the texts but because Thomas later explicitly admits his debt at *Summa* 3.12.2. Resp. Again, for Thomas's relationship in the *Scriptum* to earlier and contemporary commentators on the *Sentences,* see Gilles Emery, *La Trinité creatrice: Trinité et création dans les commentaires aux Sentences de Thomas d'Aquin et de ses précurseurs Albert le Grand et Bonaventure* (Paris: Vrin, 1995). Here Emery convincingly argues that, in the first *two* books of Thomas's *Scriptum,* Thomas both borrowed from contemporary commentators (such as Albert the Great and Bonaventure, as well as from the *Summa Halensis,* and others) *and* departed from them in significant and original ways. No study has been undertaken, analogous to Emery's, for the relationship of the third or fourth books of Thomas's *Scriptum* to its sources.

51. " . . . omnia scivit a primo instante suae conceptionis" (*Sent.* 3.14.3. Sol. V, p. 461).

52. "Crevit autem quantum ad aliquem modum certitudinis" (*Sent.* 3.14.3. Sol. V, p. 461).

53. " . . . et quantum ad hanc crevit scientia Christi, inquantum quotidie aliqua videbat sensibiliter quae prius non viderat" (*Sent.* 3.14.3. Sol. V, p. 461).

54. "Ambrosius intelligit profectum scientiae Christi quantum ad experientiam secundum novam conversionem ad sensibile praesans" (*Sent.* 3.14.3. Sol. V ad 4um, pp. 461–462).

55. "Non autem crevit ad essentiam" (*Sent.* 3.14.3. Sol. V, p. 461).

56. "Non fuit aliqua species de nova recepta in intellectu possibili ejus" (*Sent.* 3.14.3. Sol. V ad 3um, p. 462).

57. "Une Relecture," 398.

58. "Sed quantum ad ipsum habitum scientiae, manifestum est quod habitus scientiae infusae in eo non est augmentatus, cum a principio plenarie sibi fuerit omnis scientia infusa" (*Summa Theologiae* 3a.12.2., resp., in *Opera Omnia* [16 vols. to date; Rome: Typographia Polyglotta S.C. de Propaganda Fide, 1887–], 11:167).

59. Si igitur praeter habitum scientiae infusum non sit in anima Christi habitus aliquis scientiae, ut quibusdam videtur, et mihi aliquando visum est, nulla scientia in Christo augmentata fuit secundum suam essentiam sed solum per experientiam, idest per conversionem specierum intelligibilium inditarum ad phantasmata. Et secundum hoc dicunt quod scientia Christi profecit secundum experientiam, convertendo scilicet species intelligibiles inditas ad ea quae de novo per sensum accipit (*Summa* 3a.12.2. Resp., p. 142).

This remark occurs, of course, in a theological textbook, not a scriptural commentary. Nonetheless, let there be no doubt that Thomas had Luke 2:52 in mind when he wrote this article. Indeed, he explicitly cites the scriptural text in *Summa* 3.12.2 as evidence for the increase in Christ's experiential knowledge. And no less an authority than Torrell has concluded that Thomas arrives at his mature position *sous l'influence de l'Écriture*, specifically Luke 2:52. See "Une Relecture," 398–399.

60. "Sed quia inconveniens videtur quod aliqua naturalis actio intelligibilis Christo deesset, cum extrahere species intelligibiles a phantasmatibus sit quaedam naturalis actio hominis secundum intellectum, conveniens videtur hanc etiam actionem in Christo ponere" (*Summa* 3a.12.2. Resp., p. 168).

61. "Et ideo, quamvis aliter alibi scripserim, dicendum est in Christo scientiam acquisitam fuisse. Quae proprie est scientia secundum modum humanum. . . . Et ex hoc sequitur quod in anima Christi aliquis habitus scientiae fuit qui per hujusmodi abstractionem specierum potuerit augmentari; ex hoc scilicet quod intellectus agens post primas species intelligibiles abstractas a phantasmatibus, poterat etiam alias abstrahere" (*Summa* 3a.9.4. Resp., p. 144; and 3a.12.2. Resp., p. 168).

62. "Et ideo non fuit conveniens ejus dignitati ut a quocumque hominum doceretur" (*Summa* 3a.12.3. Resp., p. 169).

63. "Ad primum ergo dicendum quod scientia rerum acquiri potest non solum per experientiam ipsarum, sed etiam per experientiam quarundam aliarum rerum: cum ex virtute luminis intellectus agentis possit homo procedere ad intelligendum effectus per causas, et causas per effectus, et similia per similia, et contraria per contraria. Sic igitur, licet Christus non fuerit omnia expertus, ex his tamen quae expertus est, in omnium devenit notitiam" (*Summa* 3a.12.1 ad 1um, 166; emphasis mine).

64. "Ad tertium dicendum quod verbum Damasceni intelligitur quantum ad illos qui dicunt simpliciter factam fuisse additionem scientiae Christi: scilicet secundum quamcumque eius scientiam; et praecipue secundum infusam, quae causatur in anima Christi ex unione ad Verbum. Non autem intelligitur de augmento scientiae quae ex naturali agente causatur" (*Summa* 3.12.2 ad 3um, p. 168).

65. It has long been recognized that there are "Platonist" elements in Thomas's explanation of the beatific vision, especially, and in other of his opinions as well. Here I cite only W. R. Inge, *The Philosophy of Plotinus* (London: Longmans, Green and Co., 1929), 15; R. J. Henle, S.J., *St. Thomas and Platonism* (The Hague: M. Nijhoff, 1956); W. J. Hankey, *God in Himself* (Oxford: Oxford University Press, 1987); and, probably the clearest demonstration of Platonic influence in the realm of epistemology (especially in the beatific vision), the book recently published by Patrick Quinn, *Aquinas, Platonism and the Knowledge of God* (Aldershot, Hants, England: Avebury, 1996).

66. Few more usefully than Mark D. Jordan, *The Alleged Aristotelianism of Thomas Aquinas* (The Etienne Gilson Series 15; Toronto: Pontifical Institute of Mediaeval Studies, 1992).

67. *Aquinas, Platonism and the Knowledge of God*, 2–3.

68. See Thomas's lengthy discussion in *Summa* 1.75–79. Thomas's reservations about the limitations and unreliability of the mind's ability to know God from the world around us are, of course, famously muted in the first book of the *contra Gentiles*.

69. See, generally, *Summa* 3a. 4–5, as well as Thomas's comment at the beginning of *Summa* 3a.9.4. Resp. that the human nature assumed by God the Word lacks nothing implanted by God in human nature as such, a remark analyzed below in more detail.

70. *Summa* 3.12.2. Resp., p. 168.

71. How, then, to explain the earlier Thomistic position? I think the answer here lies, again, in Thomas's heavy dependence for *this* opinion, on other commentators on the *Sentences*, particularly Albert and Bonaventure. Thomas's position there was quite derivative, and he did not develop his own, reflective position until he revisited the question in the *Summa*. Note, again, that the argument I am trying to make about the nature of Thomas's dependence applies *only* to this opinion. Again, I am *not* trying to make a general argument about Thomas's method in the third book of the *Scriptum*. Let us remind ourselves, too, that one of the ways that we know Thomas's earlier argument is derivative is that at *Summa* 3.12.1 he explicitly acknowledges the identity of his earlier position and that of his mendicant contemporaries.

72. See, e.g., Bonaventure on this point:

Ad illud quod obiicitur, quod intellectus agens in Christo potuit abstrahere; dicendum, quod abstractio speciei a conditionibus materialibus quaedam ordinatur ad generandum habitum, quaedam vero consistit in iudicio eius quod apprehensum est per sensum, iudicio, inquam, facto ab intellectu. Et prima non fuit in Christo, cum intellectus eius haberet habitus et species rerum, illa autem abstractio ordinaretur ad acquisitionem habitus et scientiae nondum adeptae, et ita haberet annexum defectum ignorantiae. (*Sent.* 3.14.3.2. Resp., 322)

73. *De Caelo et Mundo* 1.4.27ia33.

74. *Summa* 3a.12.1. Resp., 166. See also this comment:

Si autem in aliis *Deus et natura nihil frustra* fecerunt, ut Philosphus dicit, in *I de Caelo et Mundo*, multo minus in anima Christi aliquid fuit frustra. Frustra autem est quod non habet propriam operationem.... Propria autem operatio intellectus agentis est facere species intelligibiles actu, abstrahendo eas a phantasmatibus.... Sic igitur necesse est dicere quod in Christo fuerunt aliquae species intelligibiles per actionem intellectus agentis in intellectu possibili eius receptae. (*Summa* 3.9.4. Resp., 144)

75. "Respondeo dicendum quod, sicut ex supra dictis [the reference is to *Summa* 3a.4, where Thomas taLukes at length about the humanity assumed by God the Word] patet, nihil eorum quae Deus in nostra natura plantavit, defuit humanae naturae assumptae a Verbo Dei. Manifestum est autem quod in humana natura Deus plantavit non solum intellectum possibilem, sed etiam intellectum agentem. Unde necesse est dicere quod in anima Christi non solum intellectus possibilis, sed etiam intellectus agens fuerit" (*Summa* 3a.9.4. Resp., p. 144).

76. *Summa* 3.12.2, p. 168.

77. See *Summa* 3.12.2 Resp., p. 168.

78. "Une Relecture," 399.

79.

...anima eius debuit esse deiformis, ac per hoc repleta luce sapientiae et rectitudine iustitiae; ignorantia autem privatio est scientiae et rectitudine iustitiae; ignorantia autem privatio est scientiae et potest esse via in errorem et obliquationem a rectitudine iustitiae; ignorantia autem privatio est scientiae et potest esse via in errorem et obliquationem a rectitudine iustitiae, ac per hoc Christo non competebat (*Sent.* 3. 14.3.2, p. 322). Concedendum est igitur Christum defectum ignorantiae nequaquam in se habuisse. (*Sent.* 3. 15.2.1, p. 337)

Thomas comes to a similar conclusion at *Summa* 3.15.3. Resp., p. 188. This assertion, when juxtaposed with his insistence that Christ *acquired* his omniscience, creates an unresolved tension in Thomas's thought.

80. Bonaventure concludes that Christ's active intellect did not create new knowledge because, already, *haberet habitus et species rerum* (*Sent.* 3.14.3.2 Resp. ad 4um, p. 322).

81. Duae formae ejusdem specie non possunt esse in eodem subjecto: habitus autem cognitionis omnium fuit in Christo ab instanti suae conceptionis: ergo non fuit susceptibilis alicujus habitus per cognitionem experimenti (*Sent.* 3. 13.10 sed contra 1, p. 249).

82. On this Augustinian theme and its influence, see Ernst, *Die Lehre*, esp. 29–34, 124–128, and 144–167. On the importance of the Augustinian epistemological

tradition to Bonaventure and contemporaries, see also E. Gilson, *The Philosophy of St. Bonaventure* (Paterson, N.J.: St. Anthony Guild Press, 1965). Bonaventure himself reveals his epistemological preferences in several places, nowhere more clearly in relation to Christ's knowledge than in the second and fourth of his questions *De Scientia Christi* in *Opera Omnia* 5 (1891): 6–10 and 17–27.

CHAPTER 4

1. An earlier version of this chapter was presented as "*Christus Nesciens?* Was Christ Ignorant of the Day of Judgment? Arian and Orthodox Interpretation of Mark 13:32 in the Ancient Latin West," *Harvard Theological Review* 96 (2003): 255–278. Reprinted with permission.

2. "Haec itaque corrupto deprauato que sensu inpiissime ita intellecta esse monstrantes..." (*De Trinitate* 1.30, 1:28).

3. "Omni autem modo in tantum eum a proprietate ueri Dei abesse, ut etiam testatus haec fuerit: *De die autem illa et hora nemo scit, neque angeli in caelis neque Filius, nisi Pater solus:* ut cum Filius nesciat quod Pater solus sciat, longe alienus sit nesciens a sciente, quia natura ignorationi obnoxia non sit eius uirtutis et potestatis, quae a dominatu ignorationis excerpta sit" (*De Trinitate* 1.29, 1:28).

4. "Postremo iam tamquam indissolubili abnegatae diuinitatis professione subuertisse se fidem ecclesiae gloriantur, cum relegunt: De die autem illa et hora nemo scit, neque angeli in caelis nec Filius, nisi Pater solus. Non enim uidetur exaequabilis per natiuitatem esse natura, quae ignorationis sit necessitate diuersa; et Pater sciendo ac Filius nesciendo manifestent dissimilitudinem diuinitatis: quia et ignorare Deus nihil debeat, et ignorans non conparandus sit ad scientem" (*De Trinitate* 9.2, 2:372–373).

5. *De Trinitate* 1.30, 1:28.

6. *De Trinitate* 1.30, 1:28–29.

7. "...omnes dictorum causas ex his ipsis uel interrogationum uel temporum uel dispensationum generibus adtulimus, causis potius uerba subdentes, non causas uerbis deputantes: ut cum a se dissideat Pater maior me est et Ego et Pater unum sumus, neque idem sit Nemo bonus est nisi unus Deus et Qui me uidit, uidit et Patrem, uel certe tanta a se diuersitate contraria sint Pater, omnia tua mea sunt et mea tua et Vt cognoscant te solum uerum Deum, uel illud Ego in Patre et Pater in me et De die autem et hora nemo scit, neque angeli in caelis neque Filius, nisi Pater solus, intellegantur in singulis et dispensationum praedicationes et consciae potestatis naturales professiones; et cum idem sit dicti auctor utriusque, demonstratis tamen uirtutibus generum singulorum, non pertineat ad contumeliam uerae diuinitatis quod ad sacramentum fidei euangelicae sub dispensatione et causae et temporis et natiuitatis et nominis praedicatur" (*De Trinitate* 1.30, 1:28–29).

8. "Ac primum antequam dicti ratio et causa memoratur, sensu communis iudicii sentiendum est, an credibile esse possit, ut aliquid ex omnibus nesciat, qui omnibus ad id quod sunt adque erunt auctor est. Si enim omnia per Christum et in Christo, et ita per ipsum, ut in ipso omnia sint, id quod neque extra eum neque non

per eum est, quomodo non etiam in scientia eius sit, cum plerumque scientia eius ea, quae neque in se neque per se sint, per uirtutem naturae non nesciae adpraehendat? Aduero quod causam nisi ex eo non sumit, et motum ad id quod est erit que nisi intra se non capit, quomodo extra eius naturae scientiam est, per quam et in qua id quod efficiendum sit continetur? " Cogitationes namque humanas non solum praesenti motu incitatas, sed etiam instinctu futurae uoluntatis agitandas Dominus Christus non ignorat, euangelista testante: Sciebat enim Iesus ab initio, qui essent non credentes, et qui esset traditurus eum. Naturae ergo eius uirtus, quae cognitionem rerum non extantium capit et quiescentium adhuc animorum subituras inquietudines non ignorat, id quod per se intra que se est nescisse existimabitur? . . . Cum igitur omnis in eo sit plenitudo, et omnia per ipsum et in ipso reconcilientur, et dies illa reconciliationis nostrae expectatio sit, hanc ille diem ignorat, cuius et in se tempus est et per se sacramentum est? . . . Nemo itaque quod per se et intra se est, nescit. Christus aderit, et aduentus sui diem ignorat? Dies suus est, secundum eundem apostolum: Quia dies Domini sicut fur nocte adueniet, et ignoratione eius detineri intellegendus est? Humanae naturae quod agere definiunt, quantum in se est praesciunt, et sequitur gerendorum cognitio uoluntatem agendi; Deus uero natus quod in se et per se est nescit? Per eum enim tempora et in eo dies est: quia et per ipsum futurorum constitutio est et in ipso aduentus sui dispensatio est" (*De Trinitate* 9.59, 2:438–439).

9. See the introductory remarks by G. Tissot, ed., *Traité sur 1' Évangile de S. Luc* (*SC* 45, 52 [Paris: Cerf, 1955, 1958]) for careful tracing of the commentary's sources.

10. See the critical text of the *Expositio Evangelii secundam Lucam*, in *CCL* 14, ed. M. Adriaen (Turnhout: Brepols, 1957). No other Ambrosian work presents such difficult chronological problems, and it is not impossible that the homilies which make up the commentary were delivered as early as 378. The introduction by Tissot, *ed. cit.*, is very helpful for chronological difficulties, sources, context, content, and influence. See also, for the influence of the text upon Augustine, P. Rollero, *La Expositio Evangelii secundum Lucam di Ambrogio come fonte dell'esegesi agostiniana* (Turin: University of Turin, 1958).

11. "Bene medie posuit filium; est enim idem filius hominis filius dei, ut magis dictum secundum filium hominis aestimemus, quia temporum finem non per naturam hominis, sed per naturam dei nouit. nec alienum tamen a fide est, si filium accipias dei. quid enim est quod bonus pater filium celauerit, cui omnia dedit? aut quomodo non dedit cognitionem temporis qui dedit ipsius iudicii potestatem?" (*Expositio Evangelii secundum Lucam* 8.34, p. 310).

12. "ergo unius sunt cognitionis, quia unius sunt potestatis" (*Expositio Evangelii secundum Lucam* 8.35, p. 310).

13. "deinde qui signa nouit futuri iudicii utique nouit et finem" (*Expositio Evangelii secundum Lucam* 8.35, p. 310).

14. "ergo et horam nouit, sed nouit sibi, mihi nescit" (*Expositio Evangelii secundum Lucam* 8.36, p. 310).

15. *Expositio Evangelii secundum Lucam* 8.34, p. 310.

16. "Nonne haec cottidie perstrepunt Arriani, 'scientiam omnem' in Christo esse non posse, "quia ipse, inquiunt, diei et horae est se professus ignarum"? Nonne

dicunt: Quomodo sciuit, qui eum non potuisse scire commemorant, nisi quae audierit aut uiderit,' et ea quae spectant ad diuinae unitatem naturae, ad infirmitatem sacrilega interpraetatione deriuant?" (*De Fide* 5.16. 192, p. 288).

17. See chapter 1, n. 2 for scholarship on the missing words in several early Matthean mss.

18. "Primum ueteres non habent codices graeci quia nec filius scit. Sed non mirum, si et hoc falsarunt, qui scripturas interpolauere diuinas. Sed non mirum, si et hoc falsarunt, qui scripturas interpolauere diuinas" (*De Fide* 5.16. 193, p. 289).

19. "Non ergo nesciuit diem; neque enim "sapientiae dei" est ex parte scire et ex parte nescire" (*De Fide* 5.16.196, p. 290). This text seems to have been picked up by Pseudo-Augustine, *Solutiones Diversarum Quaestionum, CCL* 90, ed. B. Schwank (Turnhout: Brepols, 1961): "Non enim est sapientiae dei ex parte scire et ex parte nescire" (*Solutio* 90, p. 222).

20. "Medium utique nomen est fili; nam et "filius hominis" dicitur, ut secundum inprudentiam adsumptionis nostrae diem futuri iudicii nescisse uideatur" (*De Fide* 5.16.194, p. 289).

21. "Et ideo non potuit creator omnium ignorare, quod fecit, nescire, quod ipse donauit" (De Fide 5.16.197, p. 291). Again, Pseudo-Augustine seems to have followed Ambrose closely here: "Et ideo non potuit creator omnium ignorare quod fecit, nescire quod ipse constituit" (*Solutio* 90, p. 222).

22. "Locum quoque etiam alibi designauit, cum sibi "structuras templi ostendentibus discipulis" diceret: Videtis haec omnia? Amen dico uobis, non relinquetur hic lapis super lapidem, qui non destruatur. De signo quoque interrogatus ab apostolis respondit: Videte ne seducamini . . . Quo autem modo uel circumdaturos exercitus Hierusalem dicat uel implenda tempora gentium et quo ordine, euangelicae utique lectionis adtestatione reseratur" (*De Fide* 5.16. 206–208, pp. 294–295).

23. "Sed quaerimus, qua ratione designare momenta noluerit. 'Si quaeramus, inueniemus' non ignorantiae esse, sed sapientiae. Nobis enim scire non proderat, ut, dum certa futuri iudicii momenta nescimus, semper tamquam in excubiis constituti et inprudentiam peccandi consuetudinem declinemus, ne nos inter uitia dies domini depraehendat. Non enim prodest scire, sed metuere, quod futurum est; scriptum est enim: Noli alta sapere, sed time. Nam si diem designasset expresse, uni aetati hominum, quae proxima erat iudicio, uideretur disciplinam praescripsisse uiuendi; superioris temporis aut iustus esset remissior aut peccator securior. Namque adulter nisi cottidianam poenam metuat, non potest ab adulterandi cupiditate desinere nec latro obsessorum saltuum secreta deserere, nisi sciat sibi momentis omnibus inminere supplicium. Plerumque enim quibus incentiuum est inpunitas, timor taedio est. Ideo ergo dixi quia scire non proderat, immo proderat ignorare, ut ignorantes timeremus, ut obseruantes emendaremur, sicut ipse dixit: Estote parati, quia nescitis, qua hora filius hominis uenturus est. Namque miles, nisi bellum in manibus esse cognoscat, praetendere non nouit in castris (*De Fide* 5.16. 209–211, 295–296).

24. "Quomodo enim nesciret diem dei filius, cum in ipso sint thensauri sapientiae et scientiae dei absconditi?" (*De Fide* 5.16.194, pp. 289–290). Colossians 2:3

was another favorite proof-text of the Nicene party in attempting to neutralize Arian exegesis of Mark 13:32.

25. "Vnde alibi quoque ipse dominus interrogatus, ab apostolis inquam, qui utique non sicut Arrius intellegebant, sed filium dei futura scire credebant—nam nisi hoc credidissent, numquam interrogassent-, interrogatus ergo, quando restitueret regnum Istrahel, non se nescire dixit, sed ait: Non est uestrum scire tempora et annos, quae pater posuit in sua potestate. Adtende, quid dixerit: Non est uestrum scire! Lege iterum: Non est uestrum dixit, non 'meum' " (Ambrose, *De Fide* 5.17.212, p. 296).

26.

> Sed dicis quia cum angelis adnumeravit et filium. Adnumeravit quidem filium, sed non adnumeravit et spiritum sanctum. Aut fatere igitur potiorem esse spiritum dei filio, ut iam non solum quasi Arrianus, sed etiam quasi Fotinianus loquaris, aut agnosce, quo referre debeas, quod nescire filium dei dixit. Etenim quasi homo adnumerari creaturis potuit, qui creatus est. (*De Spiritu Sancto* 2.11.117, p. 132)

The Photius to whom Ambrose refers seem to refer to the head of a psilosanthropic sect. See Marius Victorinus, *Adversus Arium* 1a. 21–23, 28, 25 and 2.2 for fuller description of Photius and his followers (*CSEL* 83/1, ed. P Henry and P. Hadot [Vienna: Hoelder-Pichler-Tempsky, 1971], 88–95, 102–104, 170–172).

27.

> Legi dudum cuiusdam libellos de spiritu sancto: et iuxta comici sententiam ex graecis bonis, latina uidi non bona nihil ibi dialecticum, nihil uirile atque districtum, quod lectorem uel ingratis in assensum trahat: sed totum flaccidum, molle, nitidum, atque formosum, et exquisitis hinc inde odoribus. (*Praefatio in libro Didymi Alexandri De Spiritu Sancto* [*PL* 23:104])

Rufinus quotes these words almost verbatim in his *Apologia contra Hieronymum* 2.27, ed. *CCL* 20, ed. M. Simonetti (Turnhout: Brepols, 1961), 103. See also Jerome's harsh judgment on Ambrose in *De viris inlustribus* 100, where he says:

> I shall resist giving my opinion of him, lest I be accused either of truckling or of speaking the truth about him" ("Ambrosius, mediolanensis episcopus, usque in praesentem diem scribit, de quo, quia superest, meum iudicium subtraham, ne in alterutram partem aut adulatio in me reprehendatur aut ueritas. [*PL* 23:711])

28. "Ergo unius et pater et filius et spiritus sanctus et naturae sunt et scientiae" (*De Spiritu Sancto* 2.11.116, p. 131).

29. "Eris igitur et tu 'Abdemelech,' hoc est 'adsumptus a domino,' si de profundo gentilis inprudentiae levaveris dei verbum, si credideris quia non fallitur, non praeteritur dei filius, non ignorat, quae futura sunt, non fallitur etiam spiritus sanctus, de quo dicit dominus: Cum venerit autem ille spiritus veritatis, deducet vos in omnem veritatem" (*De Spiritu Sancto* 2.11.114, p. 131).

30. "Quod si vis discere quia novit omnia et praescientiam habet dei filius omnium futurorum, quae filio incognita putas, ea de filio spiritus sanctus accepit" (*De Spiritu Sancto* 2.11.118, p. 132).

31. "Itaque ut agnoscas quia novit omnia, cum diceret filius: De die autem illa et hora nemo scit, neque angeli caelorum, excepit spiritum sanctum. Si autem exceptus est spiritus sanctus ab ignorantia, quomodo non exceptus est dei filius?" (*De Spiritu Sancto* 2.11.116, p. 131).

32. "Accipe tamen quia novit diem iudicii filius" (*De Spiritu Sancto* 2.11.119–120, pp. 132–33).

33. See J. N. D. Kelly, *Jerome: His Life, Writings and Controversies* (London: Duckworth, 1975) for the background to the commentary, not to mention a splendid biography of this great, accomplished, and ever irascible doctor of the church.

34. See the introductory material in E. Bonnard's edition and French translation of the commentary for valuable comments on context, content, sources and use (*SC* 242/259 [Paris: Cerf, 1977, 1979]. For Origen's Matthew commentary, written between 244–249, see R. Girod's edition in *SC* 162 (*SC* 162 [Paris: Cerf, 1970]; for Hilary's commentary, see J. Doignon's edition (*SC* 254/258 [Paris: Cerf, 1978, 1979]).

35. "Gaudet Arrius et Eunomius quasi ignorantia magistri gloria discipulorum sit et dicunt: non potest aequalis esse qui nouit et qui ignorat" (*Commentarii in Evangelium Matthei*, pp. 231–232). Bede must have known this commentary, or a commentary that used Jerome extensively, as he quotes frequently and *verbatim* from it in his *Commentary on Mark*. See Bede, *In Marci Evangelium Expositio* 4.13, ed. D. Hurst (*CCL* 120 [Turnhout: Brepols, 1960], 603).

36. "Contra quos breuiter ista dicenda sunt: Cum omnia tempora fecerit iesus, hoc est uerbum dei, *omnia* enim *per ipsum facta sunt, et sine ipso factum est nihil;* in omnibus autem temporibus etiam dies iudicii sit, qua consequentia potest eius ignorare partem cuius totum nouerit? Hoc quoque dicendum est: Quid est maius notitia patris an iudicii? Si maius nouit, quomodo ignorat quod minus est? Scriptum legimus: *Omnia quae patris sunt mihi tradita sunt.* Si omnia Patris filii sunt, qua ratione unius sibi diei notitiam reseruauit et noluit eam communicare cum filio? Sed et hoc inferendum: Si nouissimum diem temporum ignorat, ignorat et paene ultimum et retrorsum omnes. Non enim potest fieri ut qui primum ignorat sciat quid secundum sit. Igitur quia probauimus non ignorare filium consummationis diem" (*In Math.* 4, p. 232).

37. Again, a reference to Acts 1:7.

38. "Igitur quia probauimus non ignorare filium consummationis diem, causa reddenda est cur ignorare dicatur. Apostolus super saluatore scribit: *In quo sunt omnes thesauri sapientiae et scientiae absconditi.* Sunt ergo omnes thesauri in Christo sapientiae et scientiae sed absconditi sunt. Quare absconditi? Post resurrectionem interrogatus ab apostolis de die manifestius respondit: *Non est uestrum scire tempora et momenta quae pater posuit in sua potestate.* Quando dicit *Non est uestrum scire,* ostendit quod ipse sciat sed non expediat nosse apostolis, ut semper incerti de aduentu iudicis sic cotidie uiuant quasi die alia iudicandi sint. Denique et consequens euangelii sermo

id ipsum cogit intellegi, dicens quoque patrem solum nosse. In patre comprehendit et filium; omnis enim pater filii nomen est (*In Math.* 4, p. 232).

39. A pseudo-Hieronymian commentary on Mark was widely copied in the Middle Ages until, in the Renaissance, scholars disproved the theory that it was written by Jerome. It is published in M. Cahill, ed., *Expositio Evangelii secundum Marcum*, *CCL* 82 (Turnhout: Brepols, 1997). The commentary was probably written in the seventh century by an abbot, and is perhaps of Hibernian provenance. See Michael Cahill, *The First Commentary on Mark* (Oxford: Oxford University Press, 1998) for a fine annotated translation, with introduction treating critical problems.

40. See, e.g., Augustine's remarks in the *Harmony of the Gospels* (ca. 400):

Marcus eum subsecutus tamquam pedisequus et breviator eius uidetur. cum solo quippe Iohanne nihil dixit, solus ipse perpauca, cum solo Luca pauciora, cum Mattheo vero plurima et multa paene totidem adque ipsis uerbis siue cum solo siue cum ceteris consonante. (*De Consensu Evangelistarum* 1.2.4, in *CSEL* 43, ed. F. Weihrich [Vienna: Hoelder-Pichler-Tempsky, 1904], 4)

41. *Tractatus in Marci Evangelium*, in *CCL* 78, ed. G. Morin (Turnhout: Brepols, 1958), 496.

42. "Si enim qui accepturi sunt baptisma, credituri sunt in Patrem, Filium, et Spiritum sanctum: nunc autem *de filio dicitur de die autem illo et hora nemo scit, neque angeli in caelo, neque filius, nisi pater:* si aequaliter accipimus baptisma in Patrem, Filium, et Spiritum sanctum, et unum nomen eius, Patris et Filii et Spiritus sancti, quod est Deus, credere debemus: si unus Deus est, quomodo in una diuinitate diuersa scientia est?" (*Tractatus in Marci Evangelium*, p. 496).

43. "Si Deus est, quomodo ignorat? Dicitur enim de Domino Saluatore: 'omnia per ipsum facta sunt, et sine ipso factum est nihil.' Si omnia per ipsum facta sunt: ergo et dies iudicii, quae uentura est, per ipsum facta est. Potest ne ignorare quod fecit? Potest artifex ignorare opus suum? . . . si autem sunt in xpisto thesauri sapientiae et scientiae absconditi, debemus inquirere quare sint absconditi. Si sciremus nos homines diem iudicii, uerbi causa, quod futura esset dies iudicii post duo milia annorum, et hoc nos sciremus ita futurum, neglegentiores hinc essemus" (*Tractatus in Marci Evangelium*, p. 496).

44. Augustine probably encountered Arianism in its Homoian form. See M. Simonetti, "S. Agostino e gli Ariani," *Revue des études augustiennes* 13 (1967): 55–84; J. Zeiler, "L'arianism in Afrique avant l'invasion vandales," *Revue Historique* 73 (1934): 535–540; and see the excellent introduction to Augustine's anti-Arian corpus in Roland J. Teske, *Arianism and Other Heresies. The Works of Saint Augustine* I.18 (New York: New City, 1995), 119–132.

45. *PL* 40:683–708.

46. *PL* 42:709–742.

47. *PL* 42:743–814.

48. *CCL* 36, ed. R. Willems (Turnhout: Brepols, 1954).

49. *CCL* 50–50A, ed. W. J. Mountain (Turnhout: Brepols, 1968).

50. See, e.g., Sermons 117, 126, 135, 139, 140 (against Maximinum), 183, 330, and 341 in *PL* 38–39.

51. Est etiam inter illa quae scripsimus quoddam prolixum opus, qui tamen unus deputatur liber, cuius titulus est de diuersis quaestionibus octoginta tribus. cum autem dispersae fuissent per chartulas multas, quoniam ab ipso primo tempore conuersionis meae, posteaquam in africam uenimus, sicut interrogabar a fratribus, quando me uacantem uidebant, nulla seruata ordinatione dictatae sunt, iussi eas iam episcopus colligi et unum ex eis librum fieri adhibitis numeris, ut quod quisque legere uoluerit facile inueniat. (*Retractio* 1.26, in *Retractionum Libri Duo*, ed. A. Mutzenbecher, in *CCL* 57 [Turnhout: Brepols, 1984], 74)

For an excellent treatment of the chronological and doctrinal problems associated with this work, see. G. Bardy et al., *Oeuvres de Saint Augustin*, in *Bibliothèque Augustinenne* 10 (Paris: Etudes Augustinennes), 11–50.

52. *"De die autem et hora nemo scit, neque angeli caelorum neque filius hominis nisi pater solus.* sicut scire deus dicitur etiam cum scientem facit,—sicut scriptum est: *temtat uos dominus deus uester, ut sciat si diligitis eum;* non enim sic dictum est, quasi nesciat deus, sed ut ipsi sciant, quantum in dei dilectione profecerint, quod nisi temtationibus quae accidunt non plene ab hominibus agnoscitur; et ipsum temtat pro eo positum est, quod temtari sinit—sic et cum dicitur nescire aut pro eo dicitur quod non approbat, id est in disciplina et doctrina sua non agnoscit, sicut dictum est: nescio uos, aut pro eo quod utiliter nescientes facit, quod scire inutile est (*De Diversis Quaestionibus Octoginta Tribus*, p. 119).

53. "Unumquemque opera sua juvabunt, aut opera sua pressura sunt" (*PL* 38: 549).

54. "Ubi quidem magna quaestio est, ne carnaliter sapientes putemus aliquid Patrem scire, quod nesciat Filius. Nam utique cum dixit, *Pater scit;* ideo hoc dixit, quia in Patre et Filius scit. Quid enim est in die, quod non in Verbo factum est, per quem factus est dies? Nemo ergo quaerat novissimum diem, quando futurus sit: sed vigilemus omnes bene vivendo, ne novissimus dies cujuscumque nostrum nos inveniat imparatos, et qualis quisque hinc exierit suo novissimo die, talis inveniatur in novissimo saeculi die. Nihil te adjuvabit quod hic non feceris" (*PL* 38: 549).

55. Critical edition in *Sancti Aurelii Augustini Enarrationes in Psalmos*, ed. D. Dekkers and J. Fraipont (*CCL* 38–40 [Turnhout: Brepols, 1956). Important studies include D. de Bruyne, *Saint Augustin reviseur de la Bible* (Rome: Tipografia Poliglotta Vaticana, 1931); U. Occhialini, *La speranza della chiese pellegrina: teologia della speranza nelle "Ennarationes in Psalmos" di S. Agostino* (Assisi: Studio Teologico "Porziuncola," 1965); O. Brabant, *Le Christ, centre et source de la vie morale chez saint Augustin* (Gembloux: J. Duculog, 1971); G. Lawless, "The Monastery as a Model of the Church: Augustine's Commentary on Psalm 132, *Angelicum* 60 (1983): 258–274; A. Oden, "Dominant images for the church in Augustine's *Enarrationes in Psalmos:* a Study in Augustine's Ecclesiology (PhD diss., Southern Methodist University, 1990); and M.

Cameron, "Augustine's Construction of Figurative Exegesis Against the Donatists in the *Enarrationes in Psalmos*" (PhD diss., University of Chicago, 1996).

56. "Sed quoniam dictum est a Domino: *non est uestrum scire tempora quae Pater posuit in sua potestate,* et: *De die uero et illa hora nemo scit, neque angelus, neque uirtus, neque Filius, nisi solus Pater,* et illud quod scriptum est, tamquam furem uenire diem Domini, satis aperte ostendit neminem sibi oportere arrogare scientiam illius temporis, computatione aliqua annorum. Si enim post septem milia annorum ille dies uenturus est, omnis homo potest annis computatis aduentum eius addiscere. Ubi erit ergo, quod nec filius hoc nouit? Quod utique ideo dictum est, quia per Filium homines hoc non discunt, non quod apud se ipse non nouerit, secundum illam locutionem: *Tentat uos Dominus eus uester, ut sciat,* id est, scire faciat uos; et: *Exsurge, Domine,* id est, fac nos exsurgere. Cum ergo ita dicatur nescire filius hunc diem, non quod nesciat, sed quod nescire faciat eos quibus hoc non expedit scire, id est, non eis hoc ostendat; quid sibi uult nescio quae praesumtio, quae annis computatis certissimum sperat post septem annorum milia diem Domini!" (*CCL* 38:27).

57. "De illo enim die dictum est quod nemo eum sciret, neque angeli, nec uirtutes, neque Filius hominis. Quid ergo tam occultum, quam id quod etiam ipsi iudici occultum esse dictum est, non ad cognoscendum, sed ad prodendum? De occultis autem Filii, etiam si quisquam non Dei Filium subaudire uoluerit, sed ipsius Dauid, cuius nomini totum psalterium tribuitur, nam Dauidici utique psalmi appellantur, uoces illas audiat quibus domino dicitur: Miserere nostri, fili Dauid; atque ita etiam hoc modo eumdem Fominum Christum intellegat, de cuius occultis ipse psalmus inscriptus est" (*CCL* 38:73–74).

58. The bibliography on *De Trinitate* is immense. Seminal studies include *Die Denkform Augustins in seinem Werk De trinitate* (Munich: Verlag der Bayerischen Akademie der Wissenschaften, 1962); A. Schindler, *Wort und Analogie in Augustins Trinitätslehre* (Tübingen: Mohr, 1965); E. Hill, "St. Augustine's 'De Trinitate: ' The Doctrinal Significance of Its Structure," *Revue des études Augustiniennes* (1973): 277–286; R.J. Teske, "Properties of God and the Predicaments in *De Trinitate* V," *The Modern Schoolman* 59 (1981–82): 1–19; D. E. Daniels, "The Argument of *De Trinitate* and Augustine's Theory of Signs," *Augustinian Studies* 8 (1977): 33–54; John Cavadini, "The Structure and Intention of Augustine's *De trinitate,*" *Augustinian Studies* 23 (1992): 103–123; and idem, "The Quest for Truth in Augustine's *De trinitate,*" *Theological Studies* 58 (1997): 429–440.

59. *De Trin.* 1.11, pp. 60–61. Augustine resorted to this distinction frequently. See, e.g., *Epistle* 238, *Tractates on John* 16, 105, 108; *Enarrationes in Psalmos* 37 and 138; *Sermons* 265A and 375B; and *City of God* 10.6 and 20.30.

60. *De Trin.* 1.12, pp. 61–68.

61. Ut enim probaretur uerum corpus habere, suscepit defectus corporis: famem et sitim et huiusmodi; et ut veram animam probaretur habere, suscepit defectus animae, scilicet tristitiam, timorem, dolorem et huiusmodi. (*Sent.,* p. 93)

For a good brief discussion of this issue, see Colish, *Peter Lombard* 1:443–444.

62. "Suscepit enim de nostro ut de suo nobis tribueret, ut nostrum tolleret. Suscepit enim nostram uetustatem, ut suam nobis infunderet nouitatem" (*Sent.*, p. 93).

63. "Quos enim defectus habuit, uel ad ostensionem uerae humanitatis: Ut timorem et tristitiam, uel ad impletionem operis ad quod uenerat: Ut passibilitatem et mortalitatem, uel ab immortalitatis desperatione spem nostram erigendam: Ut mortem, suscepit" (*Sent.*, p. 93).

64. "Suscepit autem Christus sicut veram naturam hominis, ita et ueros defectus hominis, sed non omnes. Assumpsit enim defectus poenae, sed non culpae; nec tamen omnes defectus poenae, sed eos omnes quos homini eum assumere expediebat et suae dignitati non derogabat" (*Sent.*, p. 93).

65. "Non enim assumpsit ignorantiam aliquam, cum sit ignorantia quaedam quae defectus est nec peccatum est, scilicet ignorantia invincibilis . . . Constat autem in nobis esse ignorantiam atque difficultatem volendi vel faciendi bonum, quae ad miseriam nostram pertinent. . . . Haec autem Christus non habuit . . ." (*Sent.*, p. 94).

66. ". . . non igitur accepit omnes defectus nostrae infirmitatis, praeter peccatum" (*Sent.*, p. 94).

67. *Peter Lombard*, 1:442. Colish does a characteristically beautiful job contextualizing the Lombard's position with respect to other twelfth-century thinkers. Here I am mainly interested in the relation of the Lombard's thought to his commentators, but a full appreciation of that depends on the kind of analysis Colish provides.

68. ". . . dicimus animam christi per sapientiam gratis datam, in uerbo dei cui unita est, quod perfecte intelligit, omnia scire quae deus scit, sed non omnia posse quae potest deus; nec ita clare ac perspicue omnia capit ut deus; et ideo non aequatur creatori suo in scientia, etsi omnia sciat quae et ipse. Nec eius sapientia aequalis est sapientiae dei, quia illa multo est dignior, dignius que et perfectius omnia capit quam illius animae sapientia. Ergo et in scientia maiorem habet sufficientiam deus quam anima illa, quae dignior est omni creatura. . . . Omnia ergo scivit anima illa. Si enim quaedam scivit, quaedam non, non sine mensura scientiam habuit. Sed sine mensura scientiam habuit; scit igitur omnia" (*Sent.* 3.14.1, p. 90).

69. "Quarto quaeritur de hora iudicii et quaeritur, utrum alicui creaturae sit nota. Et quod non, videtur. Matthaei vigesimo quarto: *De illo autem die et hora nemo novit, neque Anglei, qui sunt in caelo, neque Filius:* ergo videtur, quod Christus non noverit: ergo multo minus noscunt alii" (*Sent.* 4.48.1.4, p. 988).

70. *Sent.* 4.48.1.4, p. 988.

71. "Christus non profecit nec potest proficere in scientia, sicut supra dicitur . . . ergo si unquam sciturus est, modo scit" (*Sent.* 4.48.1.4, p. 988).

72. "Marci, XIII, 32: *De die illa nemo scit, neque Filius, sed solus Pater.*" Sed non loquitur de Filio secundum divinam naturam, secundum quam habet eamdem scientiam cum Patre. Ergo loquitur de Filio secundum humanam naturam. Ergo Christus secundum animam non omnia scit quae scit Deus. Praeterea, Deus scit infinita. Sed anima Christi, cum sit finita, non potest comprehendere infinita. Ergo non omnia scit quae scit Deus" (*Sent.* 3.14.2.2, p. 442).

73. "Ad primum ergo dicendum quod dicitur Filius nescire, quia non facit nos scire, ex eo quod ad nos mittitur. Similter nec Spiritus sanctus, sed solus Pater scire dicitur, quia ipse non mittitur. Unde scientia Patris intelligitur quantum ad hoc quod in se scit, a qua scientia non excluditur Filius et Spiritus sanctus; ut sic intelligatur de Filio non solum inquantum homo, sed etiam inquantum Deus" (*Sent.* 3.14.2., p. 448).

CHAPTER 5

1. "Intende, lector, his verbis pia diligentia, ne sint tibi *vasa mortis*" (Peter Lombard, *Sent.* 3.17.3, 2: 111). The italicized words echo Ps. 7:14. An earlier version of this chapter was published as, "On the Reception of Hilary of Poitiers in the High Middle Ages: A Study in the Discontinuity of Tradition in Christian Thought," *Journal of Religion* 78 (1998): 213–229. "... non mediocris auctoritatis in tractatione scripturarum et assertione fidei vir exstitit" (Augustine, *De Trinitate* 6.10.11., p. 241).

2. See J. H. Reinkens, *Hilarius von Poitiers* (Schaffhausen: F. Hurter, 1864), viii. In asserting such a parallel, Reinkens spoke more truly than he knew. The view of Athanasius as saint and pillar of the Eastern church is a somewhat romantic, at best partial one which modern scholarship has done much to discredit. Out to undercut the idea that so violent a political operator could be considered a simple saint, T. D. Barnes has meticulously reviewed the evidence and then brought in a harsh verdict, severely proclaiming Saint Athanasius "a gangster" (*Constantine and Eusebius* [Cambridge: Harvard University Press, 1981, 230]). For similarly critical views of Athanasius, see the essays of Rusch, Martin, and Barnard in C. Kannengiesser, *Politique et Théologie chez Athanase d'Alexandrie.* (Actes du Colloque de Chantilly; Paris: Beauchesne, 1974). In the same volume, J. M. Leroux ("Athanase et la seconde phase de la crise arienne [345–373]," 145–156) suggests that Athanasius was too geographically and intellectually (as well as politically) isolated, even negligible, to be designated something so grandiose as a pillar of the Eastern church in his own day. In his own day, Leroux concludes, he was an important leader in Egypt, no more. A combination of factors elevated him posthumously to the status of ecclesiastical theological "pillar."

3. Thomas F. Torrance, *Divine Meaning: Studies in Patristic Hermeneutics* (Edinburgh: T & T Clark, 1995), 392.

4. G. M. Newlands, *Hilary of Poitiers: A Study in Theological Method.* European University Studies 108 (Bern: Peter Lang, 1978), vi.

5. In *In Constantium* 12, in Hilaire de Poitiers, *Contre Constance,* ed. A. Rocher, *Sources Chrétiennes* 334 (Paris, Éditions du Cerf, 1987), 192.

6. The ecclesiastical distinction is seldom absent in titles of studies of Hilary. See, e.g., J. Daniélou, "Saint Hilaire, évêque et docteur," and B. de Gaiffier, "Hilaire docteur de l'Église," in *Hilaire de Poitiers: évêque et docteur (368–1968)* (Paris: Études Augustiniennes, 1968), 17, 27–37; and P. Galtier, *Saint Hilaire de Poitiers: le premier docteur de l'Église* (Paris: Beauchesnes, 1960).

7. Peter Lombard, *Sent.* 3.15.3, 2:100–102.

8. Peter Lombard, *Sent.* 3.17.3, 2:110–111.

9. Bonaventure, *Sent.* 3.16. dub. 1, 3: 359.

10. Given how extensive Hilary's influence apparently was, there has been surprisingly little work on the high-scholastic reception of Hilary and no detailed study of
the reception of his problematic christological opinions. On Thomas Aquinas's use of
Hilary's thought in general, see Clemente Vansteenkiste, O.P., "S. Tommaso
d'Aquino e S. Ilario di Poitiers," in *Studi Tomistici*, ed. A. Piolanti (Rome: Pontificia
Accademia Romana di S. Tommaso d'Aquino, 1974), 1: 65–71. This article is
indispensable for identifying the sources of Thomas's use of Hilary and what might
be called the statistical features of that use. Valuable as this task undoubtedly is, the
author did not comment at all on *how* Hilary influenced Thomas, nor on how Thomas
shaped Hilary's thought to his own theological and exegetical ends. Vansteenkiste
usefully points out, however, that Thomas explicitly cited Hilary more than 700 times.
(More than half of the citations are found in the *Catena Aurea*, a mosaic of patristic
opinion on the four Gospels.) Vansteenkiste also notes that Thomas offers an "expositio" in his *Scriptum super libros Sententiarum* of the problematic opinions from
Hilary considered here but furnishes no analysis of the nature of the "explanation"
Thomas offers, and perpetuates thus by silence the received, unchallenged, and, in my
opinion, grossly erroneous view that Thomas was engaged in a simple explicative or
expository operation. More recently, it has been argued that Thomas was consciously
using Hilary's *De Trinitate* as a model for his own project in the *Summa contra
Gentiles*. See Joseph Wawrykow, "The *Summa contra Gentiles* Reconsidered: On
the Contribution of the *De Trinitate* of Hilary of Poitiers," *The Thomist* 58 (1994):
617–634. The most recent extensive study of Hilary's treatment of Christ's passion is
Gondreau, *The Passions*, 388–402.

11. See Athanasius, *Orations*, Books 2 and 3 especially. In these books, Athanasius answered many of the same arguments which Hilary addresses in *De Trinitate*.
Nonetheless, Hilary argued very differently than Athanasius, and, in fact, there seems
to be little evidence that Hilary directly knew any of Athanasius's works. R. P. C.
Hanson sums up the view of recent scholars when he concludes that it is "difficult to
see any clear influence of Athanasius' thought on Hilary" and "Hilary's doctrine of the
Incarnation owed nothing to Athanasius" (*The Search*, 473, 496).

12. "Passus quidem Dominus Iesus Christus, dum caeditur, dum suspenditur,
dum crucifigitur, dum moritur" (*De Trinitate* 10.23, p. 477).

13. "habens ad patiendum quidem corpus, et passus est, sed naturam non habens ad dolendum" (*De Trinitate* 10.23, p. 478).

14. "Naturae enim propriae ac suae corpus illud est" (*De Trinitate* 10.23, p. 478).

15. "Conlatis igitur dictorum adque gestorum virtutibus demonstrari non am-
biguum est, in natura eius corporis infirmitatem naturae corporeae non fuisse, cui in
virtute naturae fuerit omnem corporum depellere infirmitatem; et passionem illam,
licet inlata corpori sit, non tamen naturam dolendi corpori intulisse. Quia quamvis
forma corporis nostri esset in Domino, non tamen in vitiosae infirmitatis nostrae
esset corpore, qui non esset in origine, quod ex conceptu Spiritus sancti virgo pro-
genuit: quod licet sexus sui officio genuerit, tamen non terrenae conceptionis suscepit

elementis. Genuit etenim ex se corpus, sed quod conceptum esset ex Spiritu, habens quidem in se sui corporis veritatem, sed non habens naturae infirmitatem: dum et corpus illud corporis veritas est, quod generatur ex virgine, et extra corporis nostri infirmitatem est, quod spiritalis conceptionis sumpsit exordium" (*De Trinitate* 10.35, pp. 488–489).

16. *De Trinitate* 10.23, p. 477. A rough modern analogy might be that of a patient undergoing surgery who can feel the pressure of the scalpel and who is really wounded by its action but whose flesh has been so desensitized by the anaesthesia that, for the moment, it does not have the capability of experiencing pain. Note that at one point Hilary argues that Christ's flesh was only "like" ours: "Non fuit habitus ille tantum hominis, sed et ut hominis; neque caro illa caro peccati, sed similitudo carnis peccati" (*De Trinitate* 10.25, p. 481).

17. "Homo itaque Christus Iesus unigenitus Deus, per carnem et verbum ut hominis filius ita et Dei Filius, hominem verum secundum similitudinem nostri hominis, non deficiens a se Deo, sumpsit. In quo, quamvis aut ictus incideret, aut uulnus descenderet, aut nodi concurrerent, aut suspensio eleuaret, adferrent quidem haec inpetum passionis, non tamen dolorem passionis inferrent: ut telum aliquod aut aquam perforans aut ignem conpungens aut aera uulnerans, omnes quidem has passiones naturae suae infert, ut foret, ut conpungat, ut uulneret, sed naturam suam in haec passio inlata non retinet, dum in natura non est, uel aquam forari, uel pungi ignem, uel aerem uulnerari, quamvis naturae teli sit et uulnerare et conpungere et forare" (*De Trinitate* 10.23, p. 477).

18. Indeed, Hilary undertakes his long analysis of the body of Christ only to demonstrate that he had nothing to fear in suffering and death. See *De Trinitate* 10.13, p. 469.

> 19. Volunt enim plerique eorum ex passionis metu et ex infirmitate patiendi non in natura eum inpassibilis Dei fuisse: ut qui timuit et doluit, non fuerit uel in ea potestatis securitate quae non timet, uel in ea Spiritus incorruptione quae non dolet; sed inferioris a Deo patre naturae, et humanae passionis trepidauerit metu, et ad corporalis poenae congemuerit atrocitatem. Adque hac inpietatis suae adsertione nitantur, quia scribtum sit: *Tristis est anima mea usque ad mortem* et rursum: *Pater, si possibile est, transeat calix iste a me,* sed et illud: *Deus Deus meus, quare me dereliquisti?* Hoc quoque adiciant: *Pater, commendo in manus tuas Spiritum meum.* (*De Trinitate* 10.9, pp. 465–466)

See also: "Sed forte timuisse usque eo existimabitur, ut transferri a se calicem depraecatus sit dicens: *Abba Pater, possibilia tibi omnia sunt. Transfer calicem hunc a me*" (*De Trinitate* 10.30, p. 484).

20. "Sed forte stulta adque inpia peruersitate hinc infirmis in eo naturae praesumetur adsertio, quia *tristis sit anima eius usque ad mortem*" (*De Trinitate* 10.29, p. 484).

21. See Hilary's lament that the Arians have seized upon the scriptural passages apparently documenting Christ's fear and sorrow:

Has enim omnes piae fidei nostrae professiones ad inpietatis suae rapiunt usurpationem: ut timuerit, qui tristis est, qui et transferri a se calicem depraecatus sit; ut doluerit, qui derelictum se a Deo in passione conquaestus sit; ut infirmus quoque fuerit, qui Spiritum suum Patri commendaverit. (*De Trinitate* 10.9, p. 466)

22. "Ubi, rogo, in passione timor?" (*De Trinitate* 10.32, p. 485).

23. "Non est in uolente mori et potente non diu mori timor mortis: quia et voluntas moriendi et potestas reuiuiscendi extra naturam timoris est, dum timeri mors non potest et in uoluntate moriendi et in potestate uiuendi" (*De Trinitate* 10.12, pp. 468–469).

24. "Non ergo sibi tristis est neque sibi orat, sed illis quos monet orare peruigiles, ne in eos calix passionis incumbit: quem a se transire orat, ne in his scilicet maneat" (*De Trinitate* 10.37, p. 491).

25. *De Trinitate* 10.36, p. 489.

26. See Peter Lombard, *Sent.* 3.15.2, pp. 100–102 and 3.17.3, pp. 110–111.

27. Bonaventure, *Sent.* 3.16 dub. 1, p. 359.

28. "Dicendum, quod absque dubio, sicut Evangelium dicit, et fides catholica sentit, vera doloris passio fuit in Christo" (Bonaventure, *Sent.* 3.16.1.1 resp., p. 346).

29. "In ipso enim fuit caro passibilis et perforabilis, fuit etiam virtus sentiendi, secundum quam anima compatitur corpori laeso" (Bonaventure, *Sent.* 3.16.1.1 resp., p. 346).

30. "Quoniam ergo haec duo verum dolorem faciunt, scilicet *vera laesio* et *verus laesionis sensus*, et haec duo vere fuerunt in Christo; indubitanter tenendum est, quod in Christo fuit vera doloris passio" (Bonaventure, *Sent.* 3.16.1.1, resp., p. 346).

31. Nam si aliquis aliter dicat, secundum quod quidam haeretici dicunt, et est error antiquus Saracenorum, quod Christus, etsi videretur pati et dolere, non tamen veraciter habuit dolorem et passionis sensum. (Bonaventure, *Sent.* 3.16.1.1 resp., p. 346)

Curiously, Bonaventure refers this ancient error, not to the Manicheans, but to the Saracens. Apparently, Bonaventure is depending upon John of Damascus's description of the christological error of "the Mohammedans," who held that Christ was neither crucified nor died. Instead, the Jews seized his shadow and crucified it while God took Christ himself into heaven. John appears to be interpreting the Qur'an, Sura 4.156. See John of Damascus, *De Haeresibus Liber* 101, PG 94, col. 763–767.

32. "non solum evacuat fidem Christi et Christi Evangelium, sed etiam evacuat redemptionem nostram et dicit, Christum non esse Christum" (Bonaventure, *Sent.* 3.16.1.1 resp., p. 346).

33. "Dum enim dicit, ipsum non fuisse veraciter *passum;* dicit, ipsum non satisfecisse, ac per hoc non genus humanum esse redemptum" (Bonaventure, *Sent.* 3.1.6.1.1 resp., p. 346). This is a point made by some modern commentators as well, including Hanson: "In effect he concluded that at the very point where Christ's solidarity with humankind is most crucial, in his suffering, Christ was not really

human. Not only does this bring our redemption under question and do away explicitly with that central conviction of St. Paul, the scandal of the cross, but it leaves us uncertain as to whether such a figure can seriously act as our Mediator" (*Search*, 501–502).

34. "Dum vero dicit, ipsum *simulasse* se pati; dicit, ipsum esse mendacem, et ita nec vere fuisse Dei Filium nec Dei nuntium, et ita nec mediatorem, sed potius deceptorem. Et propterea qui dicunt, Christum non veraciter doluisse vel passum fuisse; etsi videantur ipsum exterius honorare, secundum veritatem blasphemant ipsum impiissime" (Bonaventure, *Sent.* 3.16.1.1 resp., p. 346).

35. See, for example, Albert: "Dicendum quod quidam dicunt Hilarium haec verba retractasse: et haec est meo judicio conventior solutio" (*Sent.* 3.15.G.10. Sol., p. 287).

36. Bonaventure:

Quidam enim dicunt, Hilarium verba illa retractasse. Unde audivi, Parisiensem episcopum Gulielmum referre, se librum illius retractionis vidisse et perlegisse. (*Sent.* 3.16.1.1 ad 1um, p. 346)

Moos has pointed out that in the margin of one of the manuscripts of Thomas's *Scriptum,* the same legend is reported. See *Sent.*, p. 505 n. 1. If there ever was such a book of retraction, as seems very unlikely, it has never been discovered.

37. "Sed quia librum retractionis ejus non vidimus, ideo oportet vim facere in verbis ejus" (*Sent.* 3.15.G.10. Sol., p. 287). Bonaventure:

In parte ista sunt dubitationes circa litteram, et incidit quaestio circa verba Hilarii, quae videntur esse falsa et dubia et erronea; quae si dicamus esse retractata, iuxta quod prius tactum fuit, semota erit omnis calumnia; quia tamen scriptura huius retractionis non est propalata, ideo sunt verba Hilarii secundum quod possumus, verificanda. (*Sent.* 3.16.dubium 1, p. 359)

I thank one of the anonymous readers of this manuscript, who observed that the *vim facere* can bear "an even stronger sense, suggesting that one needs to 'use force' in resolving the interpretation of Hilary." I agree, and the violence of the verb only underlines the point I am trying to make here.

38. See, e.g., Bonaventure: "Aliter potest dici, quod Hilarius in verbo praedicto et in aliis ibidem positis non excludit sensum doloris a Christo secundum *humanam* naturam, sed secundum *divinam*" (*Sent.* 3.16.1.1 ad 1um, p. 347).

39. Thomas: "Alii dicunt quod loquitur de Christo quantum ad Divinitatem" (*Sent.* 3.15.expos. textus, p. 505).

40. Albert: "Ex hoc enim accipitur, quod loquitur contra haereticos, qui dicebant Christum tantum fuisse infirmae naturae, et non potuisse de se de virtute personae repulisse hujusmodi infirmitatem" (*Sent.* 3.15.G.10. Sol., p. 287); Thomas: "quia disputat contra illos in his verbis qui Filium Dei creaturam dicebant" (*Sent.* 3.15. expos. textus, p. 505); Bonaventure: "Hilarius enim in verbis praemissis excludere voluit

errorem Arii, qui dicebat, Christum secundum se totum passum fuisse" (*Sent.* 3.16.1.1 ad 1um, p. 347).

41. See, e.g., Bonaventure: "Contra enim illos loquitur Hilarius, qui dicebant, Christum omnino succubuisse passioni et a passione esse superatum" (*Sent.* 3.16. dubium 1, p. 359).

42. "contra quod dicit Hilarius, quod etsi Christus vere passus fuerit, non tamen doluit, hoc est, passionibus non succubuisse" (*Sent.* 3.16. dub. 1, p. 359).

43. Bonaventure: "Non enim vult negare *sensum* et *experimentum* passionis, sed *vim* et *dominium* passionis" (*Sent.* 3.16. dub. 1, p. 359).

44. Thomas:

Solutio autem Magistri consistit in hoc quod non simpliciter voluit removere a Christo dolorem, sed tria quae sunt circa dolorem. Primo dominium doloris . . . Secundo autem meritum doloris . . . Tertio necessitatem doloris . . . Et secundum hoc solvuntur tria difficilia quae in verbis ejus esse videntur. Primum est quod: Poena in eo desaevit sine sensu poenae; et hoc nominat supra naturam passionis quae scilicet sensum poenae infert, qui est dolor: quod non potest intelligi de sensu exteriori, quia sic poneretur corpus illud insensibile esse; sed oportet quod intelligatur quantum ad sensum rationis qui non fuit immutatus per hujusmodi passiones a sua aequalitate. Et propter hoc dicitur, quod poena in ipso dominium non habuit. . . . (*Sent.* 3.15. expos. textus, pp. 505–506)

45. See, e.g., Bonaventure: "In Christo fuit vera tristitia, non tamen omni modo, quo in nobis est" (*Sent.* 3.15.2.2 resp., p. 338).

46. Jerome, *Comm. in Math. Libri IV*, pp. 253–254:

Illud quod supra diximus de passione et propassione etiam in praesenti capitulo ostenditur, quod Dominus, ut veritatem adsumpti probaret hominis, vere quidem contristatus sit sed, ne passio in animo illius dominaretur, per propassionem coeperit contristari. Aliud est enim contristari et aliud incipere contristari.

47. See, e.g., Thomas: "Unde dicendum, quod hoc modo fuit timor in Christo per eumdem modum sicut de tristitia et ira dictum est, inquantum scilicet ex dictamine rationis et Deitatis adjunctae" (*Sent.* 3.15.2.2 quaest. 3, p. 492).

48. See also Thomas's scattered comments at *Sent.* 3.15. expos. textus, pp. 502–506). See also his response at *Sent.* 3.15.2. sol. 1, p. 490: "Sed in Christo nunquam surgebat motus tristitiae nisi secundum dictamen superioris rationis quando scilicet dictabat ratio quod sensualitas tristaretur secundum convenientiam naturae suae."

49. These modern attempts at defending Hilary are discussed (approvingly) by E. Boularand, *L'Hérésie d'Arius et la Foi de Nicée* (Paris: Letouzey & Ané, 1972), 90–92.

50. See Borchardt, *Hilary of Poitier's Rôle in the Arian Struggle*, 117–130; P. Smulders, *La Doctrine trinitaire de S. Hilaire de Poitiers* (Rome: Analecta Gregoriana 32, 1944), 203–206; and M. M. Thomas, *The Christology of St. Hilary of Poitiers* (unpublished PhD diss., Union Theological Seminary [New York], 1964), 190, 193–194.

51. Hanson, *Search*, 501.

52. One might point out, in addition, that the medieval theologians interpreting Hilary used very little "new" technical language in interpreting him.

53. Edward Shils, *Tradition* (Chicago: University of Chicago Press, 1981), 206.

54. The term in Shils.' See *Tradition*, 206.

CHAPTER 6

1. An earlier version of this chapter was publishes as, "High-Medieval Interpretations of Jesus in Gethsemane in Patristic Context: Some Reflections on Tradition and Continuity in Christian Thought," *Harvard Theological Review* 88 (1995): 157–173. Reprinted with permission.

2. In this chapter, I will concentrate on the premodern interpretation of selected parts of the Markan and Matthean pericopes.

3. "Noli insidiatrices aperire aures, ut putes filium quasi infirmum rogare, rogare ut inpetret quod inplere non possit potestatis auctor" (*Expositio Evang. sec. Luc.* 5.42, p. 150).

4. "Sed cum Christus omnia facere posset, non videtur ei convenire quod aliquid ab aliquo peteret" (*Summa*, p. 251).

5. As virtually all ancient and medieval exegetes did. Thomas Aquinas succinctly sums up the tradition up to the thirteenth century when he declares that: "It was not that he himself was powerless" that Jesus prays, "but [he does so] for our instruction" ("non quasi ipse esset impotens, sed propter nostram instructionem") *Summa* 3a.21.1. ad 1um, p. 251.

6. See, e.g., Albertus Magnus, *Sent.* 3.17.8, p. 309.

7. In *De Fide*, p. 75.

8. Bonaventure: "Item, in quemcumque cadit dubitatio, cadere potest ignorantia et error" (*Sent.* 3.17. dub. 3, 376); Thomas: "Praeterea, ubicumque est timor, ibi est dubitatio...dubitatio...contingit ex defectu scientiae" (*Sent.* 3.17.1.4).

9. See G. Verbeke, Gérard, *The Presence of Stoicism in Medieval Thought* (Washington, D.C.: Catholic University of America Press, 1983) for an analysis of the appropriation of *apatheia* in the Alexandrian and Cappadocian fathers and others.

10. Luke 22:43–44 ("An angel from heaven appeared to him and strengthened him. And being in anguish, he prayed more earnestly, and his sweat was like drops of blood falling to the ground") are of very doubtful authenticity. The verses are absent in many ancient mss. and, in others, are marked with symbols which indicate their spuriousness. The verses may have been added from extracanonical traditions concerning the life and passion of Jesus. See Metzger, *A Textual Commentary on the Greek New Testament*, 177.

11. Ambrosius etiam in libro *De Trinitate* [sic] ait: '...Timet ergo Christus; et dum Petrus non timet, Christus timet...Ut homo turbatur, ut homo flet...turbatur anima, secundum humanae fragilitatis assumtionem turbatur...Suscepit tristitiam meam, confidenter tristitiam nomino, qui

crucem praedico. Ut homo habuit tristitiam . . . Ceterum non parum nos
movent verba Ambrosii, quibus significare videtur, Christum, secundum
humanum affectum, de potentia Patris dubitasse, sic dicens in libro II
De Trinitate [*sic*]: 'Ut homo ergo dubitat. . . .'" (*Sent.* 3.15.1, 614–15; and
Sent. 3. 17.3, 626–627)

Ambrose actually makes remarks very close to these in *De Fide* 2.5.43–7.56, pp. 71–75.

12. See, e.g., *De Trinitate* 10.25, ed479, which begins, "He had a body, but a
unique one which was of His own origin . . . He is free from the sins and the defects of
a human body" ("Habuit enim corpus, sed originis suae proprium . . . a peccatis et a
vitiis humani corporis liber").

13. "Homo itaque Christus Iesus unigenitus Deus, per carnem et verbum ut
hominis filius ita et Dei Filius, hominem verum secundum similitudinem nostri
hominis, non deficiens a se Deo, sumpsit. In quo, quamuis aut ictus incideret, aut
vulnus descenderet, aut nodi concurrerent, aut suspensio elevaret, adferrent quidem
haec inpetum passionis, non tamen dolorem passionis inferrent: ut telum aliquod aut
aquam perforans aut ignem conpungens aut aera uulnerans, omnes quidem has
passiones naturae suae infert, ut foret, ut conpungat, ut uulneret, sed naturam suam
in haec passio inlata non retinet, dum in natura non est, uel aquam forari, vel pungi
ignem, vel aerem uulnerari, quamuis naturae teli sit et uulnerare et conpungere et
forare" (*De Trinitate* 10.23, p. 477).

14. "Et interrogo eos qui hoc ita existimant, an ratione subsistat, ut mori timuerit qui, omnem ab apostolis terrorem mortis apellens, ad gloriam eos sit martyrii
adhortatus dicens: *Qui non accipit crucem suam . . .*" (*De Trinitate* 10.10, pp. 466–
467).

15. *De Trinitate* 10.26–27, pp. 481–483.

16. *Sent.* 3.15.3, 6pp. 17–20.

17. See, e.g., Bonaventure *Sent.* 3.16, pp. 345–360.

18. "Hieronymus etiam ait: 'Erubescant qui putant Salvatorem timuisse mortem,
et passionis pavore dixisse: *Transeat a me calix iste*'" (*Sent.* 3.15.1, p. 615).

19. *Enarratio* 2 in Ps. 21:3, no. 4, p. 123.

20. "Hieronymus quoque in *Explanatione fidei* ait: 'Nos ita dicimus hominem
passibilem a Dei Filio susceptum, ut Deitas impassibilis permaneret.
Passus est enim Filius Dei non putative, sed vere, omnia quae Scriptura
testatur, secundum illud quod pati poterat, scilicet secundum substantiam assumtam. Licet ergo persona Filii susceperit passibilem hominem, ita tamen eius habitatione secundum suam substantiam nil
passa est, ut tota Trinitas, quam impassibilem necesse est confiteri'.
(*Sent.* 3.15.1, 615; *Explanatio Symboli ad Damas.*, PL 30:176)

The selection extracted from Augustine is as follows:

Sed tristiam sic assumsit, quo modo carnem. Fuit enim tristis, ut Evangelium dicit. Si enim non tristis fuit, cum Evangelium dicat: *Tristis est anima
mea* etc., ergo et quando dicit: Dormivit Iesus, non dormivit; vel quando dicit

manducasse, non manducavit; et ita nihil sanum relinquetur, ut dicatur etiam, quia corpus non erat verum. Quidquid ergo de illo scriptum est, verum est, et factum est. Ergo et tristis fuit, sed voluntate tristitiam suscepit veram, quo modo voluntate carnem veram. (*Sent.* 3.15.1, pp. 616–617; *Enarrationes* 93, n. 19, p. 1321)

21. "Unde Hieronymus *Super Matthaeum*, ubi legitur: *Coepit contristari et moestus esse*, 'ut veritatem, inquit, probaret assumti hominis, vere contristatus est, sed non passio eius dominatur animo, verum propassio est. Unde ait: *Coepit contristari*. Aliud est enim contristari, aliud incipere contristari,' quod est, aliter contristatur quis per propassionem, aliter per passionem" (*Sent.* 3.15.2, p. 616; Jerome, *Comm. in Matt.* 26:37, p. 253; emphasis mine).

22. *Sent.* 3.15.2, 6pp. 16–17.

23. "Afficitur enim quis interdum timore vel tristitia, ita ut mentis intellectus non inde moveatur a rectitudine vel Dei contemplatione, et tunc propassio est; aliquando vero movetur et turbatur, et tunc passio est" (*Sent.* 3.15.2, p. 616).

24. "Habuit enim Christus verum timorem et tristitiam in natura hominis, sed non sicut nos, qui sumus membra eius. Nos enim, causa peccati nostri, his defectibus necessario subiacemus" (*Sent.* 3.15.2, p. 616).

25. "Christus vero non fuit ita turbatus in anima timore vel tristitia, ut a rectitudine vel Dei contemplatione aliquatenus declinaret" (*Sent.* 3.15.2, p. 616).

26. "Aperte noscis, eundem sibi in his verbis contradicere, nisi varias dictorum discerneret causas" (*Sent.* 3.15.2, p. 617).

27. "Ideoque secundum hanc distinctionem aliquando dicitur Christus non vere timuisse, aliquando vere timuisse" (*Sent.* 3.15.2, p. 616).

28. "Si enim discernatur intelligentiae causa praedictorum verborum, nihil occurrit contradictionis" (*Sent.* 3.15.2, p. 617).

29. "Ne autem in sacris litteris aliqua adversa diversitas esse putetur, harum auctoritatum verba in hunc modum accipienda dicimus, ut non veritatem timoris et tristitiae vel propassionem, sed timoris et tristitiae necessitatem et passionem a Christo removisse intelligantur" (*Sent.* 3.15.2, p. 616).

30. "Dicendum, quod absque dubio, sicut dicit Magister in littera, et textus etiam evangelicus confirmat, in Christo fuit vera tristitia (*Sent.* 3.15.2.2. resp., p. 338). Albert: "Dicendum, quod Christus veram tristitiam naturalem habuit" (*Sent.* 3.15.8, sol., p. 281). Thomas: "Et ideo, sicut in Christo potuit esse verus dolor, ita in eo potuit esse vera tristitia" (*Summa* 3a.15.6. resp., p. 192). For an analysis on Thomas's fear and sorry, see Gondreau, *The Passions*, 403–13.

31. *Sent.* 3.15.2.2, p. 338.

32. Bonaventure: " . . . in Christo fuit vera tristitia, non tamen omni modo, quo in nobis est" (*Sent.* 3.15.2.2. resp., p. 338). Thomas: "sed tamen aliter in ipso et in nobis" (*Sent.* 3.15.2.2, Quaestiuncula 3, Sol. 1, p. 167). See also Thomas, *Summa* 3a.15.6., resp., p. 192; and 3a.15.4. resp., p. 189: "Sciendum tamen quod hujusmodi passiones aliter fuerunt in Christo quam in nobis."

33. Albert, *Sent.* 3.15.8. sol., 287; Thomas *Sent.* 3.15.2.2, Quaestiuncula 3, Sol I, p. 490; and Bonaventure, *Sent.*, 3.15.2.2, resp., 3 p. 28.

34. Dico ergo quod in Christo fuit tantum isto tertio modo, quia de nullo tristatus fuit nisi secundum quod dictabat ei ratio" (*Sent.* 3.15.2.2. resp., p. 338). This is an idea echoed by Thomas:

> No movement of sadness ever occurred in Christ's soul unless according to the command of superior reason, when reason told the sensitive power of the soul to be sad" ("in Christo nunquam surgebat motus tristitiae nisi secundum dictamen superioris rationis, quando scilicet dictabat ratio quod sensualitas tristaretur. [*Sent.* 3.15.2.2, Quaestiuncula 3, Sol. 1, p. 490])

See also *Summa* 3.15.4. resp., p. 189: "in Christo omnes motus sensitivi appetitus oriebantur secundum dispositionem rationis."

35. "Est iterum in tertia differentia, timor scilicet naturalis, et iste est in triplici differentia: quidam est sensualitatis praevenientis rationem, quidam sensualitatis subiacentis rationi, quidam vero est ipsius partis rationalis. Primus timor est naturae corruptae et quodam modo inordinatae, similiter et tertius; secundus vero est naturae corruptae, sed tamen ordinatae. Quoniam ergo in Christo, quamvis esset defectus passibilitatis, non tamen fuit defectus inordinationis et vitiositatis, hinc est quod fuit in eo timor medio modo, non primo vel tertio" (*Sent.* 3.15. dub. 3. resp., p. 342).

36. See, e.g., Thomas Aquinas:

> Unde dicendum, quod hoc modo fuit timor in Christo per eumdem modum sicut et de tristitia et ira dictum est, inquantum scilicet ex dictamine rationis et Deitatis adjunctae, appetitus sensibilis refugiebat ea quae sunt sibi contraria. (*Sent.* 3.15.2.2, Quaestiuncula 3, Sol. 2, p. 492)

37. "Ad illud vero quod obicitur, quod timor mortis non potuit esse nisi in ratione, dicendum quod ratio praevidens mortem instantem fecit imaginationem mortis in ipsa parte sensuali, qua quidem facta, sensualitas mota fuit et horrore mortis concussa" (*Sent.* 3.15. dub. 4. resp., p. 342).

38. "...securissima enim fuit et bene noverat quod nihil poterat sibi evenire vel inferri quod ipsa prius non desideraret et vellet" (*Sent.* 3.15. dub. 4, p. 342).

39. "Alio modo potest considerari secundum incertitudinem futuri adventus: sicut quando nocte timemus ex aliquo sonitu, quasi ignorantes quid hoc sit. Et quantum ad hoc, timor non fuit in Christo" (*Sent.* 3.15.8. resp., p. 193).

40. "Et si tu dicas, quod hic non est ordo cognitionis, ut deveniatur a ratione in sensualitatem, dicendum quod hoc est verum in nobis, in quibus est scientia per acquisitionem ab inferiori" (*Sent.* 3.16. dub. 4. resp., p. 342).

41. "In Christo autem aliter esse potuit, qui fuit plenus scientia et in quo fuit obedientia perfecta virium inferiorum respectu superiorum" (*Sent.* 3.16. dub. 4. resp., p. 342). This is a point made by Thomas as well:

> in nobis inferiores vires non sunt perfecte subjectae rationi; et ideo quandoque praeter ordinem rationis insurgunt in nobis passiones tristitiae, quas quidem virtus refrenat in virtuosis, sed in aliis etiam rationi praevalent: sed in Christo numquam surgebat motus tristitiae nisi secundum dictamen superioris rationis. (*Sent.* 3.15.2.2. Quaestiuncula 3, p. 490)

42. See, e.g., Thomas, *Sent.* 3.17.1.4. Sol., p. 548: "Ad primum ergo dicendum, quod Ambrosius loquitur quantum ad sensualitatis timorem; quem dum ostendit, videbatur hominibus dubitare etiam quantum ad rationem."

43. See, e.g., Albert, *Sent.* 3.17.8. Sol., p. 309: "Dubitatio hic non exprimit nisi tremorem sensualitatis inter hoc quod sequeretur rationem, et naturalem appetitum oppositi, scilicet quod evaderet mortem." Cf. Bonaventure, *Sent.* 3.17. dub. 3, p. 376:

> Dicendum quod dubitatio proprie dicit indifferentiam iudicii rationis re-spectu utriusque partis contradictionis, ita quod neutrum praeeligat alteri; et hoc modo accipiendo dubitationem, in Christo non fuit dubitatio. Alio modo dicitur dubitatio indifferentia quaedam partis sensibilis ad sequendum af-fectum naturae inclinantem vel rationem imperantem; et talis dubitatio po-tuit esse in Christo et de hac intelligit Ambrosius.

44. *Sent.* 3.17.8. Sol., p. 309.

45. "Dicendum quod Hilarius non intendit removere timorem a Christo se-cundum quod timorem ei attribuit Scriptura et Sancti, sed secundum quod attri-buebant haeretici, qui dicebant eum timuisse ex defectu securitatis" (*Sent.* 3.16. dub. 2, p. 360).

46. "et talis est timor pusillanimitatis, de quo indubitanter verum est quod non fuit in Christo" (*Sent.* 3.16. dub. 2, p. 360).

47. "Nam omnes illae auctoritates, quae dicunt, Christum non timuisse, hoc dicunt, non quia velint a Christo omnem timore removere . . . sed quia non fuit in eo timor, qui rationem eius praeveniret, vel rationem perturbaret" (*Sent.* 3.15. dub. 3, p. 342).

CHAPTER 7

1. "Et cum nobis haec sola sit proprietas ad salutem, ut Dei Filium confiteamur ex mortuis, cur, rogo, in hac inreligiositate moriamur, ut cum Christus intra fiduciam diuinitatis suae manens, mori se per significationem adsumpti hominis cum secur-itate morientis ostenderit hoc maxime ad abnegandum eum Deum proficiat, quod se nobis Dei Filius et hominis filium est professus et mortuum?" (*De Trinitate* 10.71, 2:528).

2. See chapter 2 n. 25.

3. "Transire a se calicem rogat, utique iam se cum manentem, qui tum in san-guine noui testamenti pro multorum peccatis effundi consummabatur. Non enim rogat ne se cum sit, sed ut a se transeat. Deinde rogat ne uoluntas sua fiat, et quod uult effici, idipsum concedi sibi non uult. Ait enim: *Sed tamen non sicut ego uolo, sed sicut tu uis:* ut uoluntate calicis depraecandi humanae in se sollicitudinis significans consortium, sententiam a se unitae sibi communis que cum Patre non discerneret uoluntatis. Vt autem non pro se praecari intellegeretur et ratio significatae uoluntatis ac depraecatio non obtinendae esset in absoluto, hoc totum huiusmodi petitionis suae coepit exordiis: *Pater meus, si possibile est.* Aliquid ergo Patri relinquitur, quod ei an possibile esset incertum sit? Et si nihil Patri inpossibile est, intellegendum est ad

cuius condicionem id quod *si possibile est* sit relictum. Post huius enim orationis praecem sequitur: *et uenit ad discipulos et inuenit eos dormientes. Et ait Petro: Non potuistis una hora uigilare mecum? Spiritus quidem promptus, caro vero infirma.* Anne adhuc tristitiae causa et transeundi calicis depraecatio in obscuro est? Vigilari enim se cum ob hoc iubet et orari, ne in temptationem intrent, spiritu quidem prompto sed infirma carne. Nam qui non scandalizaturos se per constantiam fidelis conscientiae pollicebantur, in scandalo per infirmitatem carnis erant futuri. Non ergo sibi tristis est neque sibi orat, sed illis quos monet orare peruigiles, ne in eos calix passionis incumbat: quem a se transire orat, ne in his scilicet maneat.

Idcirco autem transferri eum, si possibile esset, a se praecatus est, quia cum inpossibile Deo nihil sit, sicut ipse ait: *Pater, possibilia tibi omnia sunt,* inpossibile tamen homini est passionis terrore non uinci, nec possit nisi per probationem fides nosci. Adque ideo et pro hominibus ut homo uult calicem transire, et ut Dei ex Deo uoluntas effectui paternae uoluntatis unitur. Id autem quod ait: *si possibile est,* manifeste in eo docuit quod ait Petro: *Ecce satanas expetiuit, ut uos cerneret sicut triticum. Ego autem rogaui pro te, ut non deficeret fides tua.* Per hunc enim calicem dominicae passionis temptandi omnes erant. Et pro Petro Pater rogatur, ne deficiat fides eius, ut negantis infirmitati uel dolor saltim paenitentiae non abesset: quae fides in eo non deficeret, quod paeniteret" (*De Trinitate* 10. 37–38, 2:490–92).

4. "Si itaque ad intellegentiam mortis suae ait: *deus Deus meus, quare me dereliquisti?* et: *Pater, commendo in manus tuas Spiritum meum,* numquid confessioni nostrae consulens, infirmum se esse potius confessus est, quam nos ambiguos non relinquit? Excitaturus namque Lazarum orat ad Patrem. Numquid praece eguit dicens: *Pater, gratias ago tibi quia exaudisti me. Et ego sciebam quia semper me exaudis, sed propter turbam dixi, ut credant quia tu me misisti?*

Nobis itaque orauit, ne Filius ignoraretur. Et cum sibi non proficeret depraecationis sermo, ad profectum tamen nostrae fidei loquebatur. Non inops ergo tum auxilii est, sed nos sumus inopes doctrinae. Clarificari se quoque depraecatur, ac mox de caelo uox Dei Patris clarificantis auditur. Sed ad auditae uocis admirationem ait: *non propter me uenit uox ista, sed propter uos.* Nobis Pater rogatur, nobis Pater loquitur. Totum ad effectum fit nostrae confessionis. Et cum clarificationis responsio non obsecrationi claritatis sit inpensa, sed ignorationi audientium, quomodo quaerella passionis in summa exultatione patiendi non confessionis nostrae eruditioni praestita intellegetur?" (*De Trinitate* 7.1, 2:526–27).

5. "Sed stultissimi adque inpiissimi homines, non intellegentes nihil contrarium in rebus hisdem ab eodem dictum fuisse, uerbis tantum inhaerentes causas ipsas dictorum reliquerunt" (*De Trinitate* 1.32, 1:30).

6. *Expositio Evang. sec. Luc.* 5.42, p. 150.

7. "Sed non potuit melius conteri laqueus, nisi praedam aliquam diabolo demonstrasset, ut dum ille festinat ad praedam, suis laqueis ligaretur, ut ego possem dicere: *laqueos parauerunt pedibus meis, et ipsi inciderunt in eos.* Quae potuit esse praeda nisi corpus? quae potuit esse praeda nisi corpus? Oportuit igitur hanc fraudem diabolo fieri, ut susciperet corpus dominus Iesus et corpus hoc corruptibile, corpus infirmum, ut crucifigeretur ex infirmitate. Si enim fuisset spiritale corpus, non dixisset: *spiritus*

promtus, caro autem infirma. Audi igitur utramque uocem et carnis infirmae et spiritus promti pater, si possibile est, transeat hic calix a me: haec carnis est uox. *Sed non quo ego uolo, sed quo tu uis:* habes deuotionem spiritus et uigorem. Quid repudias dignationem domini? dignationis est quod suscepit corpus meum, dignationis est quod suscepit iniurias meas, suscepit infirmitates meas, quas utique natura Dei sentire non potuit, cum etiam natura hominis contemnere didicerit uel sustinere ac perpeti. Et ideo sequamur Christum iuxta quod scriptum est: *post dominum deum tuum ambulabis et ipsi adhaerebis*. Cui adhaerebo nisi christo, sicut Paulus dixit: *qui adhaeret domino unus spiritus est?* Illius igitur, de deserto ut ad paradisum redire possimus, uestigia persequamur" (*Expositio Evang. sec. Luc.* 4.12, pp. 110–111).

    8. *De Fide* 2.5.44, p. 71.

    9. "Sed alia voluntas hominis, alia Dei" (*De Fide* 2.7.52, p. 74).

    10. Vt homo ergo dubitat, ut homo turbatur. Non turbatur ut uirtus, non turbatur eius diuinitas, sed 'turbatur anima,' turbatur secundum humanae fragilitatis adsumptionem. Et ideo quia suscepit animam, suscepit et animae passiones. Non enim eo, quod deus erat, aut turbari aut mori posset. Denique *deus, deus, inquit, meus, quare me dereliquisti?* Vt homo ergo loquitur meos circumferens metus, quod in periculis positi a deo deseri nos putamus. Ut homo turbatur, ut homo flet, ut homo crucifigitur. (*De Fide* 2.7.56, pp. 75–76)

The Arians would especially have objected to the argument *ut homo crucifigitur*. It was, as we have seen in chapter 2, essential to their soteriology that divinity was crucified and suffered on the cross. Indeed, had that not been the case, humanity would have been doomed.

    11. *De Fide* 2.7.58, 76.

    12. As Hanson argues. See *Search*, 673.

    13. " 'Scriptum est, inquiunt: *Pater, si possibile est, transfer a me calicem hunc.* Et ideo si omnipotens est, quomodo de possibilitate ambigit?' —Ergo quia omnipotentem probaui, probaui utique ambigere eum de possibilitate non posse. 'Verba, inquit, Christi sunt.' —Verum dicis. Sed quando et in qua forma loquatur, adverte. Hominis naturam gerit, hominis adsumpsit adfectum. Denique supra habes quia *progressus pusillum procidit in faciem suam orans et dicens: Pater, si possibile est*. Non ergo quasi deus, sed quasi homo loquitur. Deus enim possibile aliquid aut inpossibile nesciebat? Aut aliquid impossibile deo, cum scriptum sit: *Impossibile enim tibi nihil est?* De quo autem dubitat, de se an de patre? De eo utique, cui dicit "transfer," et dubitat hominis adfectu.—Ergo profeta non putat aliquid inpossibile deo, profeta non dubitat, et filium dubitare tu credis? Num intra homines constituis deum, et dubitat de patre deus et de morte formidat? Timet ergo Christus, et cum Petrus non timeat, Christus timet. Petrus dicit: *Animam meam pro te ponam*, Christus dicit, *Anima mea turbatur.*—Vtrumque uerum est et plenum utrumque rationis, quod et ille, qui est inferior, non timet, et ille, qui superior, est gerit timentis adfectum. Ille enim quasi homo uim mortis ignorat, iste quasi deus in corpore constitutus fragilitatem carnis exponit, ut eorum, qui sacramentum incarnationis abiurant, excluderetur impietas.

Denique et haec dixit, et Manichaeus non credidit, Valentinus negauit, Marcion fantasma iudicauit" (*De Fide* 2.5.41–44, pp. 70–71).

14. For similar examples in Ambrose's thought, see *De Sacramento* 1.7.63, p. 257; and *Enarrationes in XII Psalmos* 39, *PL* 14:1062.

15. *DFO* 3.15, *PG*: 1045–1064.

16. *DFO* 3.18, *PG*: 1071–1078.

17. *DFO* 3.24, *PG*: 1089–1094.

18. *DFO* 3.24–25 *PG*: 1089–1094

19. *De Quatuor Voluntatibus in Christo Libellus* (*PL* 176:841–846).

20. "Christus Deus fuit, et ideo voluntas divina in illo fuit. Et quia etiam homo fuit, similiter voluntas humana in illo fuit. Non dico humanam quam culpa et vitium hominis facit, sed quam natura hominis requirit. Ergo in Christo divina voluntas fuit in quantum Christus Deus fuit; et similiter humana voluntas in ipso fuit in quantum ipse homo fuit. Humana autem voluntas tripliciter consideratur; secundum rationem, secundum pietatem, secundum carnem. Ergo in Christo voluntas fuit divinitatis et voluntas rationis, et voluntas pietatis et voluntas carnis" (*PL* 176:841).

21. *PL* 176:841–842.

22. "Quocirca ambigendum non est diuersas in christo fuisse uoluntates iuxta duas naturas, diuinam scilicet uoluntatem et humanam. Et humana uoluntas est affectus rationis, uel affectus sensualitatis; et alius est affectus animae secundum rationem, alius secundum sensualitatem; uterque tamen dicitur humana uoluntas. Affectu autem rationis id uolebat quod uoluntate diuina, scilicet pati et mori; sed affectu sensualitatis non uolebat, immo refugiebat" (*Sent.* 3.17.1, p. 106).

23. Ergo et in christo secundum humanitatem, et in membris eius geminus est affectus: Unus rationis, caritate informatus, quo propter deum quis mori uult; alter sensualitatis, carnis infirmitati propinquus et ideo coniunctus, quo mors refugitur.... Secundum istum affectum [i.e., rationis] Christus mori noluit; nec obtinuit quod secundum istum affectum petiit. Ex affectu igitur humano, quem de uirgine traxit, uolebat non mori et calicem transire orabat... Hic [Beda] aperte dicit, duas in Christo fuiise uoluntates secundum quas diversa uoluit... Augustinus etiam duas in Christo asserit uoluntates, dicens: 'Quantum distat Deus ab homine, tantum uoluntas Dei a uoluntate hominis. Unde hominem gerens, Christus ostendit priuatam quandam hominis uoluntatem, in qua et suam et nostram figurauit, qui caput nostrum est, et ad eum sicut membra pertinemus. *Pater*, inquit, *si fieri potest, transeat a me calix iste.* Haec humana uoluntas erat, proprium aliquid et tamquam priuatum uolens. Sed quia rectum uult esse hominem et ad Deum dirigi, subdit: *Non quod ego uolo, sed quod tu uis;* ac si diceret: Vide te in me, quia potes aliquid proprium uelle, ut deus aliud uelit; conceditur hoc humanae fragilitati'... His testimoniis euidenter docetur in Christo duas fuisse uoluntates: Quod quia negauit Macarius archiepiscopus, in Metropolitana Synodo condemnatus est. (*Sent.* 3.17.2, pp. 107–109)

The comment made by Augustine comes in *Enarr. In Ps. 32* [CCL 38:248]). The "metropolitan council" referred to was the Sixth Ecumenical Council or Third Council of Constantinople, 680–681.

24. "Ad quid ergo petiit? Ut membris formam praeberet, imminente turbatione, clamandi ad Dominum et subiciendi uoluntatem suam diuinae uoluntati; ut si pulsante molestia tristantur, pro eiusdem amotione orent; sed si nequeunt uitare, dicant quod ipse Christus" (*Sent.* 3.17.2, p. 109).

25. "Ceterum non parum nos movent verba Ambrosii, quibus significare videtur Christum secundum humanum affectum de potentia Patris dubitasse, sic dicens in III libro *De Trinitate* [sic]: 'De quo dubitat? De se an de Patre? De eo utique cui dicit: *Transfer*... Ut homo ergo dubitat, ut homo locutus est.' His verbis innui videtur quod Christus, non in quantum Deus es vel Dei Filius, sed in quantum homo, dubitaverit affectu humano. –Ex quo sensu illud accipiendum sit. Quod ea ratione dictum accipi potest: non quia ipse dubitaverit, sed quia modum gessit dubitantis, et hominibus dubitare videbatur" (Lombard, *Sent.* 3.17.3, p. 110).

26. *The Search,* 674.

27. "Illud etiam ignorandum non est, quod Hilarius asserere uidetur christum non sibi, sed suis orasse, cum dixit: *Transeat a me* etc., sicut nec sibi, sed suis timuit; nec eum uoluisse ut sibi non esset passio, sed ut a suis transiret calix passionis, ita inquiens.... Intende, lector, his uerbis pia diligentia, ne sint tibi uasa mortis" (*Sent.* 3.17.3, p. 110).

28. *DFO* 3.24, PG 94:1000.

29. "Ad priman quaestionem dicendum quod Christo secundum quod Deus, non competit orare nec obedire, nec aliquid quod in minorationem sonat, aut quod ad diversitatem voluntatis pertinet; sed secundum quod homo, competit sibi orare propter tria, ut dicit Damascenus. Primo propter veritatem humanae naturae insinuandam, secundum quam minor est Patre et obediens ei et orans ipsum. Secundo ad exemplum orando nobis praebendum; quia omnis ejus actio nostra est instructio, cum sit nobis datus quasi exemplum virtutis. Tertio ad ostendendum quod a Deo venerat et sibi contrarius non erat, dum eum orando principium recognoscebat" (*Sent.* 3.17.3.1, p. 543).

30. "Dicendum quod, sicut dictum est in *Secunda Parte,* oratio est quaedam explicatio propriae voluntatis apud Deum, ut eam impleat. Si igitur in Christo esset una tantum voluntas, scilicet divina, nullo modo competeret sibi orare; quia voluntas divina per seipsam est effectiva eorum quae vult, secundum illum *Psalmi, Omnia quaecumque voluit Dominus, fecit* [Ps. 134 (135). 6] Sed quia in Christo est alia voluntas divina et alia humana, et voluntas humana non est per seipsam efficax ad implendum quae vult, nisi per virtutem divinam, inde est quod Christo, secundum quod est homo et humanam voluntatem habens, competit orare" (*Summa* 3.21.1).

31. *Sent.* 3.17.2.1 ad 4um, p. 372.

32. "Videtur quod Christo orare competens non fuerit. Quia, sicut dicit Damascenus: "oratio est ascensus intellectus in Deum." Sed ascendere in Deum, cum sit distantis a Deo, non competit intellectui Christi, qui semper Deo conjunctus erat. Ergo Christo non competit orare" (Thomas, *Sent.* 3.17.3.1.1, p. 540; cf. Bonaventure, *Sent.* 3.17.2.1, p. 371).

33. "Praeterea. Nullus petit aliquid a seipso. Sed, sicut Damascenus dicit: "oratio est petitio decentium a Deo." Cum igitur Christus sit Deus et non sit alius Deus praeter eum, ad eum orare non pertinet" (Thomas, *Sent.* 3.17.3.1.2, p. 540; cf. Bonaventure, *Sent.* 3.17.2.1, p. 371).

34. "Oratio est expressio voluntatis, quia est de eo quod quis absolute vult; alias est fictio. Sed Christus quidquid absolute volebat, hoc sciebat Deum velle. Ergo non oportebat quod de hoc ipsum rogaret" (Thomas, *Sent.* 3.17.3.1.3, p. 540; cf. Bonaventure, *Sent.* 3.17.2.1, p. 371).

35. "Sed contra. Augustinus de Correptione et gratia: "Nemo quaerit ab alio quod per se potest"; sed Christus omnia poterat per se: ergo nihil debebat ab alio petere, ergo nec orare" (Bonaventure, *Sent.* 3.17.2.11, p. 371). The quote from Augustine actually comes from another work of Augustine. See following note.

36. "Nam quid stultius quam orare ut facias quod in potestate habeas?" (*De natura et gratia* 18.20, in *CSEL* 60, ed. C.F. Verba and J. Zycha [Vienna: Hoelder-Pichler-Tempsky, 1913]), 246.

37. "Item, oratio est actus personae inferioris respectu eius quem orat; sed persona Christi est aequalis Patri: ergo non decuit Christum orationem fundere ad Deum" (Bonaventure, *Sent.* 3.17.2.1.2, p. 371).

38. "Item, voluntas Christi hominis erat per omnia conformis voluntati Patris, ergo nihil petebat, nisi quod sciebat Patrem velle: ergo etiam si non peteret, nihilominus quod petebat impleretur: ergo frustra petebat aliquid. Sed nihil decuit Christum frustra facere: ergo non decuit Christum orare" (*Sent.* 3.17.2.1.5, p. 371).

39. "Videtur quod Christo non competat orare. Nam, sicut Damascenus dicit, *oratio est petitio decentium a* Deo. Sed cum Christu omni facere posset, non videtur ei convenire quod aliquid ab aliquo peteret. Ergo videtur quod Christo non conveniat orare" (*Summa* 3.21.1.1).

40. "Praeterea, non oportet orando petere illud quod aliquis scit pro certo esse futurum; sicut non oramus quod sol oriatur cras. Neque etiam est conveniens quod aliquis orando petat quod scit nullo modo esse futurum. Sed Christus sciebat circa omnia quid esset futurum. Ergo non conveniebat ei aliquid orando petere" (*Summa* 3.21.1.2).

41. "Praeterea, Damascenus dicit in III libro [i.e., *DFO* 3.24], quod oratio est ascensus intellectus in Deum. Sed intellectus Christi non indigebat ascensione in Deum; quia semper intellectus ejus erat Deo conjunctus, non solum secundum unionem hypostasis, sed etiam secundum fruitionem beatitudinis. Ergo Christo non conveniebat orare" (*Summa* 3.21.1.1).

42. "Ad primum igitur dicendum quod ascendere est proprie tendere in aliquid quod supra ipsum erat. Intellectus autem Christi non tendit in aliquid quod supra ipsum esset quantum ad contemplationem, quia quidquid de Deo contemplatus est unquam, hoc contemplatus est a primo instanti conceptionis; et secundum hoc dicit Damascenus, quod 'intellectus Christi ascensione quae est in Deum non indigebat'; sed tamen potentia divina quam orando implorabat, supra ipsum erat; et sic ascendens in Deum orabat" (*Sent.* 3.17.3.1 ad 1um, p. 543).

43. "Ad tertium dicendum quod ascensio nihil est aliud quam motus in id quod est sursum. Motus autem, ut habetur in *de Anima*, dupliciter dicitur. Uno modo, proprie, secundum quod importat exitum de potentia in actum, prout est actus imperfecti. Et sic ascendere comptit ei quod est potentia sursum et non actu. Et hoc modo, ut Damascenus dicit in III lib., *Intellectus humanus Christi non eget ascension in Deum cum sit semper Deo unitus et secundum esse personale, et secundum contemplationem beatam* [*DFO* 24, p. 94:1089]. Alio modo dicitur motus actus perfecti, idest existentis in actu; sicut intelligere et sentire dicuntur quidam motus. Et hoc modo intellectus Christi semper ascendit in Deum, quia semper contemplatur ipsum ut supra se existentem" (*Summa* 3.21.1 ad 3um).

44. "Ad illud quod obiicitur, quod oratio est actus personae inferioris; dicendum, quod hoc verum est, attribuendo inferioritatem personae secundum eam naturam, secundum quam competit ei oratio. Oratio enim est actus conveniens personae ratione naturae; et sic non habet instantiam in proposito, quia quamvis persona Christi ratione Divinitatis sit aequalis Patri, secundum tamen humanitatem minor est Patre, iuxta illud Ioannis decimo quarto, *Pater maior me est*" [John 14:28] (*Sent.* 3.17.2.1 ad 2um, p. 372).

45. "Ad illud quod obiicitur, quod nemo petit ab alio, si possit illud implere, quod petit: dicendum, quod illud verum est, secundum quod petitio et impletio attribuuntur eidem ratione eiusdem naturae; sic autem non est in propositio. Name petere et orare competit Christo secundum naturam assumtam; sed posse implere debetur ei secundum naturam assumentem" (*Sent.* 3.17.2.1 ad 1um, pp. 371–372). 46. *Sent.* 3.17.1 ad 3um, p. 544.

47. "Ad illud quod obiicitur, quod Christus nihil petebat, nisi quod sciebat Deum velle; dicendum, quod verum est sed Christus bene sciebat, quod Deus quaedam volebat, quia sciebat, Christum ea nobis impetraturum per suam orationem; et ideo, orando et petendo quod Deus volebat, non frustra orabat, quia hoc ipsum, quod Deus disposuerat, nobis sua oratione impetrabat. Cum enim Deus disponit vel vult aliquid facere, non disponit in omnem eventum, sed praesuppositis congruentibus antecedentibus sicut disponit nos alvare, si tamen velimus per bona merita salutem acquirere; sic et in propositio intelligendum est" (*Sent.* 3.17.1 ad 5um, p. 372).

48. *Summa* 3.21. Earlier in the *Summa* (3.13.1), Thomas had concluded that Christ was not omnipotent as a man.

49. *Summa* 3.21.

50. "Ad praedictorum intelligentiam est notandum, quod *conformitas* voluntatis ad voluntatem in duobus consistit, videlicet *in volito* et in *ratione volendi*. Conformitatem in *volito* dico, quando diversae voluntates unum et idem volunt" (*Sent.* 3.17.1.3, pp. 368–69).

51. "Conformitatem in *ratione* volendi dico, quando idem eodem modo volunt, vel altera earum vult illud eodem modo, quo superior vult eam velle. Cum igitur ad perfectam conformitatem ista duo concurrant. . . . Possibilie est enim, quod voluntates sint conformes, ita quod una subsit alteri; et tamen non volunt idem, quia voluntas superior non vult inferiorem velle, quod ipsa vult, sed magis velle contrarium. Quoniam igitur conformitas in *ratione volendi* fuit in omnibus voluntatibus Christi, quia

sic volebat sensualitas, sicut volebat ratio eam velle; sic volebat etiam ratio Christi, sicut divina voluntas volebat ipsam velle: ideo concedendum est, quod in Christo fuit voluntatum concordia et consonantia, quamvis ex parte voliti non esset identitas, quia unaquaeque voluntas quod suum erat volebat" (*Sent.* 3.17.1.3, pp. 368–369).

52. "Ex ipsa dominica oratione, qua dicebat: *Non sicut ego volo, sed sicut tu* vis: ergo aliud volebat Christus, secundum quod homo, et oppositum, secundum quod Deus: ergo voluntas humana non erat conformis divinae" (*Sent.* 3.17.1.3, p. 367).

53. "Ad illud vero quod primo obiicitur in contrarium de oratione Domini: Non sicut ego volo, sed sicut tu vis: potest . . . dici, quod conformitas voluntatis ad voluntatem dupliciter attenditur, vel secundum *assimilationem,* vel secundum *subiectionem.* Dominus autem a voluntate sensualitatis non requirebat conformitatem assimilationis, ut idem vellet, quod ipse vellet; se conformitatem subiectionis, ut id vellet, quod Deus ordinavit eam velle; ut Dominus in praedictapetitione tollit conformitatem assimilationis, cum dicit: *Non sicut ego,* et ponit conformitatem subiectionis in hoc, quod ostendit, se velle divinae voluntati subesse. Unde in praedicto verbo insinuatur duplex voluntas in Christo, una videlicet rationis, quae erat similis et subiecta divinae voluntati; altera vero sensualitatis, quam ratio subiiciebat voluntati divinae, licet ipsa sensualitas contrarium appeteret; et ita, quamvis non esset similis, erat tamen subiecta, ac per hoc non erat contraria" (*Sent.* 17.1.3 ad 1um, p. 369).

54. "Ad illud Augustini quo dicitur, quod voluntas humana in Christo distabat a voluntate divina; dicendum, quod Augustinus intendit ibi ponere distantiam quantum ad diversitatem voluntatum et quantum ad distantiam volitorum, non autem quantum ad subiectionis ordinem in volendo; et ideo illa distantia non ponit controversiam" *(Sent.* 17.1.3 ad 2um, p. 369).

55. *Sent.* 17.1.3 ad 2um, p. 369.

56. "Item, Christus flebat de destructione Ierusalem, ergo volebat Ierusalem non destrui; et secundum divinam iustitiam volebat, eam destrui: ergo voluntas humana adversabatur divinae" (*Sent.* 3.17.1.3, p. 367).

57. "Ad illud quod obiicitur, quod Christus nolebat, Ierusalem destrui, voluntate humana; dicendum, sicut Hugo dicit, quod illa erat voluntat pietatis, quae ideo flebat, quia misericordiam diligebat; et quia Deus sic volebat eam velle, ideo divinae voluntati non repugnabat; erat enim ibi conformitas in ratione volendi, quamvis non esset in volito. Quod enim sic vellet,hoc habebat a Deo, et Deus volebat, eam sic velle" (*Sent.* 17.1.3 ad 3um, p. 369).

58. *De Trin.* 1.6.10, pp. 39–40.

59. "Item, videtur, quod voluntas rationis et sensualitatis adversentur sibi invicem, quia, secundum quod dicit Augustinus de Trinitate [11.6.10], voluntates sunt contrariae, quae sunt contrariorum volitorum; sed voluntas rationis volebat mori, voluntas sensualitatis volebat vivere: ergo sensualitatis et rationis erant voluntates contrariae" (*Sent.* 3.17.1.2, p. 368).

60. "Ad illud quod obiicitur, quod voluntas sensualitatis repugnabat rationi, quia volebat contrarium; dicendum, quod contrarietas ex parte voliti non dicit contra-

rietatem in voluntate, nisi sint tales voluntates, quae non tantum sunt natae con-
formari per subiectionem, sed etiam per identitatem ex parte voliti" (*Sent.* 17.1.3 ad
4um, p. 369).

61. "Item pavor et securitas sunt affectiones contrariae;sed in voluntate rationis
erat securitas, in voluntate sensualitatis erat timiditas: ergo contrario modo afficie-
batur voluntas rationalis et voluntas sensualis. Sed tales sunt voluntates sibi invicem
adversantes" (*Sent.* 3.17.1.3, pp. 368).

62. "Ad illud quod obiicitur, quod voluntas sensualitatis repugnabat rationi, quia
volebat contrarium; dicendum, quod contrarietas ex parte voliti non dicit contra-
rietatem in voluntate, nisi sint tales voluntates, quae non tantum sunt natae con-
formari per subiectionem, sed etiam per identitatem ex parte voliti" (*Sent.* 17.1.3 ad
5um, p. 369).

63. *Sent.* 3.17.2.1, pp. 536–538.

64. The term is usually a foil for *viator* in medieval thought. A *viator* is a human
living on earth, "on the way" to beatitude and thus limited in knowledge. A *comprehensor* enjoys the beatific vision (Christ from the first moment of his conception, the
saved after death) and thus the knowledge of all the things of God.

65. "Ex hoc licet nobis aliud velle quam Deus vult, quia nescimus quid
Deus velit in aliquibus. Sed Christus sciebat in omnibus quid Deus vellet. Ergo
quantum ad omnia volita voluntatem humanam divinae conformabat" (*Sent.* 3.17.2.1,
p. 534).

66. "Ad tertium dicendum quod quamvis Christus sciret quid Deus vellet in
quolibet, non tamen qualibet sua vi apprehendebat divinam voluntatem, nec rationem
quare Deus id vellet secundum ordinem ad finem aliquem. Et ideo non oportebat
quod quaelibet vis ejus conformaretur divinae voluntati in volito" (*Sent.* 3.17.2.1 ad
3um, p. 538).

67. "Dicendum, quod cum oratio...ad ostensionem benignitatis et mis-
ericordiae" (*Sent.* 3.17.2. resp., pp. 373–374). Thomas: *Sent.* 545–546.

68. "Ad secundam quaestionem dicendum quod oratio semper est ad supplen-
dum aliquem defectum. Christus autem non patiebatur aliquem defectum quantum
ad bona spiritualia quia beatus erat; patiebatur autem defectum, inquantum erat
passibilis in anima et in corpore. Unde omnis oratio Christi quae erat pro bonis
spiritualibus, non erat pro se, sed pro aliis.... Sed oratio quae erat pro his quae
pertinent ad corpus, erat etiam ipsi pro seipso" (*Sent.* 3.17.2, p. 544).

69. "Tertio quaeritur, utrum illa oratio, qua oravit in passione, ut calix transfer-
retur a se, fuerit a ratione, an a sensualitate. Et quod a sensualitate, videtur: "Auctoritate
Magistri [i.e., Peter Lombard] in littera: 'Secundum affectum sensualitatis Christus
mori noluit, nec obtinuit quod secundum istum affectum petiit': ergo videtur, quod
petitio illa ex coluntate sensualitatis processerit.

Item, hoc ipsum ostenditur ex ordine verborum, cum dicit: *Non sicut ego volo, sed
sicut tu;* aut hoc dicit ratione voluntatis sensualitatis, aut rationis. Quantum ad voluntatem rationis non dicit, quia ill erat per omnia divinae voluntati conformis: ergo
hos dicit quantum ad voluntatem sensualitatis: ex illa ergo voluntate procedebat
postulatio orationis propositae.

Item, nullus sapiens petit vel orat contrarium eius quod vult; se ratio volebat mori: ergo petitio de evasione mortis non erat petitio rationis: et erat rationis, vel sensualitatis: ergo sensualitatis" (*Sent.* 3. 17.3, p. 374).

70. "Dicendum, quod de praedicta oratione est loqui dupliciter: aut quantum ad materiam, aut quantum ad formam. Si loquamur de ipsa quantum ad materiam; cum materia orationis respiciat desiderium petentis, talis petitiio fuit petitio fuit petitio sensualitatis, cuius desiderium erat non moriendum" (*Sent.* 3.17.3. resp., p. 375).

71. "Si autem loquamur de praedicta oratione quantum ad formam; sic, cum forma petitionis respiciat discretionem proponentis, et talis modus proponendi sit ad discretionem rationis, concedendum est, quod talis oratio fuerit voluntatis rationalis" (*Sent.* 3.17.3. resp., p. 375).

72. "Et per hot patet responsio ad quaestionem propositam et etiam ad obiecta; ad quaestionem propositam, quia non est simpliciter concedendum, quod talis oratio fuerit simpliciter rationis, vel simpliciter sensualitatis, sed quodam modo huius, quodam modo illius: sensualitatis quantum ad materiam, sed rationis quantum ad formam" (*Sent.* 3.17.3. resp., p. 375).

73. "Ejus enim orare, cujus est velle. Sed non mori in Chisto absolute non volebat nisi sensualitas. Ergo oratio qua mortem petebat a se excludi, erat actu sensualitatis" (*Sent.* 17.3.3, p. 542).

74. "Alio modo dicitur sensualitatis ut objecti, idest de eo quod sensualitas volebat; et sic erat aliqua ejus oratio sensualitatis, quia ratio orans erat quasi advocatus sensualitatis, proponens Deo sensualitatis appetitum. Hoc autem non faciebat quasi ratio vellet hoc quod pro sensualitate petevat, sed ut doceret omnem hominis voluntatem Deo subdendam esse, et in omnibus necessitatibus ad eum recurrendum" (*Sent.* 3.17.3, p. 545).

75. "Illud quaeritur de illo verbo Ambrosii, *Ut homo dubitat, ut homo locutus est.* Videtur enim esse falsum: quia Christus habuit scientiam omnium futurorum sub certitudine: ergo videtur, quod de nul.lo potuerit dubitare.—Item, in quemcumque cadit dubitatio, cadere potest ignorantia et error; sed nullum istorum potuit in Christo cadere: ergo videtur, quod non potuerit dubitare" (*Sent.* 3.17. dub. 3, p. 376).

76. "Dicendum, quod dubitatio proprie dicit indifferentiam iudicii rationis respectu utriusque partis contradictionis, ita quod neutrum praeeligat alteri; et hoc modo accipiendo dubitationem, in Christo non fuit dubitatio. Alio modo dicitur dubitatio indifferentia quaedam partis sensibilis ad sequendum affectum naturae inclinantem, vel rationem imperantem; et talis dubitatio potuit esse in Christo; et de hac intelligit Ambrosius, de alia vero currit obiectio" (*Sent.* 3.17. dub. 3, p. 376).

77. "Dicendum quod dubitatio dupliciter dicitur. Primo enim et principaliter significat motum rationis super utraque parte contradictionis cum formidine determinandi alterum. . . . Primo autem modo dicta dubitatio contingit ex defectu medii sufficientis ad veritatem inveniendam; et ideo contingit ex defectu scientiae; et propter hoc in Christo non fuit" (*Sent.* 3.17.4, pp. 547–548).

78. "Secundo translatum fuit hoc nomen ad significandum formidinem affectus in aggrediendo vel sustinendo aliquod terribile . . . Secundo autem modo dicta contingit ex infirmitate ejus quod laesivum imminens evadendi facultatem non videt. Et

quia Christus habebat infirmitatem in carne, ut supra dictum est, et laesivum mortis imminens, sensualitas trepidabat; ideo erat talis dubitatio in Christo quantum ad sensualitatem, quamvis esset summa securitas quantum ad rationem quae auxilium divinum imminere videbat: quod sensualitas apprehendere non poterat" (*Sent.* 3.17.4, p. 548).

CHAPTER 8

1. *An Essay on the Development of Christian Doctrine.* I use the final, 1878 edition here, with a foreword by Ian Ker (Notre Dame: University of Notre Dame Press, 1989), 1.1.2, p. 35. The essay was published first in November 1845. Hereafter abbreviated as *Essay.*

2. *Essay,* 1.1.5, p. 38.

3. *Essay,* 1.9.9, p. 53.

4. *Essay* 2.9.5, p.64.

5. "This process, whether it be longer or shorter in point of time, by which the aspects of an idea are brought into consistency and form, I call its *development,* being the germination and maturation of some truth or apparent truth on a large mental field" (*Essay* 1.15, p. 38; emphasis added).

6. *Essay,* 2.4.3., 2.4.6, 2.9.5, pp. 59–60, 60–62, 64–65 et passim.

Index